CODE PYTHON: BEGINNERS

Jenif D Souza W S

Dedicated to
Gentry George

CONTENTS

DETAILED CONTENTS

PREFACE

It gives me immense pleasure to bring this book "CODE PYTHON: BEGINNERS". This book is written in simple programming which makes the beginners to understand easily. This book covers all the basic concepts and additional solved programs which will be helpful for all the learners and readers.

Why python?
- It is simple
- Easy to learn and understand
- Fun to use
- Powerful
- Object Oriented programming language
- Free open source software
- Can deploy on any platform

Why this book?

"CODE PYTHON: BEGINNERS" will be more helpful for the beginners to understand the concepts very easily. It contain many solved programs for reference. This book explained all the concepts with simple example programs for readers to understand easily and consist of different question patterns for students and job seekers.

Use of python in Engineering Domain
- To develop web application
- Develop GUI based application
- In networking and security
- In automation testing
- In IoT and embedded applications
- In image processing
- To perform complex mathematical calculation
- In gaming
- Used by data scientist to process large volume of data

ACKNOWLEDGEMENT

Teaching is the source of inspiration for this book and it planted the idea to share my knowledge with the world. I am indebted to my husband, Mr. Gentry George for his unconditional love, support and encouragement in the whole process of writing, editing and publishing this book.

I owe a great debt to my parents, Mrs. Maria Selvi Dsouza and Mr. Wilson Dsouza who encouraged me to write this book. Wish to express my love to my siblings Shani Dsouza and Josfer Dsouza. Furthermore, I would like to thank my friends and colleagues of St. Joseph's College of Engineering, for their invaluable help and productive environment to work. Am also thankful to all my family for backing me up.

Finally, I would like to express my gratitude to all my well-wishers, reviewers and readers, who had supported me to become author of this book.

-Jenif D souza

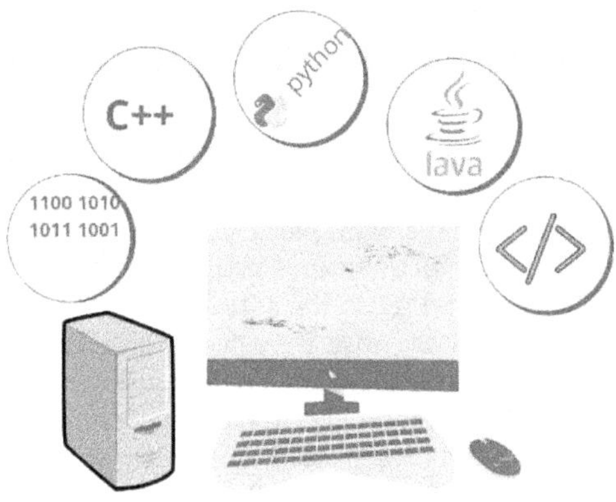

CHAPTER 1: INTRODUCTION TO COMPUTER AND PROGRAMMING LANGUAGE

Computer plays a vital role in our daily life, in education, research, networking, e-commerce, gaming, etc,. As the technology develops, the interaction of computer with humans has become more comprehensive. In this chapter we will discuss and recollect the basics of computer, components of computer, generation of computers, generation of programming language.

CHAPTER OUTLINE

Computer basics – Characteristics of computer – Operations of a computer – History of computers – Generation of computers – Classification of computers – Components of a computer – Programming Language – History of programming language – Software

OBJECTIVE

After covering the chapter, the student will be in a position:

- To know about computer.
- To understand the basics of computer and its generations.
- To understand characteristics of computer and its advantages.
- To known about Von Neumann concepts.
- To know about basic operations of computer.
- To know about the history of computers.
- To learn about various components of computer.
- To learn about the classifications of computer.
- To know what programming languages are and its generation.

- To define what are software and its types.

1.1 WHAT IS COMPUTER?

A computer is an electronic device that can accept data as input, process that data and produce information as output, and store that information for future use. The word computer is derived from the Latin word 'computare' which means 'to calculate'. It accepts the input and perform various arithmetic and logical actions which results to provide an optimum and recurring solution. The computer was originally defined as a super fast calculator as it had the capacity to solve complex arithmetic and scientific problems at very high speed and precision. But, in addition to handling complex arithmetic computations, computer has become more vital in day to day life, it plays major role in all the sophisticated scenarios. Computer is used in most of the industries starting from agriculture to space. The figure 1.1 shows working of the computer.

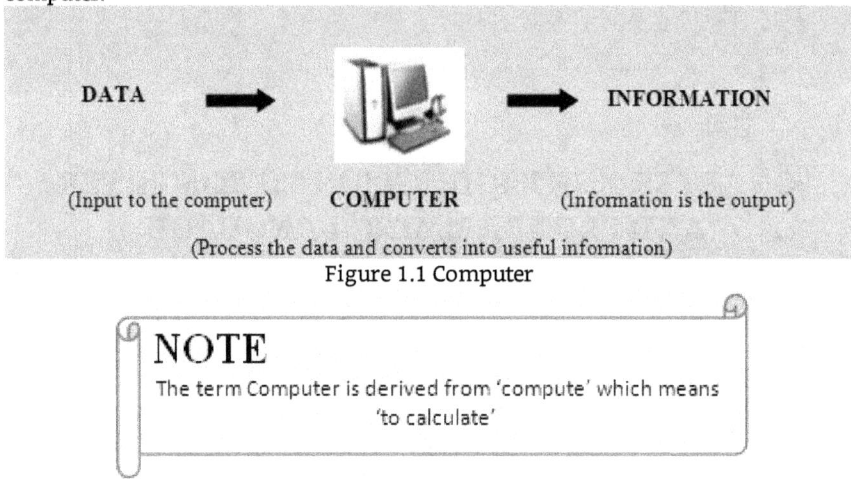

Figure 1.1 Computer

> **NOTE**
> The term Computer is derived from 'compute' which means 'to calculate'

1.2 CHARACTERISTICS OF COMPUTERS

Speed, accuracy, storage capability, diligence and versatility are some of the characteristics which make a computer unique and powerful. Brief overviews of these characteristics are:

a) Speed: The computer is able to process the data and gives the output in fractions of seconds. A powerful computer is capable of executing billions of instruction per second. The speed of computer is calculated in Hz (Hertz) like MHz, GHz, and THz.

b) Accuracy: The accuracy of computers is consistently high enough which avoids any errors. For example, the computer can accurately give the result of division of any two numbers up to 10-15 decimal places. The errors are mostly due to errors in instructions during programming.

c) Storage Capacity: The computer has a provision to store large volumes of data in the small storage devices. It has capacity to store huge amount of data and help in the retrieval of data as an easy task. A limited amount of data can be stored temporarily in the primary memory. Secondary storage devices like compact disk, hard disk can store a large amount of data permanently.

d) Versatile: Computers are very flexible and multipurpose machines. It flexible, easily adaptable and can perform multiple tasks. It can perform different types of tasks with the same ease. At one moment you can use the computer to prepare a letter document and in the same moment you may play music or print a document or browse through the internet. All this makes them versatile in nature.

e) Diligence: When used for a longer period of time, the computer does not get tired or fatigued. It can perform long and complex calculations with the same speed and accuracy through start till the end.

f) Sharing: Nowadays the computers can be interconnected and share data to any point. The data can be shared within a limited group or can be shared with public based on the requirement. We can also reduce the cost by connecting a network of systems to a single server or devices.

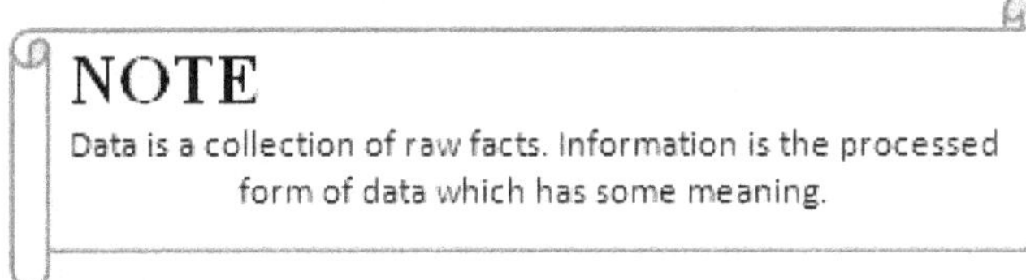

1.3 BASIC OPERATIONS OF COMPUTER

The basic operations done by a computer are input, output, process and storage. The figure 1.2 shows the operations of computer.

Input: The data or input is send by the user using some input devices for processing to the computer. The inputs are entered to the computer by using the input devices such as keyboard, mouse, scanner, MICR, OCR etc.

Process: The processing of data is done by Central Processing Unit (CPU). The CPU can only execute the instructions which are in binary form.

Output: In this process, useful information is obtained from the processing devices. Finally, output is displayed by using output devices such as monitor, printer etc. This output can be stored for further processing.

Storage: The information will be stored in primary or secondary memory for future use. Primary memory involves RAM and ROM, whereas secondary memory are in the form of Magnetic disk, Magnetic tape, CD's, Memory cards, Pen drives etc.

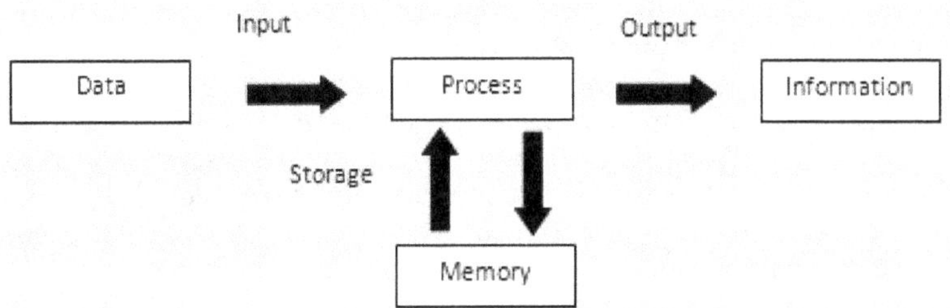

Figure 1.2 Operations of computer

NOTE

The origin of computing started with the early man who uses fingers, stones sticks, etc.

1.4 HISTORY OF COMPUTERS

The evolution of computer started from 16th century. The first use of the word "computer" was recorded in 1613, means person who do calculations. The manual method of computing was slow and error prone. This led to the creation of the first calculating device Abacus to today's high speed calculating devices. During the last 50 years computer had undergone many rapid changes. The period of evolution of computer can be divided into five different phases. The major key developments for the generations of computers are:

• **Abacus**: The foundation of computing device starts with Abacus. Abacus was introduced 5000 years ago. It is an old and simple framed device with rows of wires in which beads are arranged. It is used to perform basic arithmetic operations. The Abacus is shown in figure 1.3.

Figure 1.3 Abacus

Figure:1.4 Napier's Bones

• **Napier's Bones:** Napier's bones was invented by John Napier in 1617. It can perform multiplication, division and calculate square and cube roots by moving the rods around and placing them in specially constructed boards. Here values and numbers are written on strips of boxes, ivory, silver or wood. The Napier's bones is shown in figure 1.4.

• **Slide Rule**: The slide rule was developed by William Oughtred in 1622. It is an analog device works based on lograthims. It provides an accuracy for 3 digits.

• **Pascaline**: Blaise Pascal, a French mathematician invented the first mechanical machine, called Pascaline. It is also known as Pascal's calculator. It was designed and built in 1642 to 1644. It is used in 17th century. It is a rectangular brass box, which uses eight movable dials. It could perform addition and subtraction on whole numbers. The Pascaline is shown in figure 1.6.

Figure: 1.5 Pascaline

• **Stepped Reckoner:** It was developed by German mathematician G.W. Von Leibniz in 1694. It performs addition, subtraction, multiplication and division. The multiplication and division is done by repeated addition and subtraction.

• **Difference Engine:** The Difference Engine was developed by Charles Babbage in 1822. It can perform dieferential equation.

• **Analytical engine:** The first analytical engine was invented by Charles Babbage, at Cambridge University in 1833. It is the first system to have input, process and output.

Figure 1.6 Analytical engine

This machine is programmed by instructions on punch cards and output is stored in mechanical memory. The Analytical engine is shown in figure 1.6.

Figure: 1.7 Arithmometer

• **Arithmometer:** Arithmometer is the first digital mechanical calculator which was invented by a Frenchman Colmar. Arithmometer can perform four basic arithmetic operations such as addition, subtraction, multiplication and division. It is invented by a Frenchman Colmar. The figure 1.7 shows Arithmonmeter.

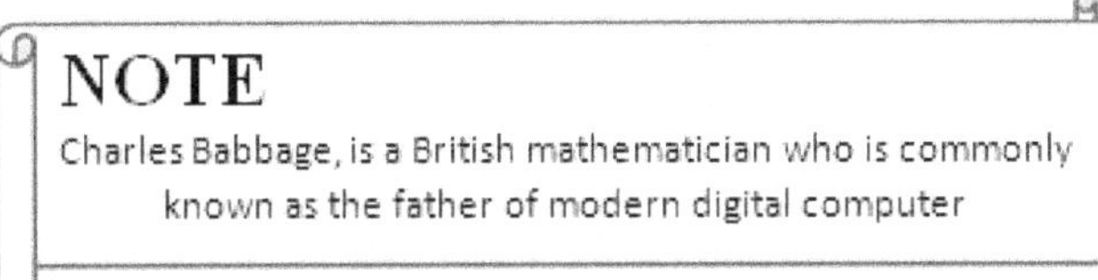

• **Mark I:** This was the first fully automatic calculating machine and was an electronic relay computer. Mark I can perform basic arithmetic and complex equations. It took about 3-5 seconds per calculation. Mark I has complex design and large size.

• **ABC:** Atanasoff-Berry Computer (ABC). This computer developed by John Atanasoff and Clifford Berry was the world's first general purpose automatic electronic digital computer.

1.5 GENERATION OF COMPUTERS

Based on the different time era the generation of computers are classified into :
• The First Generation (1942-1955)
• Second Generation computers (1955-1964)
• Third Generation computers (1964-1975)
• Fourth Generation computers (1975-1980)
• Fifth Generation computers (1980-present)

1.5.1 The First Generation: (1942-1955)

The first generation uses **vacuum tube** based machines. The vacuum tube is a glass tube that contains electrodes for controlling electron flow. They were very expensive to operate. Vacuum tube utilization of large amount of electricity and produce a lot of heat. It often causes malfunctions. The figure 1.8 shows Vacuum tubes. The table 1.1 shows the technology of First Generation Computer.

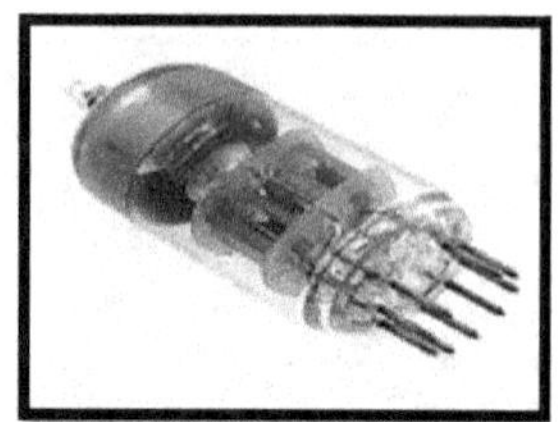

Figure:1.8 Vacuum tubes

Hardware: Vacuum tube, punched cards, magnetic tapes

Software: Programming is done by using machine language

Input: Punched cards for data input

Output: Punched cards and paper tape for output

Storage: Magnetic tapes and drums for external storage

Used for: Scientific purpose

Example: ENIAC, EDVAC, EDSAC, UNIVAC I

Table 1.1 Technology of First Generation Computer

The first generation computers are:

- **ENIAC:** Electronic Numerical Integrator and Calculator. It is an electronic general purpose computer. It was built using 70,000 resistors, 18,000 vacuum tubes, 10,000 capacitors and 1,500 relays. It consumes around 160 kilowatts of electrical power. The ENIAC computation speed is high when compared to Mark I but, it can store only a limited data.

- **EDVAC:** In the mid 1940's Dr. John Von Neumann designed the Electronic Discrete Variable Automatic Computer. It is an earliest electronic computer. The stored program concept was first adopted in this machine.

- **UNIVAC I:** The Universal Automatic Computer I was the first general purpose commercially available computer. It is a first commercial computer which was designed specifically for business data processing applications.

Disadvantages:

- Bulky in size.
- They required big storage space and very difficult to handle.
- It emitted large amount of heat which required air conditioning.
- It required constant maintenance.
- Manual assembly required and had limited commercial use.
- Consumes more power
- Non portable

1.5.2 The Second Generation: (1955-1964)

The second generation computer was evolved in the year 1955-1964. These Supercomputers used transistor technology. The stored program concept was introduced during this era. The second generation computers paved the way for software industries. The TX-0 is the first transistorized computer. The Transistors is shown in figure 1.9. The Second generation computers are IBM 1620, IBM 7094, CDC 1604, UNIVAC 1107, Honeywell 400, etc. The Table 1.2 shows the technology used by second Gener-

Figure:1.9 Transistor

ation Computers.

Hardware: Transistors

Software: Programming is done by using Machine level, Assembly Language

Input: Punched cards

Output: Printouts

Storage: Magnetic core technology

Used for: Scientific and commercial purposes

Used in: Honeywell, IBM

Table 1.2 Technology of Second Generation Computer

Advantages:
- Vacuum tube technology was replaced by transistors
- Assembly language practiced instead of machine language
- Size of the computers got reduced
- High level languages were invented
- They were smaller, faster, more reliable than first generation computers
- It consumes less power than first generation computers and energy efficient

Disadvantages:
- Big in size and required complete room for installation
- Required air conditioning
- Difficult to use

1.5.3 The Third Generation: (1964-1975)

The third generation computer is evolved in the year 1964 – 1975. In this generation, semiconductor is developed which reduced the size even further. It's now light in weight with very low power consumption. Computer's execution speed is millions of instructions per second. Commercial production became easier and cheaper. Higher level languages like Pascal and Report Program Generator (RPG) and applications oriented languages like FORTRAN, COBOL, and PL/1 were developed. This generation was characterized by the invention of Integrated Circuits (ICs). The IC combined electronic components are mounted to a small chip made out of quartz. The Integrated circuit is shown in figure 1.10. The Table 1.3 shows the technology used by third Generation Computers.

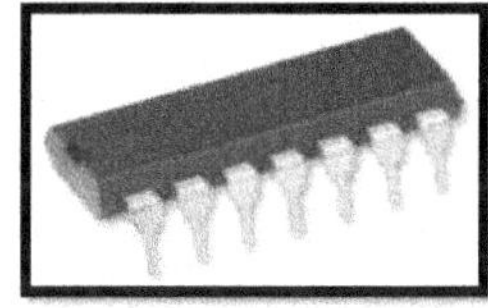

Figure:1.10IntegratedCircuit

Hardware: Integrated circuits

Software: High level programming languages such as FORTAN, COBOL, Pascal and BASIC are used

Storage: Magnetic tapes and drums for external storage

Input: Keyboard

Output: Display

Used for Scientific, commercial, online purposes

Used in: IBM 360/370, PDP-8, PADP-11, CDC6600, B6500

Table 1.3: Technology of third generation computer

Advantages:
- Computation speed had increased when compared to second generation.
- Size and power consumption of the machines had reduced.
- Design-of Operating systems and new higher level languages

- Easy to use and to upgrade

Disadvantages:
- Bulky in size and required complete room for installation.
- Required air conditioned room
- Costly

1.5.4 The Fourth Generation: (1975-1980)

The fourth generation computers are evolved in the year 1975. The Microprocessor is used in fourth generation computers. The Microprocessor is an electronic component used by a computer to do its work. It's like a CPU on a single IC chip with millions of components including transistors, resistors, and diodes that work together. The microprocessor is shown in figure 1.11. The general features of the fourth generation computers Explained in table 1.4

Figure:1.11 Microprocessor

Hardware:	Microprocessors
Software:	Programming languages such as C, C++, GUI based operating systems are used
Storage:	RAM,ROM, External storage devices
Input:	Keyboard, Mouse
Output:	Monitor/Screen
Used for	Scientific, commercial, online, networking purposes
Used in:	IBM PC, VAX 9000, CRAY

Table 1.4: Technology of Fourth generation computers

Fourth generation technologies includes:

- **Small Scale Integration (SSI):** The third generation computers made use of 'Integrated Circuits that has 1020 components on each chip. It has a very few transistors embed on it.
- **Large Scale Integration:** It is a process of embedding thousands of transistors on a single chip.
- **Very Large Scale integration:** It is a process of embedding millions of transistors on a single chip.
- **PCs:** Computer production became inexpensive and the era of Personal Computers (PCs) commenced. These computers can be placed in tables or desks and can be used for single-user tasks. Fourth generation languages emerged and applications software's started becoming popular.
- **Networks:** As the computers started becoming more and more powerful, they could be linked together or networked to share not only data but also memory space and software. The local area network (LAN) connects number of devices together. Web is a global network which links computers across world under a single network of information.

Advantages:
- Faster, cheaper and powerful.
- It is easier to use than previous generations.
- Microcomputers and personal computers are introduced.
- Mainframes, supercomputers were used and personal computers were widespread.

- High speed network such as LAN, WAN, SAN are introduced.
- Use of Large Scale Integration (LSI) and later Very Large Scale Integration (VLSI).

1.5.5 The Fifth Generation: (1980 – present)

Defining the fifth generation computers are somewhat difficult because this field is still growing. The computer uses Artificial Intelligence (AI) which is Expert Systems. Computers which could think and reason in much the same way as humans and even have voice recognition system. These computers use parallel processing, optic fiber technology and superconductors to handle Artificial Intelligence, expert systems, Robotics etc., and have high processing speeds and are more reliable. Quantum mechanism and nanotechnology will also radically change the phase of computers. The table 1.5 shows the technology used in fifth generation computer.

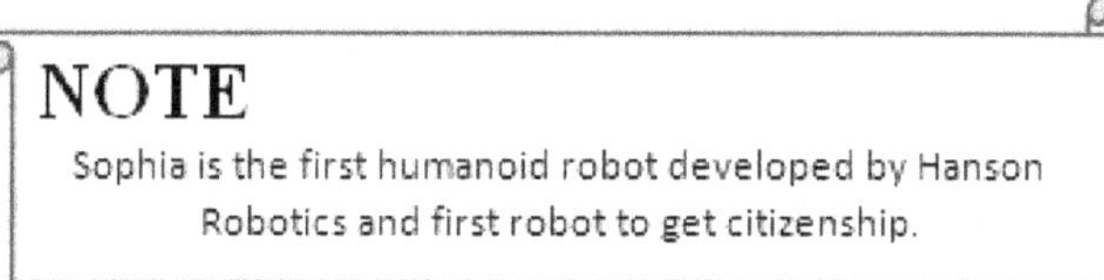

Hardware:	Artificial Intelligence, Integrated circuits with ULSI/SLSI
Software:	High level programming languages such as Java, python, C#
Storage:	Primary and secondary storage devices
Input:	Multiple devices
Output:	Monitor/Screen/Virtual Display
Used for:	Scientific, commercial, online, multimedia, networking purposes
Used in:	IBM notebooks, IOS-Siri, Android- Google Assist, Alexa

Table 1.5: Technology of fifth generation computer

Advantages:

- Faster, powerful, reliable and easy to use.
- The processors works in quantum speed
- Consumes less power
- Air conditioning is not necessary
- Can recognize Image and Graphics

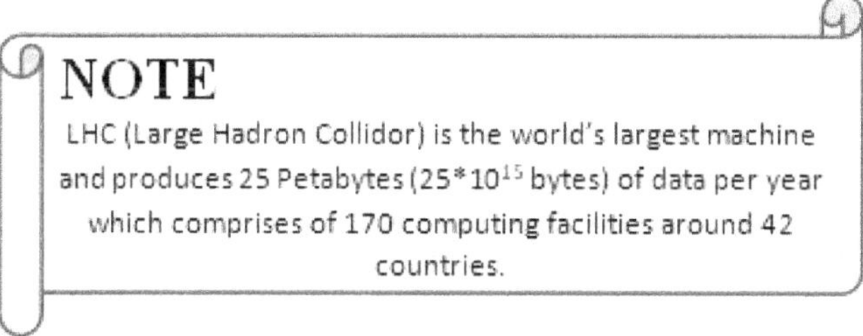

1.6 CLASSIFICATION OF COMPUTERS

The computers are classified into various categories depends on their purpose, operation and size. The figure 1.12 shows the pictorial representation of classification of computers.

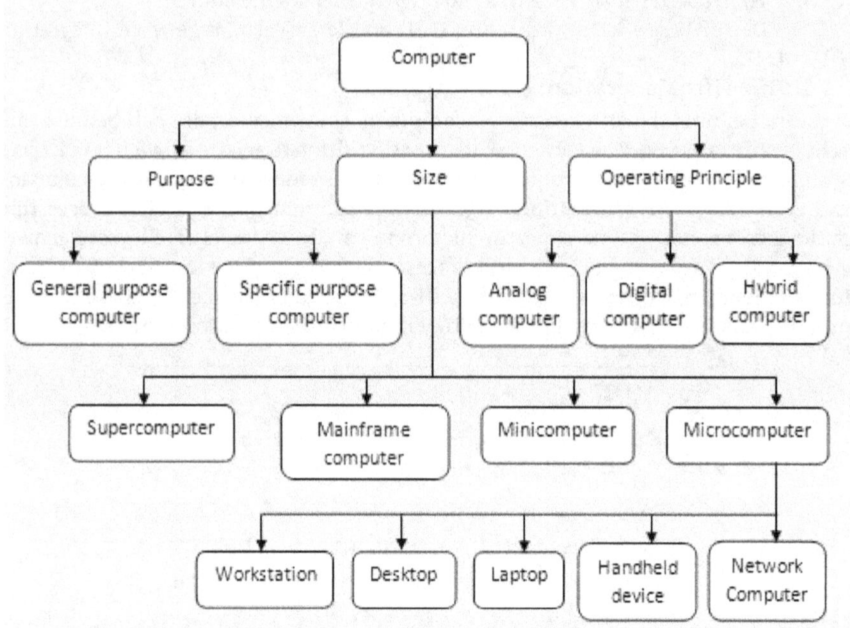

Figure 1.12: Classification of computer

1.6.1 Classification according purpose of the computer

Based on the purpose and application, computers are classified into two: General purpose and special purpose computers.

a) General Purpose Computers: The General Purpose Computers used for any kind of applications. These computers can be used in solving a business Problem and mathematical equations with same accuracy and consistency. Nowadays general purpose digital computers play vital role in major applications such as accounts management, payroll, data processing, etc.

b) Special Purpose Computers: When it comes to specific jobs or tasks, the special purpose computers are usually used. Specific jobs or tasks like Satellite launching, weather forecasting, automobiles, microwaves, etc was done using these computer. The purposes are critical and need great accuracy and response in these computers.

1.6.2 Classification according operational principles

According to the operational principle or logic of computers, the computer are categorized as analog, digital and hybrid computers.

a) Analog Computers: These computers represent data in the form of continuous electrical signals. These computers are used in early days. Analog computer can perform several mathematical operations. They are used for measuring of parameters that vary continuously in real time, such as pressure, temperature and voltage.

b) Digital Computers: Data on these computers is represented as a series of 0s and 1s. They are suitable for higher processing speeds and complex computation. The digital computers are programmable computers. They can be general purpose computers or special purpose computers. The computers used at our homes and offices are the example for digital computers.

c)   Hybrid Computers: Hybrid Computers are a combination of Analog and Digital computers and with speed of analog and accuracy of digital computers. In specialized applications where the input data is in an analog form which is converted into digital form for further processing.

1.6.3 Classification according to size

Based on sizes of the computers, the computers are classified into:

- Supercomputers
- Mainframe computers
- Minicomputers
- Microcomputers

a)   Supercomputers

They are extremely fast computers that can perform hundreds of millions of instructions per second. It is most expensive and powerful computer which is used for complex tasks so that, it requires a lot of computational power. Super computers have multiple .processors which processes multiple instructions at the same time. This is known as parallel processing. They process the data generally in two approaches, distributed computing or dedicated processing. In distributed computing large number of discrete devices will be connected together via a network and each device perform its own piece of task and sent to a central server which integrates and process the final result. In dedicated processing, the central processing servers arranged in mesh or hypercube architectures, processes the data which reduces the time as the system works in close proximity. These computers are mostly used in very advanced applications like processing geological data, weather forecasting, etc.

Example: CRAY-2, NEC - 500, PARAM.

b)   Mainframe Computers:

Main frame computers are very large computers which process data at very high speeds of the order of several million instructions per second. They have high-end processors connected with related peripheral devices. These are powerful multi-user computer capable of supporting many hundreds or thousands of users simultaneously. The mainframes are used in highly critical applications such as bulk data processing and in large organizations, banks, industry, etc. These computers can be linked into a network with micro computers, smaller computers and with each other.

Example: IBM4381, CDC.

c)   Minicomputers

These computers are more powerful than the microcomputers. It has higher memory capacity and high storage capacity. The minicomputer is a multi-user computer which is capable of supporting 10 to 100 users simultaneously. Minicomputers are also known as workstations or mid-range systems. They are mainly used in applications like financial accounting, payrolls, Computer Aided Design etc.

Example: VAX 7500, PDP-11.

d)   Microcomputers

Microcomputers are generally referred to as Personal Computers (PCs). Microcomputers are computer with a microprocessor and its central processing unit (CPU). These systems do not occupy space as much like mainframe computers. Along with a keyboard and a mouse, microcomputers can be called Personal Computers (PCs). Microcomputer is packed with I/O devices such as monitor, a keyboard, Memory in the form of RAM and a power supply unit. These computers can be placed in tables or desks and can be used for single-user tasks. It has a smallest memory and less power. These microcomputers include Desktops, Laptops, Workstations, Handheld devices,

Network computers.

Workstations: It is a single-user, powerful computer. A workstation is like a personal computer, but it has a higher-quality monitor and a more powerful microprocessor.

Desktops: A desktop is proposed to be used on one single location. The components of a desktop computer are available at comparatively lower costs. The Power consumption of desktop is not as critical as that in laptops. In workplace and households the desktops are widely popular.

Laptops: The Laptops are developed for mobile use. The operation of laptop is similar to desktops. Laptops run on an inbuilt single battery and an external adapter to charge that computer batteries. They are enabled with an inbuilt mouse, keyboard and a liquid crystal display (LED) display. Devices like CDs, pen drives, printers, etc can be connected to these computers. The Notebook computers are smaller in size than laptop computers. However, laptop and notebook have powerful processors, support graphics, etc.

Handheld Device: A mobile device is basically any handheld computer. It is designed in such a way that to be extremely portable, often fit in pocket or palm. The mobile devices are more powerful, and it can do many works simultaneously like desktop or laptop computer. Some of the handheld devices are:

• **Tablet Computers:** The tablet computers are designed to be portable like laptops. The major difference of tablet computers than other device is that, it doesn't have keyboards or touchpad.

• **Smartphone:** A Smartphone is a most powerful mobile phone which is designed to run a many different applications in addition to phone service. They are small tablet computers and they can be used for watching videos, web browsing, reading documents, playing games and more.

• **Personal Digital Assistants (PDAs):** A PDA is a handheld computer and popularly known as a palmtop. It has a memory card for storage of data a touch screen. PDAs can also be used as web browsers, portable audio players and smart phones. Most of the PDAs can access to the Internet with the help of Bluetooth or Wi-Fi communication.

1.7 APPLICATIONS OF COMPUTER

Computers play a vital role in our day to day life, from booking an appointment to forecasting the weather. Some key areas where its applications are widely used are:

Education: It is an effective tool for teaching and learning. Smart classes are now common across where children can visually watch what they are learning which made class room learning more interactive.

Medicine and healthcare: The diagnosing of diseases now becomes more efficient and accurate with newly advanced bio-technology.

Science: Developing, analysis and testing of emerging theories have now become more smooth and swift. The studies and prediction of natural calamities like earthquakes, pollution etc becomes more comprehensive.

Banking: Computation and transactions become fast with the introduction of new generation banking technology like internet banking and mobile banking.

Publishing: Creation of jobs and publishing a job can be done in shorter duration with the help of computers.

Engineering/ Architecture/ Manufacturing: The calculations, designing, drawings, modeling became easy with the coming up of different software. Planning, designing and execution also are now in accurate and with less time consumption

Business Applications: The entire business functionality from decision making to funding can now be controlled and recorded using the advanced systems.

Entertainment: Animations, Graphics, audio and video and effects are now its verge with the advancement in technology. The feel of a movie is now become more realistic.

Communication: Contacting a person in any part of the world or even in the space is now possible with fraction of seconds. Communication is done by email, e-fax, etc.

Advertisement: It is used in different advertising fields such as education, movie, business, etc.

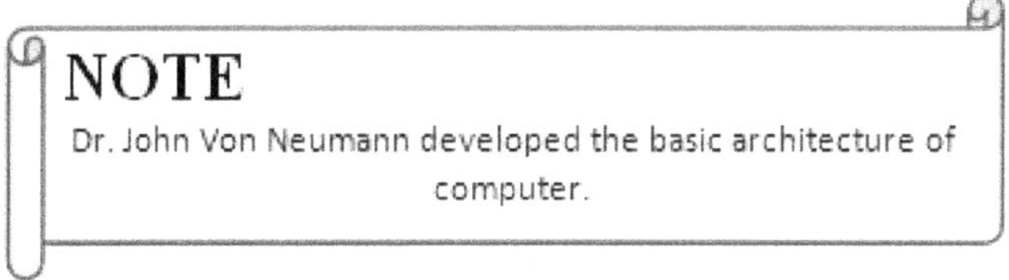

1.8 VON NEUMANN CONCEPT

Dr. John Von Neumann in the mid 1940's designed the Von Neumann concept. The Von Neumann architecture introduced the concept of stored program, in this the instructions or program are stored in memory. The EDVAC is the first machine which used the stored program concept. The EDVAC is Electronic Discrete Variable Automatic Computer, is an earliest electronic computer. This architecture performs operations in lesser time. The hardware component of this system includes Memory (RAM), ALU, Control unit, and Input and Output devices.

- The data is given as input by some input devices.
- This data are processed into information by Control unit and perform some operations using Arithmetic and Logic Unit (ALU)
- This information is displayed in output devices and stored in memory.

1.9 COMPONENTS OF A COMPUTER

The computer is the combination of hardware and software. The physical components such as keyboard, mouse, monitor etc, are called hardware and set of programs or instructions are called as software. The components of computer are shown in figure 1.13. The components of computer includes:

a) Input Unit
b) Central Processing Unit
c) Output Unit
d) Memory Unit

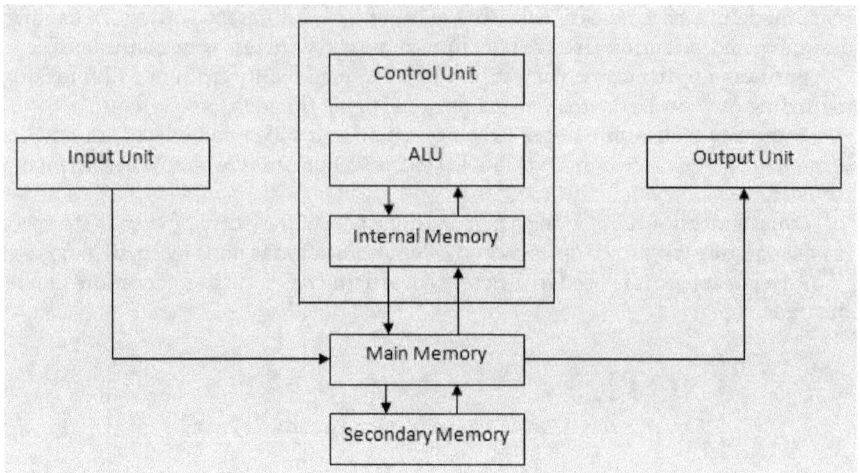

Figure: 1.13 Components of a Computer

1.9.1 Input Unit

The input unit is to feed any input data to the computer. Some of the input devices are keyboard, mouse, scanner, etc. These input devices are electromechanical devices are used to feed in the data into the computer for processing, deriving and storing of outputs. We can feed in data in two ways:

- Manual entry: Where we input data via keyboard or mouse.
- Direct entry: Here the data is feed in via a source document.

1.9.2 Central Processing Unit (CPU)

CPU interprets and executes input data into meaningful output or information. The CPU is considered as the brain of the computer which controls all the operation of input, output and memory units. It performs both arithmetic and logical operations, and controls the usage of main memory. It performs four phrases of actions like fetching information, decoding the instructions, executing the instructions and storing results back in the memory. The three main subsystems of CPU are:

- Arithmetic/Logic Unit (ALU)
- Control Unit (CU)
- Registers

i) Arithmetic Logic Unit (ALU): It does both arithmetic and logical calculations. Arithmetic unit is responsible for performing the arithmetic operations like addition, subtraction, multiplication and division. Logical unit does all the logical operations like greater than (>), less than (<), equal to (=), not equal to (!=), AND, OR, NOR etc. The result of the operation is stored in internal memory.

ii) Control Unit: Control unit controls the flow of data between memory, CPU and I/O devices. It fetches or extracts the instructions from the memory, interprets them and executes them. The control unit checks the errors and correctness of instruction.

iii) Registers: These are high speed temporary memory which holds information like data, instruction, addresses etc. The instruction is fetched using Program Counter (PC) and Instruction Register (IR) and the MAR (Memory Address Resister) and MDR (Memory Data Register) will handle data transfer between main memory and processor. Operands for arithmetic and logical unit are handled by Accumulated register (A) and some other registers also present to contain partial results and memory addresses.

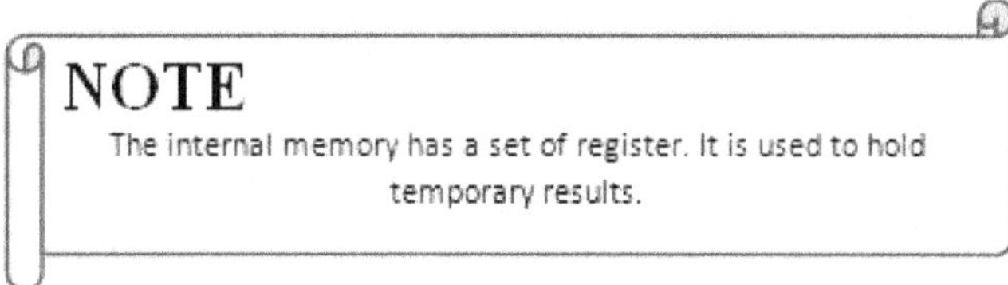

NOTE

The internal memory has a set of register. It is used to hold temporary results.

1.9.3 Memory Unit

The place for holding the instructions, data and output in a computer is its memory unit. They are classified into two categories:

- Primary Memory
- Secondary Memory

i) Primary Memory

The main memory part of the computer is known as Primary memory and classified basically as RAM (Random Access Memory) and ROM (Read Only Memory). ROM is the read only memory and is the non-volatile memory. They can hold data even after the power goes off. We cannot write data in this memory. So they are used to store binary codes for the look up table for processing the sequence of instruction. There are four types of ROM – Masked ROM, P ROM, EP ROM, EEP ROM.

RAM is the random access memory and we can read and write into the RAM. These memory locations cannot hold the data after power goes off. We use these memory locations to store data that changes frequently and are then read by the microprocessor to store it back in the storage. There are two types of RAM- Static RAM and Dynamic RAM. The difference between RAM and ROM are discussed in table 1.6.

No.	RAM	ROM
1	RAM is known as Random Access Memory	ROM is known as Read Only Memory
2	In RAM data can be read and write	In ROM data can be only read
3	Data is stored temporarily	Data are stored permanently
4	There are two types of RAM- Static RAM and Dynamic RAM.	There are four types of ROM – Masked ROM, P ROM, EP ROM, EEP ROM.
5	Contents are lost when the device is off so it is known as volatile memory	Contents are retained even if the device is off so it is known as non- volatile memory.

Table 1.6: Difference between RAM and ROM

ii) Secondary Memory

These memory locations stores huge junk of data and are also known as auxiliary memory or external memory. These are used to store the software programs and data. They are classified as Magnetic devices, Optic devices and Magneto Optical devices. Examples are Hard disk, Floppy disk, CD/DVD-ROM, USB etc.

1.9.4 Output Unit

The output unit gives information to the user. Some of the output devices are printer, monitor, etc. The output devices are the key players which help to convert the output results processed by the CPU into human readable format. They can help to display or print the results based on its properties. The output devices are classified into two types

i) Soft Copy Devices

These devices help in keeping the soft copy of the output in audio, video or visual forms. They are stored basically within the storage devices. Devices such as Monitor, Projectors etc show the softcopy output.

ii) Hard Copy devices

The hard copy device manages to provide the data into a paper. They quality of the print may depend upon the number of dots per inch or pixels. More the pixel density more the quality of the print we get. Devices such as Dot Matrix Printers, Laser Printers etc gives the hard copy output.

1.10 PROGRAMMING LANGUAGE

A Program is a set of instructions to a computer to perform a specific task. The process of telling computers what to do is known as Programming. Many programming language are used to a write programs. The computer program is a set of instructions given to the computer to perform various tasks or operations. Programming languages are broadly categorized into three:

- Machine language
- Assembly language
- High level language

1.10.1 Machine language

Machine Language is the only language understands to computer but it is difficult for the programmer to understand. In machine language the information is stored in the form of 0's and 1's so this language is also known as binary language. In a computer system smallest unit of data is known as bit. The bit means binary digit which is 0's and 1's. A byte consists of 8 bits.

For example:

00010001 11001001

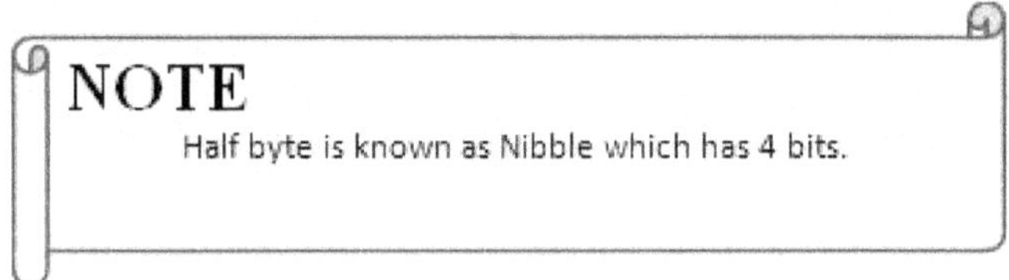

1.10.2 Assembly Language

The Assembly Language is an intermediate of high-level language and machine language. The assembly language is similar to machine language, but it is easier to program. The 0s and 1s of the machine language were substituted by letters and symbols in assembly languages. The assembly language program uses symbolic representation of machine codes.

For example:

    MOV B, A
    ADD B, A

The computer does not understand assembly code. The program which is written in assembly language has to be converted into machine code using a translator known as assembler.

1.10.3 High-level Language

High-level languages are easier for human to understand but difficult for the computer to understand. The program in a high-level language is written in English-like language. Since the machine language and assembly language both are dependent on the hardware, they are referred to as low level programming languages. Both these languages require a deep understanding of the internal structure of the computer. Some of the high level languages are C++, Java, Python, etc.

1.11 GENERATION OF PROGRAMMING LANGUAGES

Programming languages are characterized from what computer do and how close they are to what people do. Programming languages are categorized into five generation.

- First generation – Machine language
- Second generation – Assembly language
- Third generation – Uses interpreter and compiler to translate to machine language
- Fourth generation – Language which is closer to human language
- Fifth generation – Natural language

First and second generation languages are low level language. Whereas, third and fourth generation languages are High-level language that is easily explicable to human. There are five generations of computer language. The history of programming language is shown in figure 1.14.

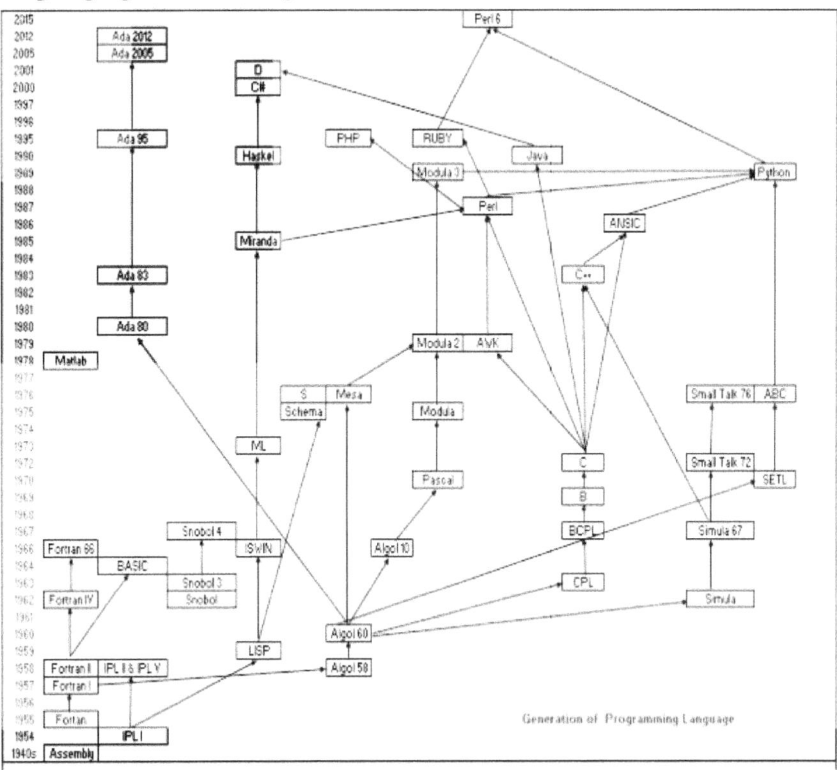

Figure 1.14 History of Programming languages

1.11.1 First generation: (1946 – 1958)

It is the Low-level language used for communication with computer hardware directly. It is written in binary machine code directly. It is written in strings of 0 and 1, the only language the computer understands. This language is hardware dependent.

Machine Language: The only language which is can understand by the computer is machine language. The programs in this language are written in binary code i.e. the combination of binary digits 0 and 1. Machine languages execute the fastest since they are immediately understood by the computer. No translation of the programs is required. Also they make efficient use of primary memory. But it is very difficult to program in this binary or machine language. It is also very tedious and time consuming, since all the instructions have to represent as a series of 0s and 1 s. Therefore there is always a possibility of errors.

Example:

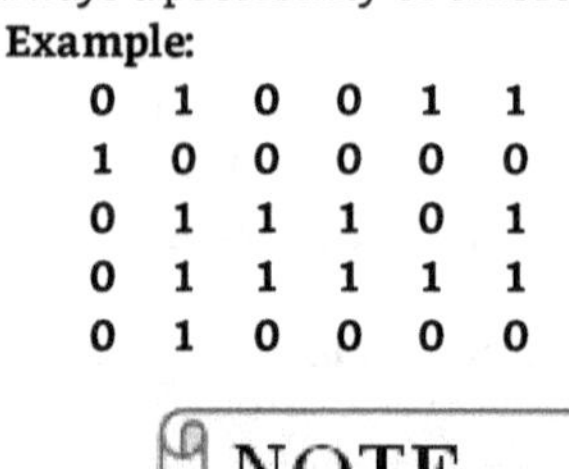

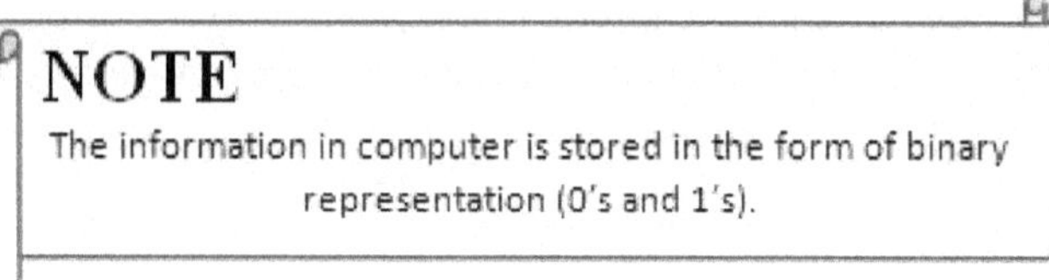

1.11.2 Second generation: (1959 – 1964)

2GL is Procedural Languages which use mnemonic system for representing machine instructions. The 2GL programming language is an assembly language. This language is hardware dependent. Translate instruction into machine operation codes (op-codes). The table 1.7 shows the binary code and Hexadecimal code for the Opcode and operand.

Example:

MOV C, A

ADD B

HLT

Opcode	Operand	Binary code	Hex code
MOV	C,A	0100 1111	4FH
ADD	B	1000 0000	80H
HLT		0111 0110	76H

Table 1.7: Opcode and operand to binary code and Hex code

Assembly Language: The 0s and 1s of the machine language were substituted by letters and symbols in assembly languages. The assembly languages use mnemonics in place of operation codes. The language uses symbols instead of numbers to write programs. A program written using such symbols in the assembly language is called the source program. The program written in assembly language has to be converted into machine language for the computer. To translate the assembly language to machine language, system program assembler is used. Each assembly language instruction is converted into a corresponding machine code using assembler. It is easy to write programs in assembly language when compared to machine language and can be easily modified. However, like the machine language, assembly languages are also hardware dependant.

1.11.3 Third generation (1954-1990)

3GL is a procedural Language and is mostly Machine independent. This generation use interpreter and compiler to translate to machine language. Some of the third generation languages are FORTRAN, COBOL, C, BASIC, C++, Pascal, and java. Some languages supported by compiler are FORTRAN, COBOL. Some languages are supported by Interpreter are Java, BASIC, JVM (Java virtual machine), Python. The table 1.8 shows the description of third generation languages.

NAME	YEAR	DESCRIPTION
FORTRAN (FORmula TRANslator)	1954-1958	It is used to represent complex mathematical formula.
COBOL: (COmmon Business Oriented Language)	1960	It is used in Business for large complex data files. It is a classical procedural language. It introduced the data structure record. It was designed especially for business applications.
BASIC (Beginners All-purpose Symbolic Instruction Code)	1964	It is easy to learn and uses little memory. It also creates complex report quickly. BASIC is one of one most popular language for use in microcomputer systems. The BASIC can be used for both scientific and business applications.
Pascal	1970	It was named from Blaise Pascal, French mathematician. The features of PASCAL allow it to be used for both scientific and business applications. It is a very powerful language.
C	1972	It is efficient code and it is the language of UNIX. The C is the successor of programming language B, which is the successor of BCPL. It was developed by Dennis Ritchie. It is a block structured language which allows the use of various concepts of structured programming. C is also very portable. C is the most popular language used for systems programming like designing compilers and operating systems.
C++ (Enhancement of C)	1981-1986	C++ uses both Object Oriented and structured code.
Java (coffee)	1991	Java is Cross-platform which use object oriented concept. In the year 1994 it has been rewritten for Internet and renamed as Java.

Table 1.8: Third generation languages

1.11.4 Fourth generation: (1971 – today)

4GL is a very high level language. It is a Standard Query Languages which retrieve information from databases. It is Easy to learn and use. It is a Nonprocedural Languages. Types of fourth generation are Database Query Languages, Decision Support Systems, Statistics, Simulation, Optimization, Decision Analysis, Presentation Graphics Systems, etc. Unlike procedural languages which require that a programmer writes all the steps to complete the program and generate output, which are related to a more structural approach towards programming. It is the first standardized language.

SQL: Structured Query Language (SQL) a typical Data Base Management System (DBMS) allows users to store, access, and modify data in an organized, efficient way. Originally, the users of DBMSs were programmers.

1.11.5 Fifth generation: (Today to future)

5GL is a Nonprocedural Natural language. Some of the examples of fifth-generation languages of 5GL are Prolog, OPS5 and Mercury.

PROLOG: The Prolog is a general-purpose logic programming language. It is associated with computational linguistics and artificial intelligence. Prolog is derived from first-order logic, has a formal logic not like many other programming languages. This language has been used for expert systems, theorem proving, term rewriting, automated planning and type-inference.

1.12 SOFTWARE

Software is a collection of data and instructions which is responsible for controlling and managing the hardware components to accomplish a specified task. Software can be classified as two

- System Software
- Application Software

1.12.1 System Software

These are collection of data or instruction used to run the computer systems. This software is not always noticed by the user as they interact basically with the hardware and application directly. They are:

- Operating System
- Device Drivers
- Language Translators
- System Utilities.

i) Operating System

OS acts as the main interface between the user and the hardware. They are the first set of software loaded into the main memory during startup. There functionalities include device management, memory management, CPU management etc.

Examples: Windows, LINUX, IOS.

ii) Device Drivers

A device driver acts as the translator between a device and the operating system. When we connect a new device into the system, the device drivers detect it and install necessary driver software so that the device can function smoothly. The failure of the device driver results in malfunction of the device.

Examples: Printer driver software, Wi-Fi driver software.

iii) Language Translators

The language translator helps to convert the high level language into machine language as the computer by its nature understands only machine language consisting of 0s and 1s. The language translators are classified into 3 types:

a) **Compiler:** The compiler converts the source code or the high level language into binary form or machine language.

b) **Interpreter:** The interpreter does the translation of high level code to machine code and executes the program line by line.

c) **Assembler:** The program in assembly language is converted into machine language by the help of assembler.

iv) System Utility

The day to day tasks related to the maintenance of the computer are carried out by system utility programs. They are responsible for securing and maintaining the rest of the system activities like time, date, help etc.

1.12.2 Application Software

Application software is the ones which the user interacts with the most and is used to accomplish a specific task. They are available in packages or just as a single program. The most common application software's are MS-Office Suite, Adobe Photoshop, Microsoft word, Microsoft excel, etc.

SUMMARY

- A computer is an electronic device that can accept data as input, process the data and produce information as output, and store the information for future use.
- The basic characteristics of computer include speed, accuracy, reliable, storage capacity, versatile, diligence and sharing.
- The basic operations in a computer includes – input, output, process and storage.
- First generation computers were vacuum tubes based machines. These were huge size.
- Second generation computers were transistor based machines. They used the stored program concept.
- Third generation computers were characterized based on the use of IC. They required low maintenance and consumed less power compared to their predecessors.
- Fourth generation computers used microprocessors which is designed using the VLSI and LSI technology. The computers became portable, small, reliable and cheap.
- Fifth generation computers are capable of learning in its own and self organization. They use parallel processing and are based on Artificial Intelligence.
- Based on their sizes and types computers are broadly classified as minicomputers, microcomputers, mainframe computers, and supercomputers.
- Computers are used in various areas such as advertising, medicine, education, entertainment, sports, government, science and engineering, office and home.
- System Software and Application Software are two categories of Software.
- Operating System (OS) intermediates between user of computer and computer hardware. Windows XP, Windows 7, UNIX, MS-DOS and Mac OS X, are some examples of OS.
- Translator is used to convert a program written in high-level language and assembly language into machine language. Compiler, Assembler, and interpreter are the three kinds of translator software.

- The components of computer consist of input devices, CPU, output devices and memory.
- Program is a set of instructions to a computer to perform a specific task. The process of telling computers what to do is known as Programming.
- The types of programming language are high level language, machine language, and assembly language.

REVIEW QUESTIONS

1. What is computer?
2. What are the characteristics of computer?
3. What is data and information?
4. What are the components of computer?
5. What are the categories of computer?

6. What are the generations of computer? Explain briefly.
7. Differentiate RAM and ROM.
8. Write down the advantages of computer.
9. What are devices? What are its types?
10. Explain static RAM and Dynamic RAM.
11. What is program? Explain about programming languages.
12. What are the generations of programming languages?
13. What is memory? Explain its types.
14. What are the types of software?
15. Explain about system software and application software with example.
16. Explain about Von Neumann architecture.
17. What is translator? What is its type?
18. Differentiate compiler and interpreter.
19. What are the types of system software?
20. Give some example for application software.

MUTIPLE CHOICE QUESTIONS

1. Who is known as father of computer?
   a. Blaise Pascal
   b. John Von Neumann
   c. Charles Babbage
   d. Mark
2. The processed data is known as __________.
   a. datum
   b. Information
   c. Process
   d. Instruction
3. Which is the only language understand to computer?
   a. Assembly language
   b. Human language
   c. Binary language
   d. High level language
4. Which of the following is known as permanent storage?
   a. Primary storage
   b. Secondary storage
   c. All the above
   d. None of these
5. How the memory of computer is measured?
   a. Bytes
   b. Hertz
   c. Watt
   d. None of these
6. Which of the following convert assembly language into machine language?
   a. Compiler
   b. Interpreter
   c. Assembler
   d. None of these
7. Which of the following act as main interface between the user and the hardware?

     a. CPU
     b. Memory
     c. Hardware
     d. Operating system
8. What hardware is used in first generation of computer?
     a. Vacuum tubes
     b. Integrated circuits
     c. Transistors
     d. Microprocessors
9. Which is the first machine used the stored program concept?
     a. UNIVAC I
     b. EDVAC
     c. ENIAC
     d. MARK I
10. Which of the following is the first general purpose commercially available computer?
     a. UNIVAC I
     b. ENIAC
     c. Analytical Engine
     d. EDSAC

TRUE OR FALSE

1. Computer processes the data into information and store the information for future use.
2. Information is a collection of raw facts.
3. The computer can read and understand any languages.
4. In memory 1 byte is equal to 8 bits.
5. Computer only understands 0's and 1's.
6. The transistor is the hardware used in fifth generation of computer.
7. The process of writing the program by using some programming language is known as programming.
8. The ROM is the secondary storage memory.
9. The first generation computers are bulky and emit more heat.
10. Supercomputers used transistor technology.
11. The CPU can only execute the instructions which are in binary form.

FILL IN THE BLANKS

1. Computer is a __________ device.
2. __________ accept data as input then process the data and produce information as output.
3. The set of instruction to perform certain task is known as __________.
4. The process of writing the program is known as __________.
5. The speed of the computer is calculated in __________.
6. __________ is used to translate source program into machine language.
7. The __________ architecture is known as stored program architecture.
8. The ALU is for __________ and __________ operations.
9. The __________ and __________ are the primary memory.
10. __________ is known as brain of the computer.

ANSWERS

MUTIPLE CHOICE QUESTIONS
1. c
2. b
3. c
4. b
5. a
6. c
7. d
8. a
9. b
10. a

TRUE OR FALSE
1. True
2. False
3. False
4. True
5. True
6. False
7. True
8. False
9. True
10. True
11. True

FILL IN THE BLANKS
1. electronic
2. Computer
3. program
4. programming
5. Hertz
6. Translator
7. Von Neumann
8. arithmetic, logic
9. RAM, ROM
10. CPU

CHAPTER 2: INTRODUCTION TO PROBLEM SOLVING

A problem can be divided into two phases such as problem solving phase and Implementation phase. The problem solving phase produces an ordered sequence of steps that describe solution of problem. This sequence of steps is called an algorithm. The implementation phase is implementing the program in some programming language. This chapter discusses about the problem solving phase and various strategies solve the problem. This chapter includes methodologies, design, building blocks and concepts such as flowchart, algorithm and pseudocode.

CHAPTER OUTLINE

Algorithm – Flow chart – Pseudocode – programming language Control flow – Function– Sequence – Selection – Iteration – Recursion – Algorithmic problem solving – Strategies for developing algorithm

OBJECTIVE

After covering the chapter, the student will be in a position:

- To create an ability to design algorithmic solution to problem.
- To understand the basics of algorithmic problem solving
- To learn about algorithm and notations
- To know about characteristics of an algorithm and method for developing an algorithm
- To known the guidelines to develop algorithm, its advantage and disadvantages
- Flowchart, notations advantages, disadvantage and guidelines to create flow-

chart
- Strategies for developing an algorithm

2.1 PROBLEM SOLVING

The process of analyzing, understanding and solving the problem is known as problem solving. The problem solving includes activities such as:

Step 1: Analyzing the problem

Step 2: Understanding the problem

Step 3: Generating algorithms for the problem

Step 4: Verifying the algorithm that whether all the requirements of the problem are met.

Step 5: Finally the algorithm is implemented by using some programming language.

2.2 ALGORITHM

The term algorithm was derived from the name **Mohammed ibn-Musa al-Khwarizmi**, a mathematician in the ninth century who created algorithm. In Latin Al-Khwarizmi is known as Algorismus later it is changed as Algorithm. It is often used for calculation, data processing and programming. Algorithms can be expressed in any language.

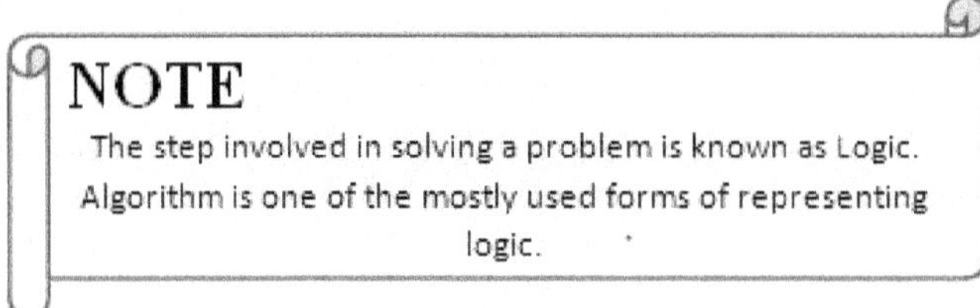

Algorithm is a sequence of steps that tells us how to do something. Algorithm gives the logic of the program that is a step-by-step description of how to arrive at a solution. An algorithm provides a blueprint for writing a problem and to solve a particular problem. In general, Algorithm is a set of instruction for performing a task. Algorithm is a procedural solution to problems. The solutions of algorithm are not answers but specific instructions for getting answers. Algorithm is a procedure or formula for solving that problem.

The step of algorithm are finite in number, has sequential flow and unambiguous. It follows English like representation. Algorithms for making things will often be divided into sections; Input, process, output. The parts/ components/ ingredients required to accomplish the task is known as input. The actions/ steps/ methods are known as processing and the required outcome is the output.

Example:

To build a model of a car the parts (Inputs) are needed, instructions on how to assemble the car (Processing) and the result is the car (Output).

2.2.1 Rules for writing step by step algorithm
- Algorithm is a step by step procedure, should be in sequence

- Use start and stop to begin and terminate the process
- Should be finite
- Follows English like representation
- Should be well defined

Example:

Algorithm to find greatest among three numbers

Step 1: Start
Step 2: Read three number A, B, C
Step 3: Compare A is greater than B and A is greater than C. If A is greater, Print A is greater else perform step 4.
Step 4: Compare B is greater than C. If B is greater Print B is greater else Print C is greater
Step 5: Stop

This algorithm follows sequential logic and from step 3 selection logic is followed by using IF-ELSE construct.

2.2.2 Features of Algorithm

- Algorithm should be written in sequence.
- Instructions are finite in number.
- It looks like normal English.
- Each instruction in an algorithm is well defined.
- An algorithm describes a process that eventually halts after arriving at a solution to a problem.

2.2.3 Characteristics of algorithm

- Specific: The algorithm should be precise. After the algorithm gets terminated, desired result must be obtained.
- Definite: The algorithm should be clear and unambiguous.
- Finiteness: It has finite number of steps.
- Effectiveness: It takes less time and memory.
- Generality: It should be applied for different set of inputs.
- Correctness: Good algorithm is measured by using its efficiency and correctness.
- Language independent: We can convert algorithm into any programming language.

2.2.4 Representation of Algorithm

An algorithm can be represented in following ways:

- Normal English
- Flowcharts
- Pseudo code
- Programming language

2.2.5 Advantages of algorithm

- It is step by step procedure to solve problem, so it is easy to understand.
- It is not depended on programming language.

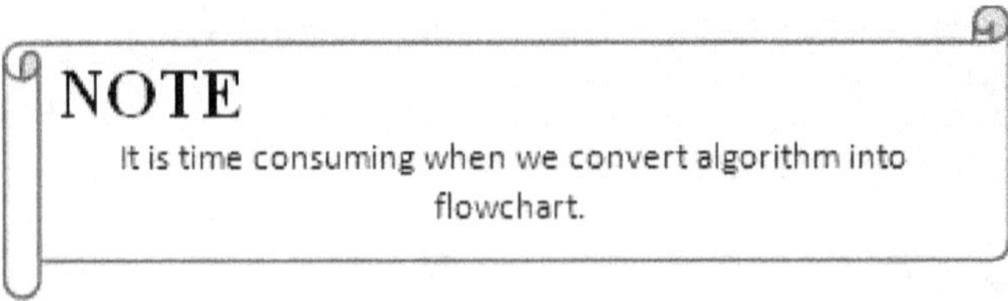

2.3 NOTATION DEVELOPING ALGORITHMS

Notation is a set of characters, expressions, symbols, designs used in problem solving to represent technical facts. There are various notations for developing a program:

- Pseudo code
- Flow chart
- Programming language

2.3.1 Pseudocode

Pseudocode looks like programming language but it is not a real programming code. Pseudocode is a formal design tool developed with the structural programming. The pseudocode is also known as Program Design Language (PDL). It is also known as False code because it has some resemblance to real code. Pseudocode is a type of structured English that is used for describing an algorithm. Pseudocode can be neither compiled nor executed. Keywords used in pseudocode are,

- Start and Finish - BEGIN MAINPROGRAM and END MAINPROGRAM, or simply BEGIN and END
- Initialization - SET, INITIALIZE, INITIALIZATION and END INITIALIZATION
- Subprogram - BEGIN SUBPROGRAM and END SUBPROGRAM
- Selection - IF, THEN, ELSE, ENDIF
- Repetition - WHILE, END WHILE, FOR, END FOR
- Input - READ, GET, OBTAIN, PROMPT
- Output - PRINT, SHOW, DISPLAY
- Process - COMPUTE, DTERMINE, CALCULATE

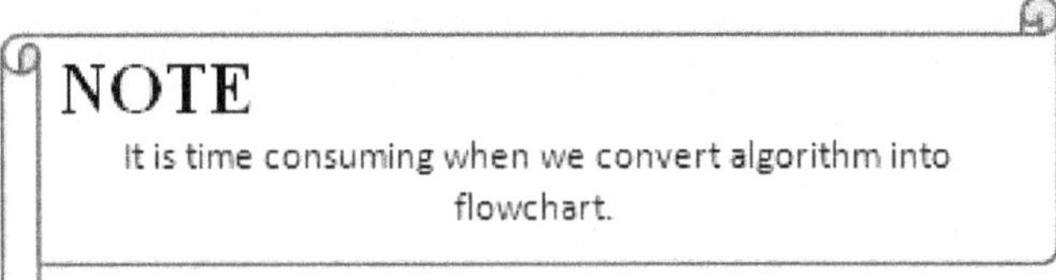

Rules for writing pseudocode:

- Statement should be written in English
- Write one statement per line.
- Capitalize the keywords.
- Indent to show hierarchy
- End multiline structure
- It should follow top to bottom approach.

Example: Pseudocode to add two numbers

```
BEGIN
    READ a,b
```

```
    add=a+b
    WRITE add
END
```
Example: Pseudocode to find greatest among two numbers
```
BEGIN
    READ a,b
    IF (a>b) THEN
        PRINT a is greater
    ELSE
        PRINT b is greater
    ENDIF
END
```
Advantages:

- It is language independent.
- It is done easily in any word processor
- Converting pseudocode to programming language is very easy as compared with flowcharts.
- It helps even non-programmers to understand the logic of the designed solution.
- It is easy to modify

Disadvantages:

- It is not visual representation.
- It does not have any standardized style or format.
- For beginner, it is more difficult to follow the logic or write pseudocode.

2.3.2 Flowchart

Flowchart is a diagrammatic or symbolic representation of process that illustrates the sequence of operations to be performed to arrive at a solution. It is pictorial representation of an algorithm. It uses different shaped symbols to denote different appropriate instructions. It is basically used to design and document processes to help the viewers to visualize the logic of the process, so that they get better understanding of the process.

The process of drawing flowchart is known as flowcharting. Flowcharting has many standard symbols. The actual instruction is written in the box. Flowchart uses different shaped symbols to denote the instructions and it is connected by lines having arrows to indicate the flow of operations. The boxes which are used in flowcharts are standardized to have specific meanings. These flowchart symbols have been standardized by the American National Standards Institute (ANSI). The following are the flowchart symbols:

NAME	SYMBOL	SHAPE	DESCRIPTION
Flow lines		Lines having arrow head	The flow line indicates the exact sequence or direction in which the statements flow or executed. An arrow comes from one symbol and ends at another symbol.
Terminal symbol	Start Stop	Oval shape	Terminators show the start and end of the process. This symbol is always placed at the beginning and ends of the flowchart.
Input/ Output Symbol		Parallelogram	This is also known as Data. This is used for both input (read) and output (write). It is used to denote any function of an I/O device in the program.
Process		Rectangle	This is used for calculations and initialization of memory locations. This indicates the process or action.
Decision	False True	Diamond	It is used for decision making and branching statements. It is used to indicate a point at which decision has to be made. It has one entry and 2 exits.
Connectors	n n	Circle and a letter or digit inside	Letter or digit is placed inside the circle to specify the link. Connectors are used when the flowchart is exceeds more than one page.

NOTE

The direction of flow in flow chart should always be from left to right or from top to bottom.

Additional symbols:

NAME	SYMBOL	DESCRIPTION
Document	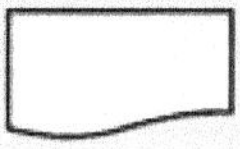	It specifies that either input to the process or output from the process is in the form of printed document.
Display		It is used to show output in the monitor.
Magnetic disk		It is used for data storage location (database)
Predefined process		This denotes predefined process (subroutines). This symbol is commonly used for subprograms.
Sort		It is used to specify a process that arranges a specific set of items in sequence. To arrange in order.
Merge	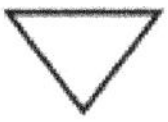	It is used to combine one or more items together.
Manual Input		It denotes input given by the user manually.
Off page connector		To create a hyperlink and cross-reference from a process on one page to another page.

Guidelines for drawing flowchart:

- Start with Terminal symbol 'start'.

- Give input by using the input symbol.

- Process should be mentioned by using process symbol.

- Display output by using the output symbol.

- End with the terminal symbol 'end'.

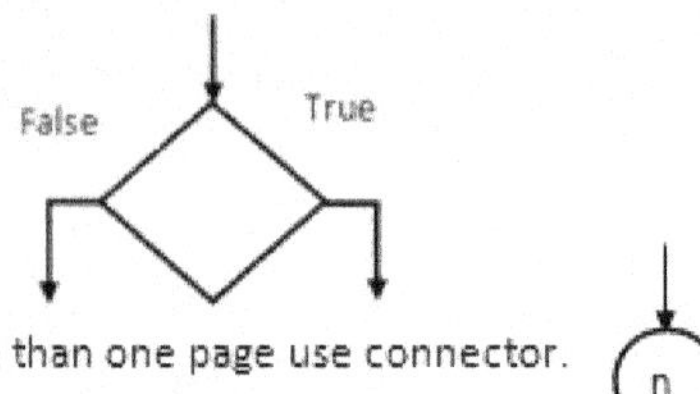

- If there is a possibility of multiple solution use decision symbol. It should have only one input and two or more output.

- If the program continue in more than one page use connector.

- Use proper flowchart symbol wherever necessary.

Advantages:

- Can understand logic clearly.
- It uses various standard symbols for better readability and understandability.
- Better communication
- Effective Analysis and coding
- Proper program documentation
- Effective program maintenance
- Good visual clarity
- The process can be explained clearly by using various symbols.

Disadvantages:

- For complex logic, it is difficult to use
- Drawing flowchart is a time consuming process
- For alteration and modifications, flowchart may require redrawing completely
- For large application the time and cost of drawing flowchart becomes high.
- Over usage of symbols may leads to confusion.
- Updating the flowchart is difficult.

Example:

Flowchart to add two numbers

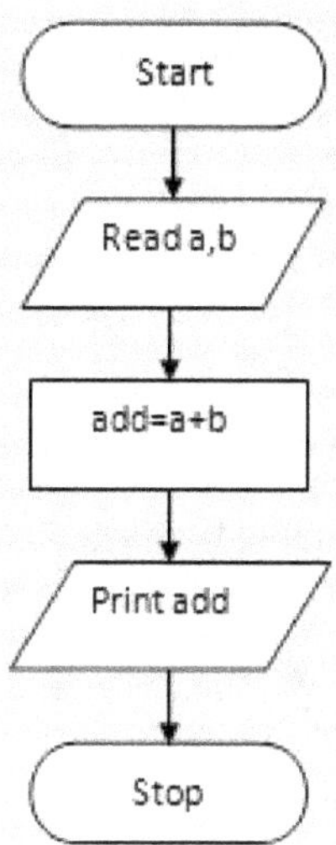

NOTE

The flowchart can also be drawn using Raptor. Raptor is a flowchart based programming environment.

Example: Flowchart to find greatest among two numbers

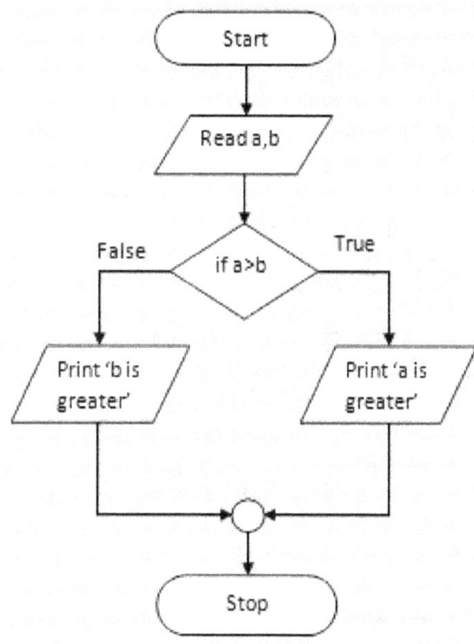

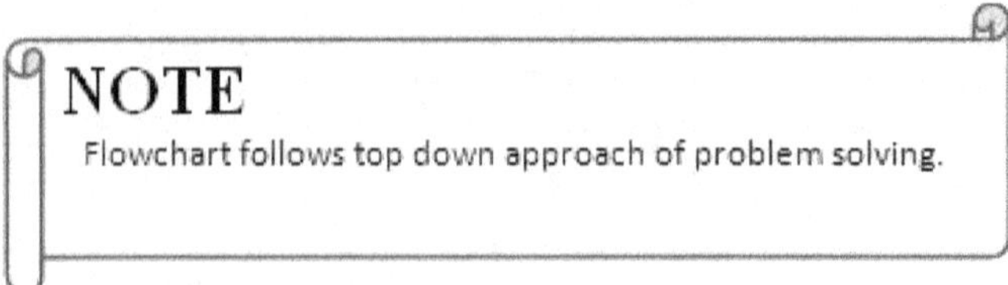

2.3.3 Programming Languages

Computer won't understand algorithm, so algorithms are translated into code. This code is written in programming languages. There are many programming languages available. Some of them are C, C++, java, Python, etc. In this book, programming is done using python programming language. Programming languages are categorized into many types.

1. **Interpreted programming languages:**
   - BASIC (Beginner's All Purpose Symbolic Instruction Code)
   - Lisp (List processing language)
   - Pascal (procedural programming language)
   - python (Interpreted programming language)
   - REXX (Restructured Extended Executor)
   - Perl (High level interpreted programming language)
2. **Functional programming languages:**
   - clean (purely functional programming language)
   - curry (functional logic programming language)
   - f# (both functional and iterative object oriented programming)
   - Haskell (purely functional language)
   - Q (interpreted functional language)
3. **Compiled programming language:**
   - Ada (structured language based on Pascal)
   - ALGOL (Algorithmic Language)
   - C (procedural and general purpose language)
   - C++ (Object oriented Language)
   - C# (multi-paradigm programming language)
   - COBOL (Common Business Oriented Language)
   - Fortran (General purpose and procedural language)
   - Java (general purpose, object oriented language)
   - VB (Event driven programming language)
4. **Procedural programming language:**
   - CLIST (Procedural programming language)
   - Hyper Talk (high level programming language)
   - Modula-2 (General purpose procedural language)
   - MATLAB
   - PL/I
5. **Scripting Language:** The scripting languages are Apple Script. Awt, PHP, VB Script, Windows powershell
6. **Markup Language:** The markup languages such as Curl, HTML, XML, XHTML, SGML
7. **Logic based programming language:** The logic based programming such as Fril, prolog
8. **Concurrent programming language:** Concurrent programming languages such

as ABCL (Actor-Based Concurrent Language), Concurrent Pascal, E, Joule, etc.

9. **Object oriented language:** The object oriented language such as Agora, BETA, Moto, Object-Z, REBOL (Relative Expression Based object Language), Scala, Lava, etc.

2.4 BUILDING BLOCKS OF ALGORITHM

Algorithm can be designed using the below basic methods.

- Statements
- State
- Control Flows
- Functions

2.4.1 Statement

Each and every line in an algorithm is known as statements. It is also known as instruction.

Example:

Read two numbers 'a' and 'b'

Add 'a' and 'b'

2.4.2 State

How the stored data will be, in each processing time or in a particular time period this is known as state of a value or variable. State shows the current value or contents.

Example: For addition of two numbers

Read two numbers 'a' and 'b' -> Reading state

Add 'a' and 'b' result=a+b -> Processing state

Print result -> Output state

In time period 1(t1) 'a' and 'b' are in reading state, in time period 2(t2) 'a' and 'b' are in processing state and in period 3(t3) 'a' and 'b' are in output state.

2.4.3 Control Flow

Control flow (Flow of control) is the order in which individual statement, instruction or function of algorithm is executed. This logic is used for creating loops in program logic, when one or more instructions want to be executed several times or depending on some conditions. Normally an algorithm has three control flows:

- Sequence (Sequential control)
- Selection (condition Control)
- Iteration (Repetition)

2.4.3.1 Sequence

A sequence is a series of steps that occur one after other, in same order every time. Steps are executed in sequence that follow top to bottom or left to right approach.

Example:

Algorithm for addition of two numbers

Step 1: Start

Step 2: Read two numbers 'a' and 'b'
Step 3: Add two numbers, Set sum= a+b
Step 4: Print Sum.
Step 5: Stop

This algorithm follows sequential order to add two numbers. These steps process one after other in same order.

2.4.3.2 Selection

A selection is a decision that has to be made. In selection only one alternative steps is executed based on the condition. Selection is a decision making process.

Example:

Algorithm to find greatest among two numbers

Step 1: Start
Step 2: Read two numbers 'a' and 'b'.
Step 3: If 'a' is greater than 'b' go to step 4 else go to step 5
Step 4: print 'a' is greater go to step 6
Step 5: Print 'b' is greater.
Step 6: Stop.

This algorithm follows IF-ELSE construct to find greatest among two numbers. If the condition is true step 4 is executed else step 5 gets executed. This type of flow of control is known as selection.

2.4.3.3 Repetition

Repetition means a set of steps which are repeated over and over until some event occurs. It is commonly known as iteration. Set of steps processed again and again until the conditions fails. 'FOR' loop and 'WHILE' loop are used to perform iteration.

Example:

Compute and print average of ten numbers

Step 1: Start
Step 2: Initialize total=0 and i = 0
Step 3: While i =<10
    Step 3.1: Read number 'n'
    Step 3.2: total = total + n
Step 4: Calculate average, average= total/10
Step 5: Print average
Step 6: Stop

This algorithm follows repetition of step 3.1 and step 3.2 until step 3 fails. This type of flow of control is known repetition or iteration.

2.4.4 Functions

Function is a block of organized, reusable code that is used to perform some related action. Function provides better modularity and high degree of code reusability. Function is mainly for breaking problem into sub problems. Function is also known as methods, subroutines, procedures.

Pseudocode   Flowchart

BEGIN subprogram

    Statement(s)

END subprogram

Example:

Algorithm to find factorial of a number using function

Step 1: Start
Step 2: Read number 'n'
Step 3: Call factorial(n)
Step 4: Print factorial
Step 5: Stop
Subroutine; factorial(n)
Step 1: factorial(a)
Step 1.1: If a = =1 then return 1 else go to step 1.2
Step 1.2: return a*factorial(n-1)
    In this above algorithm factorial(n) is a function call that calls factorial(a). This is used for code reusability.

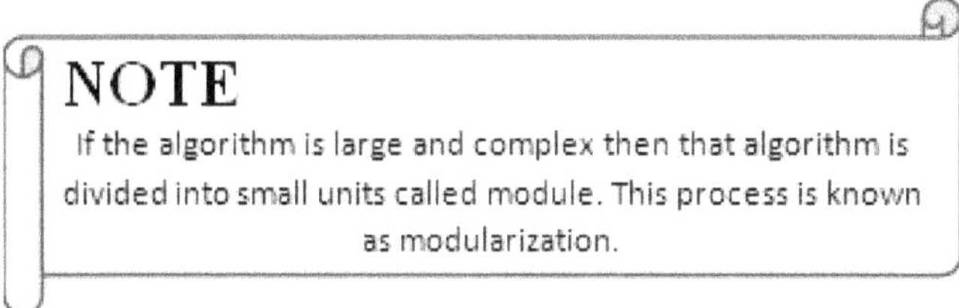

2.5 METHODOLOGIES / APPROACHES FOR DESIGNING ALGORITHM

There are two main methodologies or approaches used to design an algorithm. They are:

- Top down approach
- Bottom up approach

2.5.1 Top down approach

This approach starts from top to bottom dividing the algorithm. In this approach a complex or large problems are divided into one or more modules or function. This process of diving large problem into some small modules is called as modularization. This makes the complex problem easy to design and implement. The flowchart follow top down approach of solving the problem.

2.5.2 Bottom up approach

This approach is the reverse of top down approach which starts from bottom and move towards the top of the algorithm. This algorithm groups or combine all the sub modules or function to form a final algorithm.

2.6 ALGORITHMIC PROBLEM SOLVING

Algorithm is a procedural solution to problems. It is not answers for the problem. It is about formulation and solution where the solution includes possibly implicitly, the principles and techniques that have been developed to assist in construction of correct algorithm. The steps that are taken in consideration for solving a problem are,

- Define the problem in very simple and precise language.
- Analyze the problem to find out different solution for the problem
- Evaluate all the possible solution and choose the best possible solution
- Clearly define the step by step procedure for the chosen solution
- Finally, write these procedures in some programming language and execute it

There are many sequences of steps for algorithmic solving problem. They are,

1. Understanding the problem: The Problem given has to be understood completely and clearly. Check if it is similar to some standard problems or existing algorithm. If not exist then a new algorithm has to be developed else make use of the existing one.

2. Find the capabilities of the computational devices: Once problem is understood, we need to know the capabilities of the computing devices such as, speed and memory space of Input and output devices.

3. Finding the solution: The solution or the problem is analyzed. Once algorithm is developed, it is necessary to show that it computes answer for all the possible legal solutions (inputs). The solution may be exact or approximate solution.

4. Decide the data structure: Some algorithms are predicted on ingenious data structure. Basic data structures are arrays, records, sets can also be used, if needed.

5. Selecting the Algorithm Design techniques: Some important design techniques are linear and non linear programming. Dynamic programming is one such technique.

6. Methods of specifying an algorithm: Algorithms can be specified by using natural language, pseudo code and flowcharts. These are the various representation of algorithm.

7. Evaluating algorithms correctness: Once algorithm is developed, it is necessary to show that it computes answer for all the possible legal inputs. This process is known as validation.

8. Analyzing algorithm's performance: As an algorithm is executed, it uses the computer's CPU to perform operation and it memory to hold the program and data. The Analysis is done to determining computing time and storage an algorithm requires. It checks whether the software meet any efficiency constraint that exists.

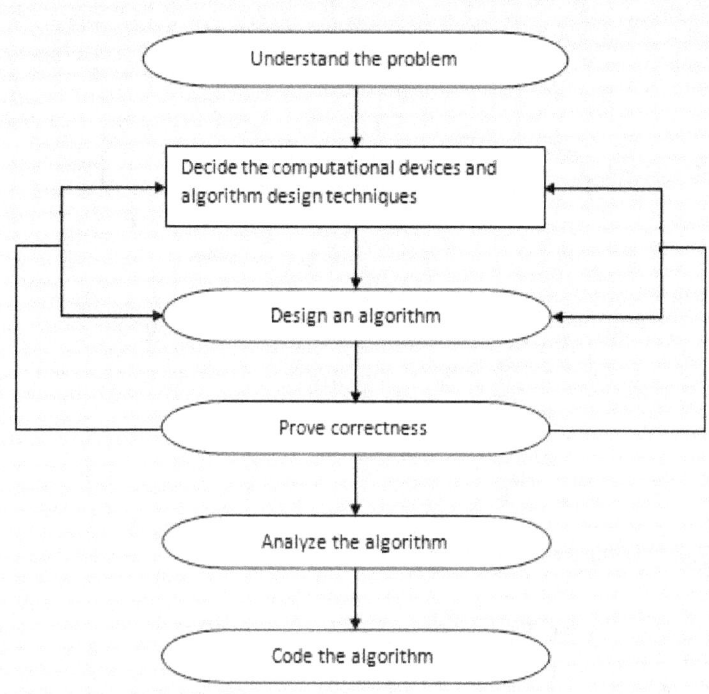

2.7 STRATEGIES FOR DEVELOPING ALGORITHM

The various strategies used for developing algorithms are:

1. Sequence
2. Selection
3. Repetition
   - Iteration
   - Recursion

2.7.1 Sequence

A sequence is a series of steps that occur one after other, in same order every time. Steps are executed in sequence that follow top to bottom or left to right approach. The sequence structure is a case where the steps in an algorithm are constructed in such a way that, no condition step is required.

Pseudocode	Flowchart

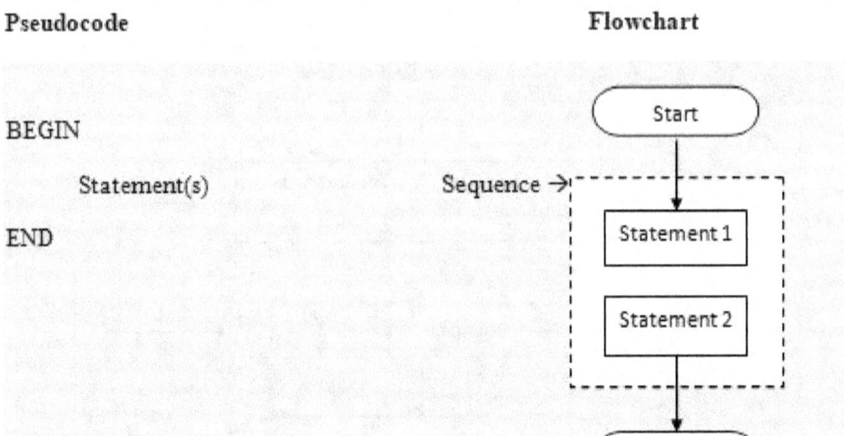

BEGIN

    Statement(s)

END

Example:

Algorithm for addition of two numbers

Step 1: Start
Step 2: Read two numbers 'a' and 'b'
Step 3: Add two numbers, Set sum= a+b
Step 4: Print Sum.
Step 5: Stop

      This algorithm follows sequential order to add two numbers. These steps process one after other in same order.

2.7.2   Selection

      A selection is a decision that has to be made which has many alternative steps. In selection only one alternative steps is executed based on the condition. Selection is a decision making process. This is also known as condition control. The if- else construct is mostly used for these type of control flow. Once the condition is evaluated, the control flows into one of two paths. The selection structures are also known as Case selection structures.

Pseudocode   **Flowchart**

BEGIN

Statement(s)

IF (condition)

       Statement(s)

ELSE

       Statement(s)

ENDIF

END

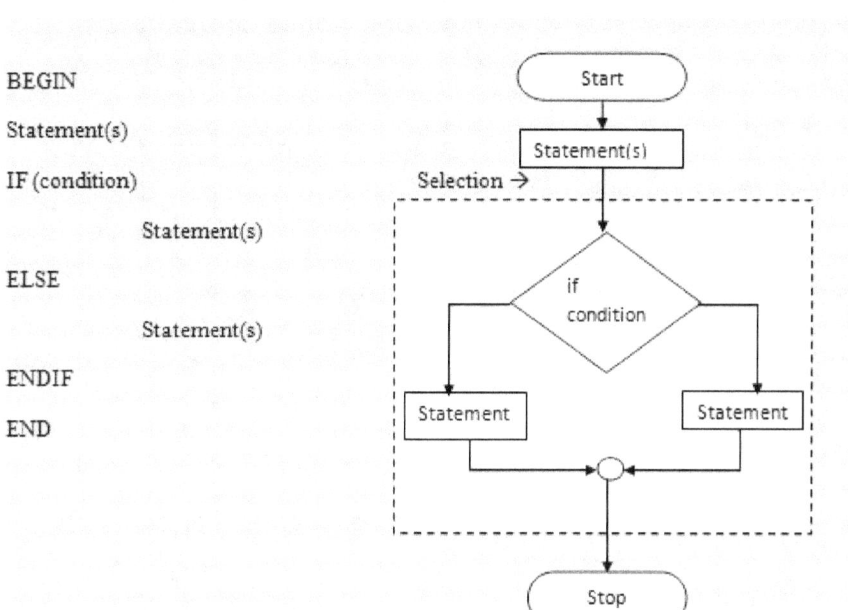

Example:

Algorithm to find greatest among two numbers

Step 1: Start
Step 2: Read two numbers 'a' and 'b'.
Step 3: If 'a' is greater than 'b' go to step 4 else go to step 5
Step 4: print 'a' is greater go to step 6
Step 5: Print 'b' is greater.
Step 6: Stop.

       This algorithm follows IF-ELSE construct to find greatest among two numbers. If the condition is true step 4 is executed else step 5 gets executed. This type of flow of control is known as selection.

2.7.3 Repetition

       Repetition means a set of steps which are repeated over and over until some event occurs. It is commonly known as iteration. Set of steps processed again and again until the conditions fails. 'FOR' loop and 'WHILE' loop are used to perform iteration. It either repeats the processing or the control leaves the structure.

Pseudocode	Flowchart

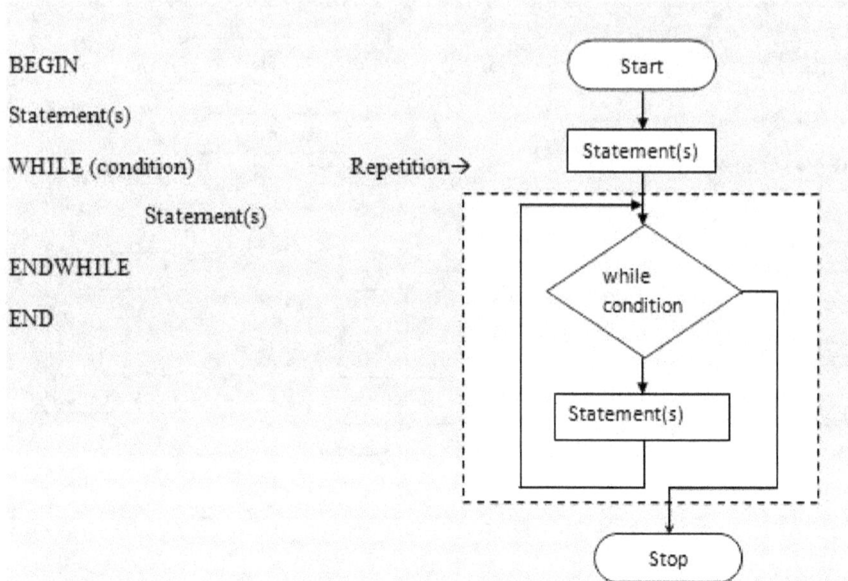

BEGIN

Statement(s)

WHILE (condition)   Repetition→

        Statement(s)

ENDWHILE

END

Example:

Compute and print average of ten numbers

Step 1: Start
Step 2: Initialize total=0 and i = 0
Step 3: While i =<10
    Step 3.1: Read number 'n'
    Step 3.2: total = total + n
Step 4: Calculate average, average= total/10
Step 5: Print average
Step 6: Stop

2.7.3.1 Iteration

Iteration means repetition. It is a repetition of a set statement some particular number of times. Here, a set of steps which are repeated over and over again until some event occurs.

Algorithm for iteration (Syntax)

    Step 1: start
    Step 2: Statement(s)
    Step 3: Use control flow condition. Repeat the step inside the loop till it not satisfy the condition
    Step 4: Statement(s)
    Step 5: Stop
Example:

To find average of 10 numbers

```
BEGIN

     READ a,b

     total=0

     FOR 1 to 10
```

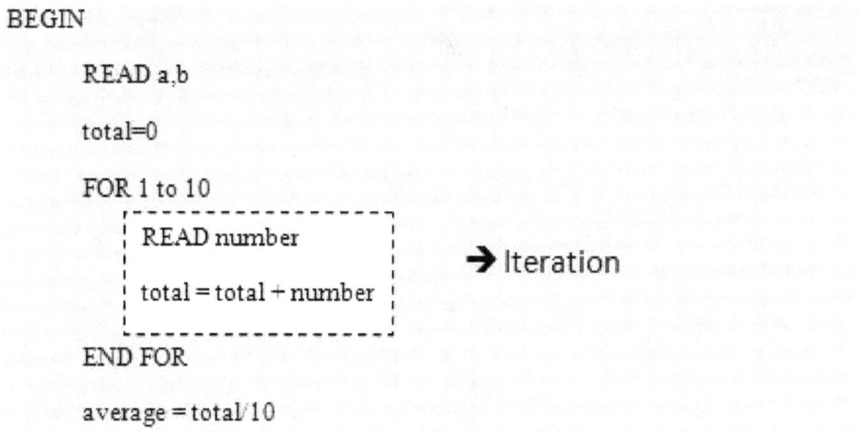


```
     END FOR

     average = total/10

END
```

Repetition of instruction is done till the range of the FOR loop reaches 10. This type of looping is known as iteration.

2.7.3.2 Recursion

A recursion algorithm is an algorithm that calls itself with a value. Function calling itself until the base condition is reached is known as recursion. In recursion there are two cases i.e., Base case and recursive case.

Base Case:

It is a case for which the solution can be stated non-recursively.

Recursive Case:

Recursive case is a case for which the solution can be stated in terms of smaller version of itself.

Algorithm for recursion (Syntax)

Step 1: start
Step 2: Statement(s)
Step 3: call subprogram (argument)
Step 4: Statement(s)
Step 5: stop
Algorithm for subprogram

Step 1: start subprogram (parameter)
        Step 1.1: It Base Case then go to step 1.1.1 else 1.1.2
                Step 1.1.1: return base solution
                Step 1.1.2: return recursive solution, which includes call subprogram
(small version of argument)
Step 2: Stop subprogram
Example:

Algorithm to find factorial of a number using recursive function:

Step 1: start

Step 2: Read number 'n'
Step 3: Call factorial(n) and print factorial
Step 4: Stop
Algorithm for subprogram 'factorial(n)'

Step1: factorial(n)
    Step 1.1: if n = = 1 then go to step 1.1.1 else go to step 1.1.2
        Step 1.1.1: return 1
        Step 1.1.2: return n*factorial(n-1)
Flowchart to find factorial of a number using recursive function

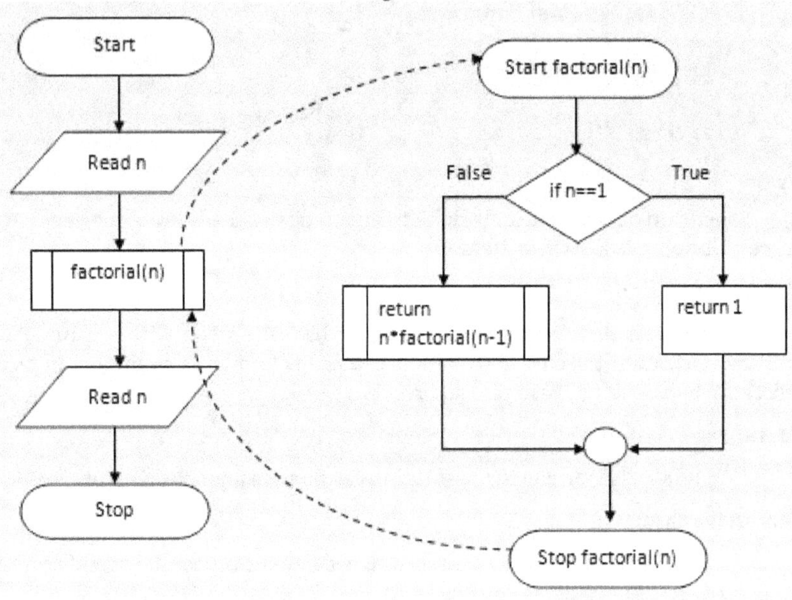

Here, Base case is n = = 1
    Base case solution is return 1
    Recursive case is n = = 1 is false
    Recursive case solution is return n*factorial(n-1)

SUMMARY

•   A problem can be divided into two phases such as problem solving phase and Implementation phase.

•   Algorithm is a sequence of steps that tells us how to do something. Algorithm gives the logic of the program that is a step-by-step description of how to arrive at a solution.

•   Algorithm is often used for calculation, data processing and programming.

•   Pseudocode looks like programming language but it is not a real programming code. Pseudocode is a formal design tool developed with the structural programming.

•   Flowchart is a diagrammatic or symbolic representation of process that illustrates the sequence of operations to be performed to arrive at a solution.

•   Top down approach a complex or large problems are divided into one or more modules. The flowchart follow top down approach of solving the problem.

- A Flowchart is a pictorial or symbolic representation of a solution to a given task.
- Flowchart uses many symbols/ shapes to denote different task of instructions.
- These flowchart symbols have been standardized by the American National Standards Institute (ANSI).
- Computer won't understand your algorithm, so algorithms are translated into code, which the computer understands. This code is written in programming languages.

ILLUSTRATIVE PROGRAMS

1. Write algorithm, pseudocode and flowchart to find product and sum of two numbers and display it.

Algorithm:

Step 1: Start

Step 2: Get two numbers a, b

Step 3: Add two numbers

    sum=a+b

Step 4: Product of two numbers

    product=a*b

Step 5: Display sum, product

Step 6: Stop

Pseudocode:

BEGIN

    READ a,b

    COMPUTE sum=a+b

    COMPUTE product = a*b

    DISPLAY sum, product

END

Flowchart:

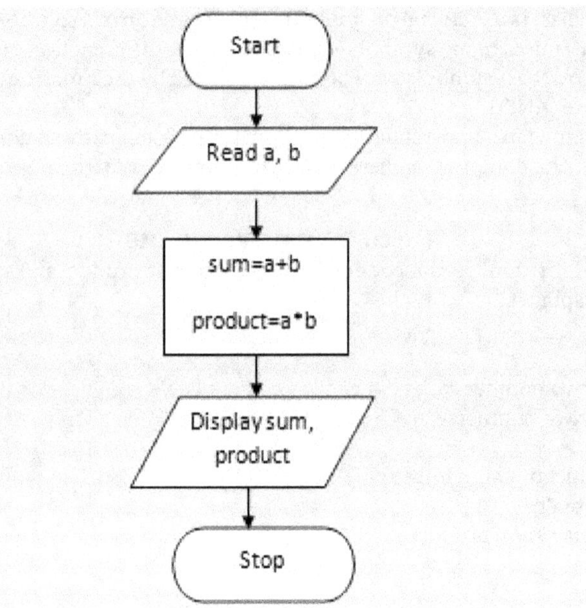

2.   Write an algorithm, pseudocode and flowchart to calculate the roots of a quadratic equation

Algorithm
Step 1:Start
Step 1: Read a, b, c
Step 3: $d = \sqrt{(b \times b - 4 \times a \times c)}$
Step 4: $x1 = (-b + d) / (2 \times a)$
Step 5: $x2 = (-b - d) / (2 \times a)$
Step 6: Print x1, x2
Step 7: Stop

Pseudocode
BEGIN
READ a, b, c
$d = \sqrt{(b \times b - 4 \times a \times c)}$
$x1 = (-b + d) / (2 \times a)$
$x2 = (-b - d) / (2 \times a)$
PRINT x1, x2
END

Flowchart:

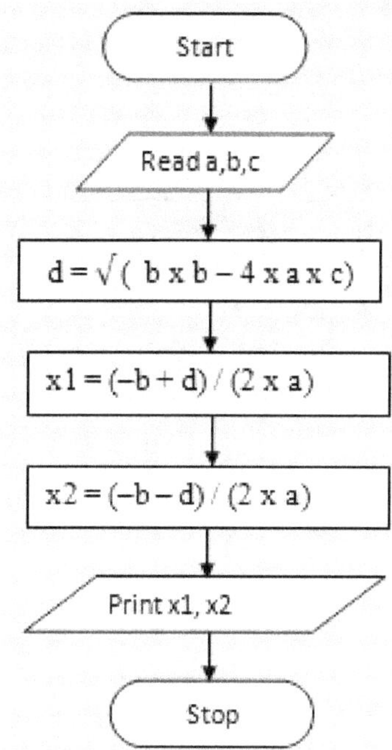

3.   Write an algorithm, pseudocode and flowchart to convert feet to centimeter.

Algorithm:

Step 1: Start

Step 2: Read feet

Step 3: centimeter = feet x 30

Step 4: Print centimeter

Step 5: Stop

Pseudocode:

BEGIN

    READ feet

    centimeter = feet x 30

    PRINT centimeter

END

Flowchart:

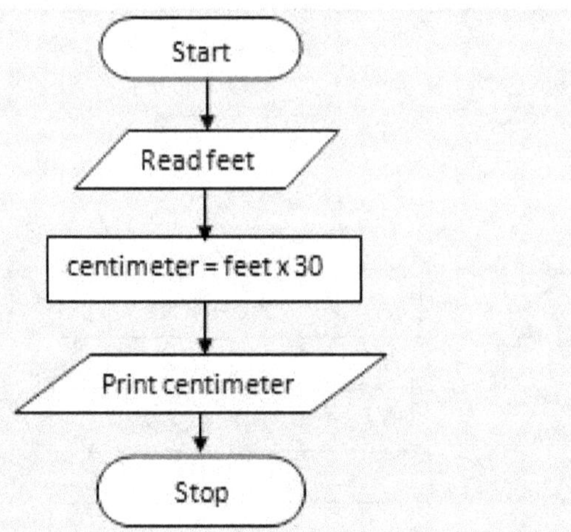

4. Write an algorithm to calculate the average of four marks of a student and indicate whether it is Pass or Fail.

Algorithm:

Step 1: Stop

Step 2: Input M1,M2, M3, M4

Step 3: GRADE = (M1+M2+M3+M4)/4

Step 4: if (GRADE < 50) then Print "FAIL" else perform step 5

Step 5: Print "PASS"

Step 6: Stop

Pseudocode

BEGIN

READ 4 marks M1, M2, M3, M4

 Calculate GRADE = (M1+M2+M3+M4)/4

 IF GRADE < 50

    Print "FAIL"

ELSE

    Print "PASS"

    END IF

END

Flowchart:

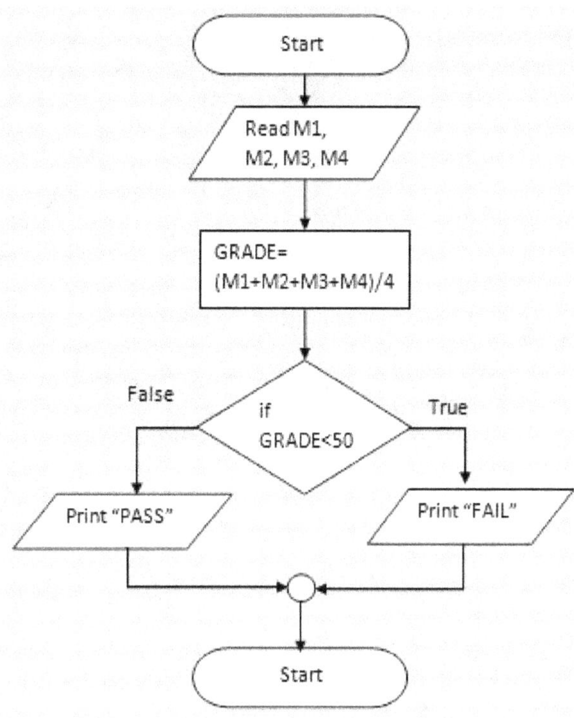

5. Write algorithm, pseudocode and flowchart to swap two numbers

Algorithm:

Step 1:Start

Step 1: Read a, b

Step 3: temp=a

Step 4: a=b

Step 5: b=temp

Step 6: Print swapped values a, b

Step 7: Stop

Pseudocode:

BEGIN

    READ a, b

    temp = a

    a = b

    b = temp

    PRINT a, b

END

Flowchart:

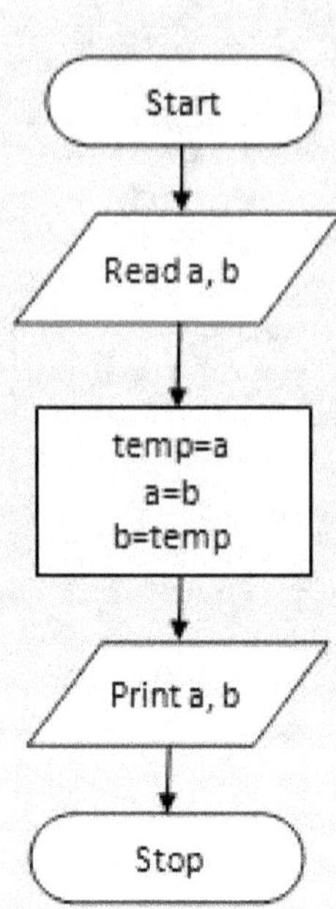

6. Write algorithm, pseudocode and flowchart to convert temperature Celsius to Fahrenheit

Algorithm

Step1: Start

Step 2: Read Temperature in Celsius C

Step 3: F = C*(9/5)+32

Step 4: Print Temperature in Fahrenheit F

Step5: Stop

Pseudocode

BEGIN

    READ Celius C

    F=C*(9/5)+32

    PRINT F

END

Flowchart

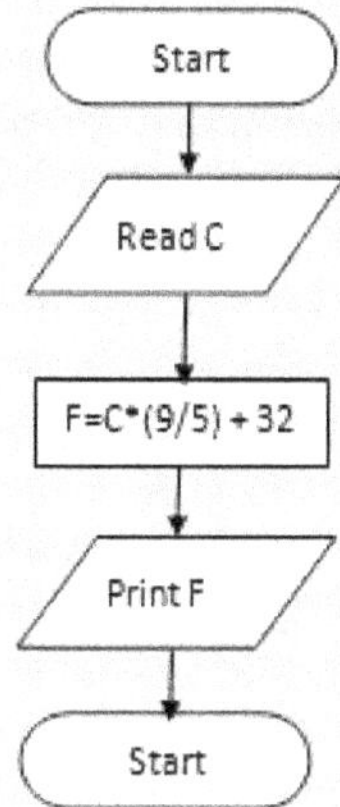

7. Write algorithm, pseudocode and flowchart to find whether the number is odd or even.

Algorithm:

Step 1: Start

Step 2: Read the number n

Step 3: If n is modulo 2 is not equal to zero then Print ODD and go to Step 5else go to Step 4

Step 4: Print EVEN

Step 5: Stop

Pseudocode:

BEGIN

    READ number n

    IF n% 2 != 0 DISPLAY Odd

    ELSE DISPLAY Even

END

Flowchart:

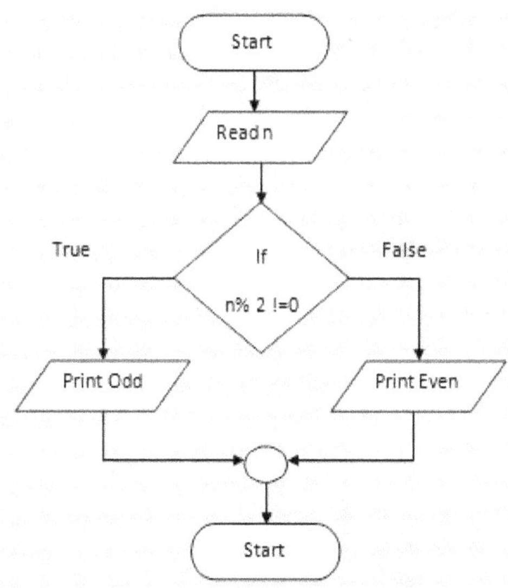

8. Write algorithm, pseudocode and flowchart to find area of circle.

Algorithm:

Step 1: Start

Step 2: Read radius r

Step3: Initialize pi as 3.14

Step 4: Calculate area= pi* r * r

Step 5: Display area

Step 6: Stop

Pseudocode:

BEGIN

    READ r

    INITIALIZE pi=3.14

    area=pi*r*r

    PRINT area

END

Flowchart:

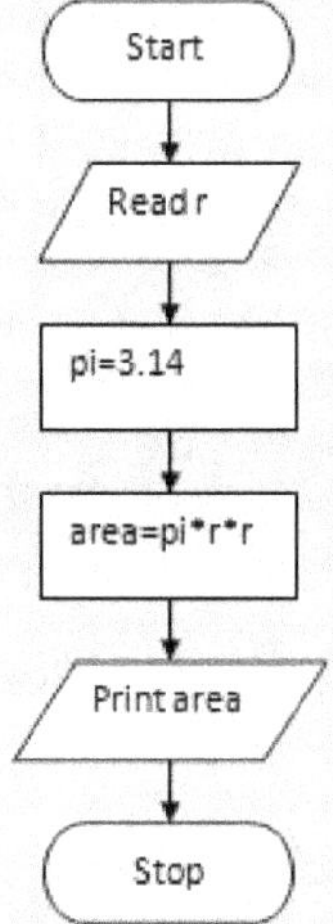

9. Write algorithm, pseudocode and flowchart to find sum of n numbers.

Algorithm:

Step 1: Start

Step 2: Read n

Step 3: sum=0, i=0

Step 4: if i<=n repeat step 5 else go to step 6

Step 5: sum=sum+i

Step 6: i=i+1

Step7: Go to step 4

Step8: Print sum

Step 9: Stop

Pseudocode:

BEGIN

    READ n

    INITIALIZE sum=0, i=0

    REPEAT

```
        sum=sum+i
        i=i+1
        UNTIL i<=n
        PRINT sum
END
```

Flowchart:

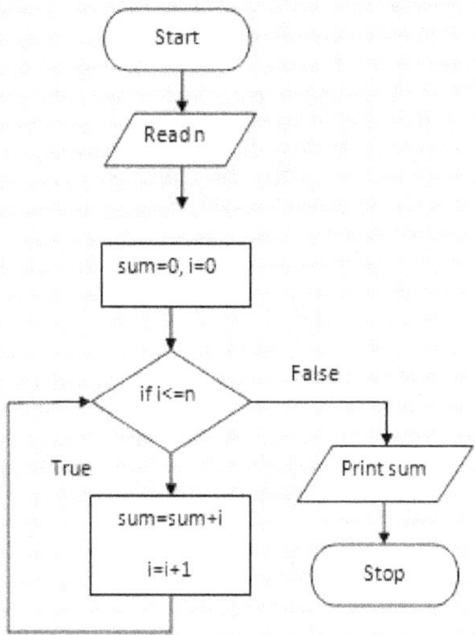

10. Write algorithm, pseudocode and flowchart to find minimum number in a list.

Algorithm:

Step 1: Start
Step 2: Read the total number of elements n
Step 3: Initialize i=0
Step 4: Read the first element and assign it as MIN
Step 5: If i<n-1 then go to step 6 else go to 11
Step 6: Read next element a
Step 7: If MIN > a then go to step 8 else go to step 9
Step 8: Assign MIN=a
Step 9: Set i=i+1
Step 10: Go to step 5
Step 11: Print MIN
Step 12: Stop

Pseudocode:

```
BEGIN
    READ n
    INITALIZE i=0
    READ first element as MIN
    WHILE i<n-1
        Read next number as a
        IF MIN>a
            ASSIGN MIN=a
        END IF
```

```
        SET i=i+1
PRINT MIN
END
```

Flowchart:

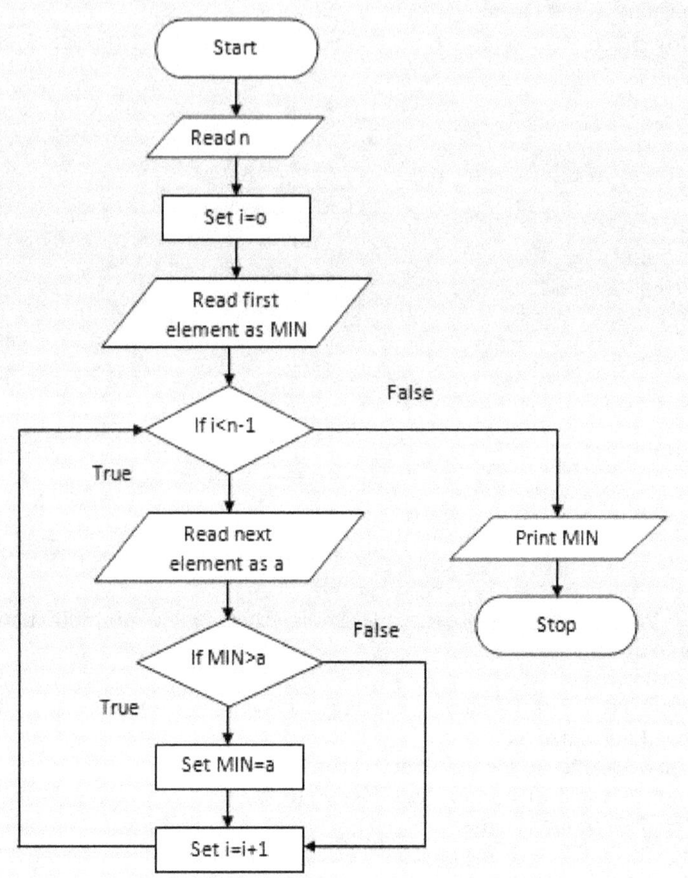

11. Write algorithm, pseudocode and flowchart to guess a number in a range.

Algorithm:

Step 1: Start

Step 2: Read the range n

Step 3: Get a random number from system r

Step 4: Read value from user x

Step 5: If x = r go to step 8 else go to step 6.

Step 6: If x< r then Print 'Your guess is low' else Print 'Your guess is high'

Step 7: Go to step 4

Step 8: Print 'Your guess is correct'

Step 9: Stop

Pseudocode:

```
BEGIN
    READ range n
```

```
GET random number r
READ value from user x
WHILE x=r
    PRINT 'Your guess is correct"
ELSE
    IF x<r
        PRINT 'Your guess is low'
    ELSE
        PRINT 'Your guess is high'
    ENDIF
END
```

Flowchart:

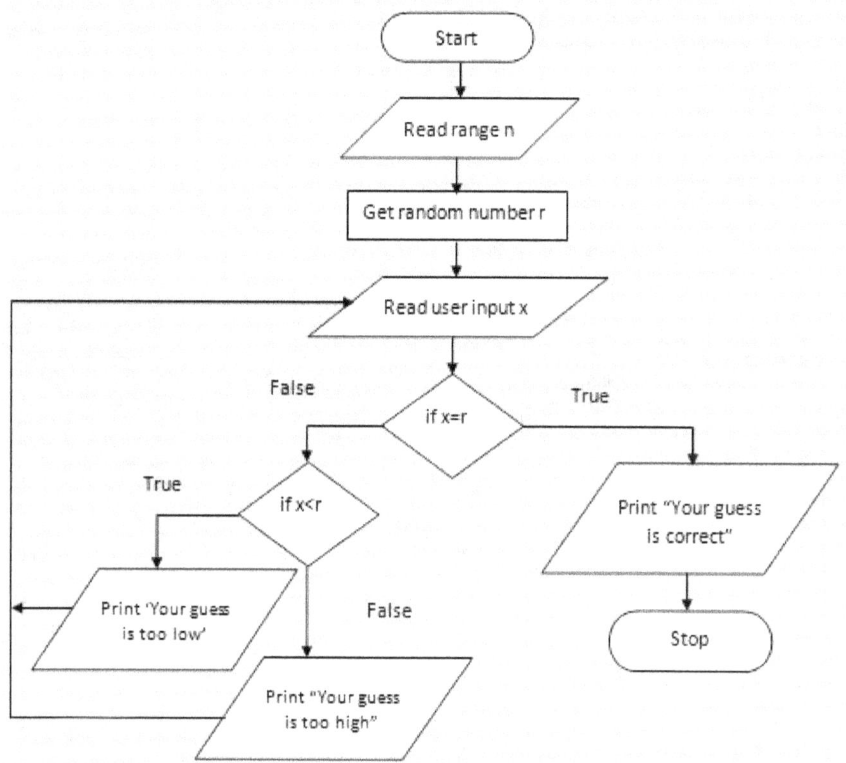

12. Write algorithm, pseudocode and flowchart for Tower of Hanoi problem.

Algorithm:

Step 1: Start

Step 2: Move n-1 disks from source to auxiliary

Step 3: Move nth disk from source to destination

Step 4: Move n-1 disks from auxiliary to destination

Step 5: Procedure Hanoi(disk, source, destination, auxiliary)

Step 6: If disk = =0, Then

    Step 6.1: Move disk from source to destination

Step 7: Else
    Step 7.1: Hanoi(disk-1, source, auxiliary, destination)
    Step 7.2: Move disk from source to destination
    Step 7.3: Hanoi(disk-1, auxiliary, destination, source)
Step 8: END IF
Step 9: END procedure
Step 10: Stop

Pseudocode:
BEGIN
    FUNCTION Hanoi(disk, source, destination, auxiliary)
    IF disk = = 1
        move disk from source to destination
    ELSE
        Hanoi(disk-1, source, auxiliary, destination)
        move disk from source to destination
        Hanoi(disk-1, auxiliary, destination, source)
    ENDIF
END

Flowchart:

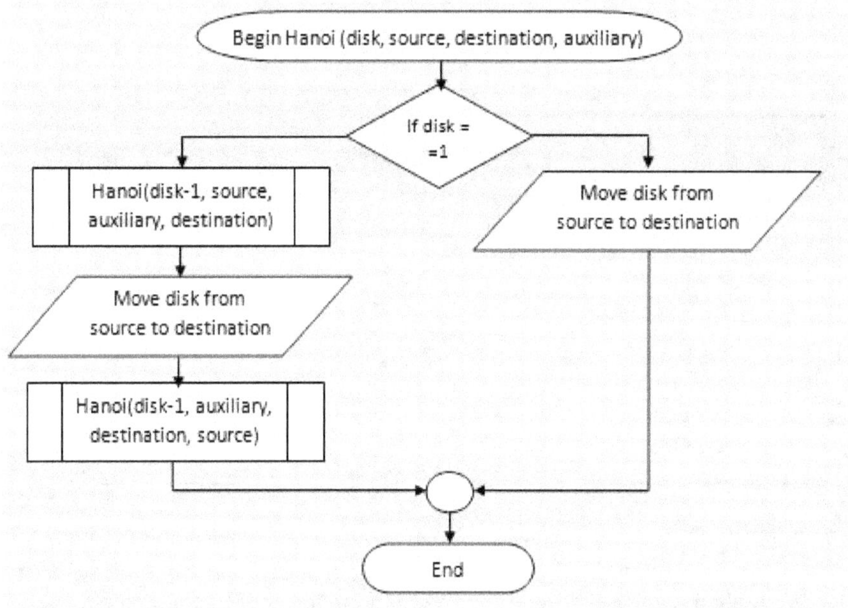

13. Write algorithm, pseudocode and flowchart to find Fibonacci series using recursion.

Algorithm:
Step 1: Start
Step 2: Read the number of terms n
Step 3: Initialize F=0, F1=1, i=2
Step 4: Print F, F1
Step 5: While i<=n

Step 5.1: F2=F+F1
Step 5.2: F=F1
Step 5.3: F1=F2
Step 5.4: i=i+1
Step 5.5: Print F2
Step 6: Stop
Pseudocode:
BEGIN
    INITIALIZE F=0, F1=1, i=2
    PRINT F, F1
    GET number of terms n
    WHILE i <=n
        F2=F+F1
        PRINT F2
        F=F1
        F1=F2
        i=i+1
    END WHILE
END
Flowchart:

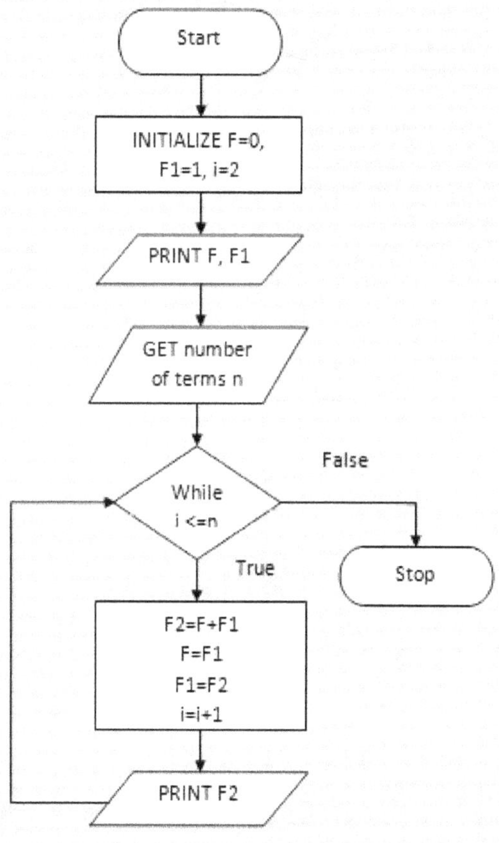

ADDITIONAL PROGRAMS

1. Write algorithm, pseudocode and flowchart to find whether the number is prime or not.
2. Write algorithm, pseudocode and flowchart to find sum of digits of a number.
3. Write algorithm, pseudocode and flowchart to positive, negative or zero.
4. Write algorithm, pseudocode and flowchart to display the percentage and average mark scored by a student.
5. Write algorithm, pseudocode and flowchart to display n even numbers.
6. Write algorithm, pseudocode and flowchart to sort the number is ascending order.
7. Write algorithm, pseudocode and flowchart to check whether the two inputs are equal or not.
8. Write algorithm, pseudocode and flowchart to sort cards in list.
9. Write algorithm, pseudocode and flowchart to check whether the number is divisible by 6 or not.
10. Write algorithm, pseudocode and flowchart to check whether the person is eligible to vote.

REVIEW QUESTIONS

1. What is algorithm? Give its advantages.
2. What are the characteristics of algorithm?
3. What is pseudocode? Write guidelines to write pseudocode.
4. What is flowchart? Explain with example.
5. Discuss the advantage and disadvantage of flowchart.
6. What is flowcharting?
7. Explain some basic symbols used in flowchart.
8. Explain the guidelines to draw a flowchart.
9. What are the strategies used to develop algorithm?
10. What is iteration? Give example.
11. What is recursion? Give example.
12. Difference between iteration and recursion.
13. What are the building blocks of algorithm?
14. What is function?
15. What is control flow? What are its types?

MUTIPLE CHOICE QUESTIONS

1. Which symbol is used for decision making in flowchart?

   a.   c.

   b.   d.

2. Which symbol is used for process and calculation purposes?

   a.

   b.   c.

              d.

3. Which of the following are correct about algorithm?
   a. It has finite number of steps
   b. It should produce result in a finite amount of time

    c. It solves only simple and general problem

    d. None of these

4. Which of the following is correct about algorithm?

    a. Write one statement per line.

    b. Capitalize the keywords.

    c. Indent to show hierarchy

    d. All the above

5. The diamond symbol in flow chart is used for ____________

    a. Get input

    b. Decision making

    c. Displaying output

    d. Processing

TRUE OR FALSE

1. Algorithm can have any number of steps.
2. The while loop continues to iterate until its condition becomes false.
3. Flowchart gives good visual clarity.
4. It consumes less time when we convert algorithm into flowchart.
5. Pseudocode is not visual representation.
6. Algorithm follows English like representation to solve the problem.
7. The implementation phase is implementing the program in some programming language.
8. Function provides less degree of code reusability.
9. Converting pseudocode to programming language is very easy as compared with flowcharts.
10. Pseudocode is easy to understand for beginners.

FILL IN THE BLANKS

1. The process of dividing the problem into module is known as ____________.
2. The pictorial representation of process is known as __________.
3. The Pseudocode is also known as ____________.
4. The direction of flow in flow chart is represented by using __________.
5. ____________ is a step by step procedure to solve a given problem.
6. __________ is an informal and English-like representation of an algorithm.
7. A problem can be divided into two phases such as __________ problem solving phase and __________.
8. The process of analyzing, understanding and solving the problem is known as __________.
9. Pseudocode follows ______________ approach.
10. The process of drawing flowchart is known as __________.

ANSWERS

MUTIPLE CHOICE QUESTIONS

1. d
2. c
3. a
4. d
5. b

TRUE OR FALSE

1. False
2. True
3. True

4. False
5. True
6. True
7. True
8. False
9. True
10. False

FILL IN THE BLANKS

1. modularization
2. Flowchart
3. Program Design Language (PDL)
4. Flow line
5. Algorithm
6. Pseudocode
7. problem solving phase,implementation phase
8. problem solving
9. top to bottom
10. Flowcharting

CHAPTER 3: INTRODUCTION TO PYTHON PROGRAMMING

This chapter discuss about history and evolution, important features and application of python language. It also discuss about how to download and install python IDLE. This chapter also discusses the difference between complier and interpreter and also about interactive mode and scripting mode. This chapter explains variables, expression, statement, keywords, comments, basic operators, values and data types concepts with example.

CHAPTER OUTLINE

Introduction to python: history, evolution, timeline, features, advantages, application – Download and install python – Compiler and interpreter, interactive and scripting mode – variables – statement – expression – keywords – comments – indentation – operators – values – data types: precedence, associativity

OBJECTIVE

After covering the chapter, the student will be in a position:

- To known the history and evolution of python programming
- To known about the Features of python and installation of python programming.
- Difference between compiler and interpreter.
- To known about modes of python.
- To know about values and data types
- To understand about variables, expressions, statements

- To known about basic operators and their precedence in python
- To understand comments and keywords in python
- To known about comments and indentation.

3.1 WHAT IS PROGRAM AND PROGRAMMING?

A program is a collection or sequence of instructions that perform a specific task or computation when executed by a computer. It is a sequence of instructions that tell a computer what to do. The programming is a process of writing a program. In this book we are going to learn about python programming language.

3.2 INTRODUCTION TO PYTHON

Python is a high level general purpose, object-oriented scripting programming language which follows object oriented concept. It is an interactive and interpreted reliable programming language. It is used for program scripting, database programming, etc.

3.2.1History of Python

Python was developed during the year 1985- 1990 by Guido van Rossum. He was a computer programmer at CWI (Center for Wisdom and Informatics), a National Research Institute for Mathematics and Computer science in Netherland. It was developed as a scripting language for administrative works. Python got its name from a comedy series Monty Python's flying circus telecasted in BBC. Python was released in the year 1991.Python is derived from All Basic Code (ABC), modula-3, C, C++, Algol-68, Small talk and UNIX shell and many other scripting languages. The figure 3.1 shows the evolution of python programming. from other programming languages.

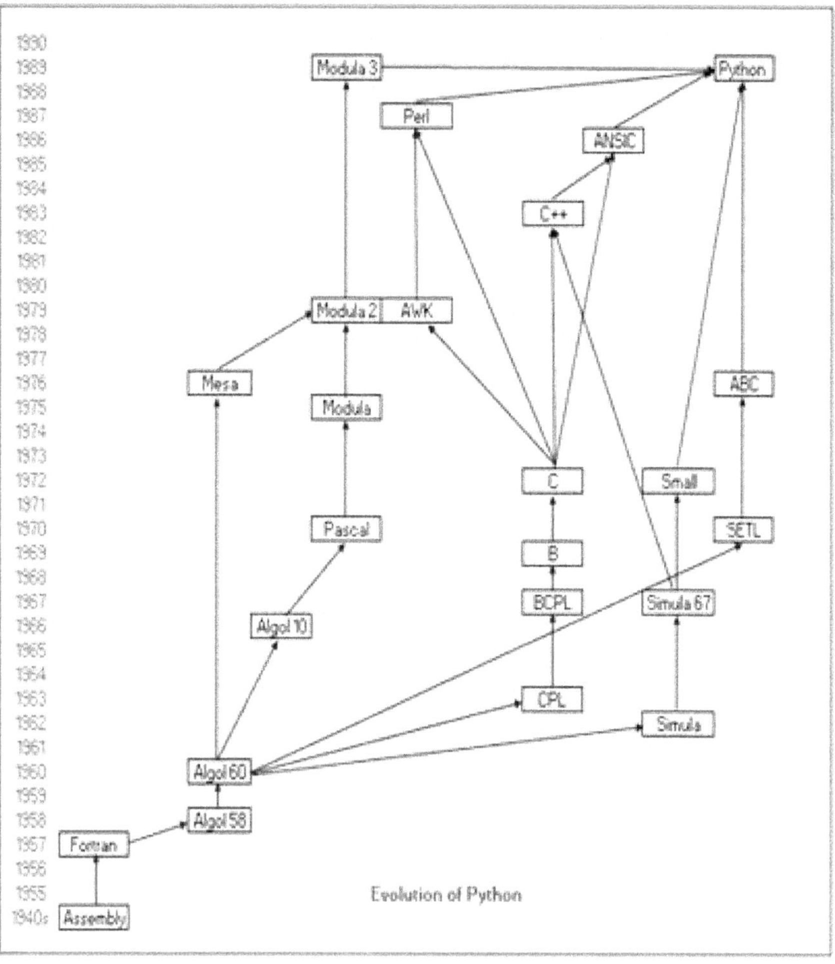

Figure 3.1: Evolution of python programming

3.2.2 Timeline of Python

Python was implementation in the year 1989. The Python's labeled version 0.9.0 was released in1991. This version has various features like inheritance, exception handling, and data types such as list, dictionary, string, etc. The first version of python "Python1.0" was released in 1994 which has functional programming tools. Python 2.0 Version was released in 2000 which includes list comprehensions. The Python 3 was released in 2008, it is also known as Python3000 or Py3K. The figure 3.2 shows the time line of python programming.

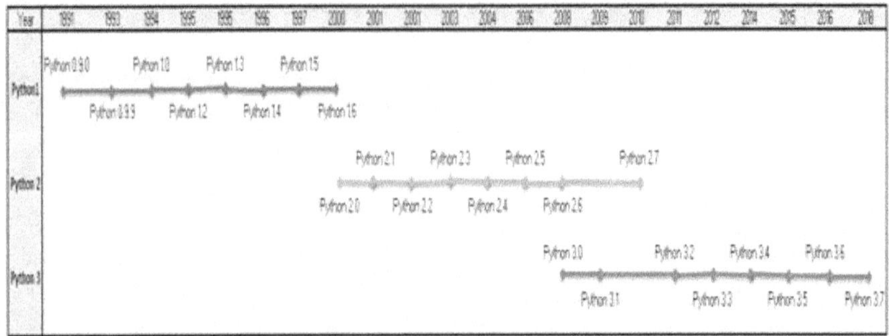

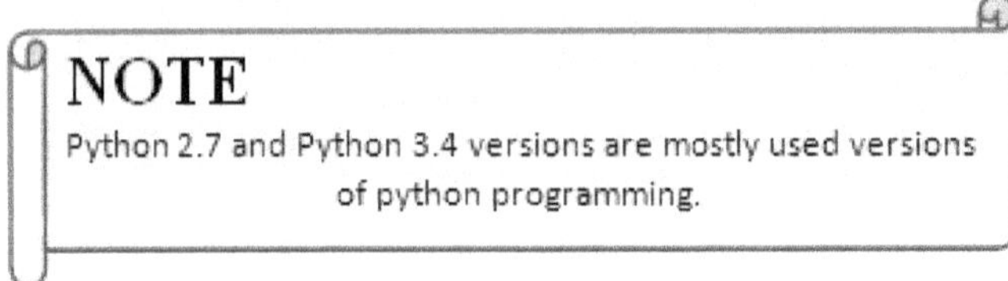

Figure 3.2: Timeline of python programming

> **NOTE**
>
> Python 2.7 and Python 3.4 versions are mostly used versions of python programming.

3.2.3 Feature of Python

- **Simple syntax:** It is very simple and small language, it has clearly defined syntax.
- **Easy to learn:** It is clearly defined and easily readable. It use English like words.
- **Interactive:** It is an interactive language which gives immediate feedback to user.
- **Free and Open source:** It is constructed under OSI approved open source license so it is free to use.
- **Versatile:** It supports many applications such as computation, gaming and text processing.
- **Maintainability:** Easy to maintain the code
- **Portable and platform independent:** Compiled and run virtually in many platforms so it is portable. It is platform independent.
- **Embedded:** Python is embedded and integrated with other languages such as C, C++, java, etc.
- **Extensible:** Python can extend or add low level modules.
- **Interpreted:** Python is process by interpreter.
- **Object oriented:** It uses both procedural oriented approach which has procedures or functions and has object oriented approach such as polymorphism, inheritance, etc.
- **Dynamically typed:** The datatype of the variables do not have to be predefined. The variable's type is defined during runtime based on the value entered.
- **Garbage collection:** Python has garbage collector for collecting object which is no longer referred.
- **Multi-paradigm programming language:** Python follows object oriented and structural programming paradigms.
- **Library support:** Python support many libraries on various platforms.

Additional features:

- Python has many built-in data types.
- It support many control statements.
- It is easier programming with the use of functions, classes, modules and package.
- It is multithreaded.
- Easy to use and it has no intermediate compilation steps.
- It is robust.
- It has automatic garbage collection.
- It supports functional, structural and object oriented programming.
- It can be used as scripting language.

Language features

- It is a beginners language
- Python uses Indentation instead of braces
- It can perform subscripting (slicing)
- Python has Exceptions as in Java
- It uses object oriented approach
- Python uses files

3.2.4 Advantage of Python

- Python is easy to learn and use.
- It is free and open-source
- It is cross platform, which can be run in all major operating systems.
- It has large number of built-in functions, libraries and modules.
- It uses object oriented concepts and has built-in dictionary, list data structures.
- Python does not have pointer like other programming language.

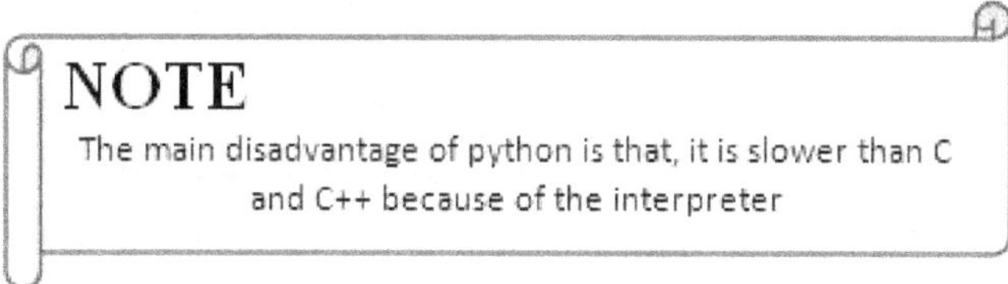

3.2.5 Application of Python

- It is mainly used in gaming and robotics.
- It is used in Graphical user interface (GUI) programming.
- It is also used for database programming and network programming.
- It is a language in machine learning and deep learning.
- It is used in text processing and scientific computing.
- It is used in data science projects.

3.3 DOWNLOADING AND INSTALLING PYTHON IDLE

Python interpreter is downloaded from https://www.python.org/downloads/ . Based on the operating system, the version of python is chosen.

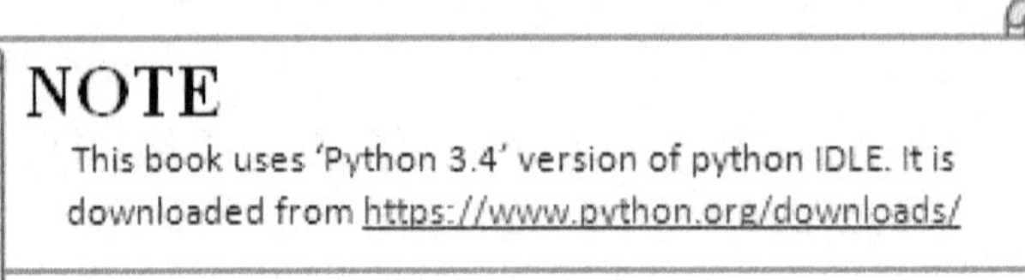

1) On Linux:

Python comes pre-installed with Linux. Type 'idle ' at the command prompt this should start up the Python development environment IDLE. User can also install Python and IDLE directly from the command line, by typing into your terminal:

>>>sudo aptget install python3.4

>>>sudo aptget install idle

This will install both python and IDLE in Linux. We can run the program from the python editor by pressing the F5 function key or from the editor's Run menu: Run→Run Module. The output will be appeared in the IDLE interactive shell window. To start IDLE, open your terminal and type   >>> idle and interactive shell will be displayed.

2) On Windows:

Go to https://www.python.org/downloads/ and download the windows MSI installer for either x86 or x86-64, depending on which version of Windows you are running.

1) Go to www.python.org

2) Click "Downloads" Link at the top of the page. Select the release based on the operating system. The figure 3.3 shows the version of python for windows.

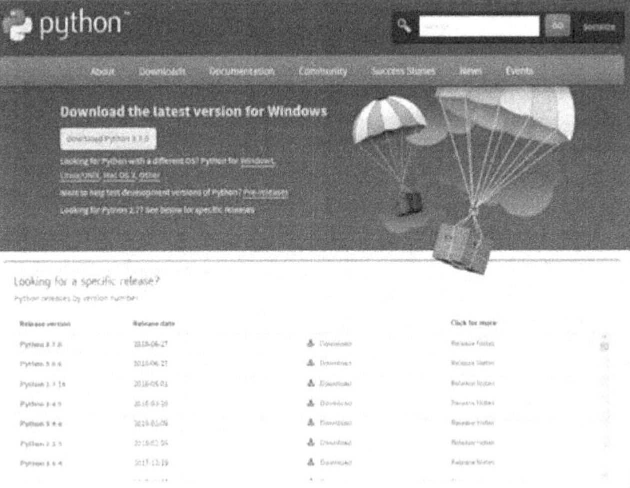

Figure 3.3: Download version of python

3)   Download .msi file from the version you selected. The last two lines in figure 3.4 shown the MSI Installer, now click that installer and download it.

Files

Version	Operating System	Description	MD5 Sum
Gzipped source tarball	Source release		e80a0c1c71763ff6b5a91f8cc9bb3d50
XZ compressed source tarball	Source release		8d526b7128affed5fbe72ceac8d2fc63
Mac OS X 32-bit i386/PPC installer	Mac OS X	for Mac OS X 10.5 and later	8491d013826252228ffcdeda0d9348d6
Mac OS X 64-bit/32-bit installer	Mac OS X	for Mac OS X 10.6 and later	349c61e374f6aeb44ca85481ee14d2f5
Windows debug information files	Windows		d6ffch8cdabd93ed7f2feff661816511
Windows debug information files for 64-bit binaries	Windows		a5eea5b374295ac1ed02bddf30a07101
Windows help file	Windows		5faae75ddaedc25e33e5613c7x46cd15
Windows x86-64 MSI installer	Windows	for AMD64/EM64T/x64	9638671196305447fad72e60cc561c713
Windows x86 MSI installer	Windows		e9626d7042d2a33147fe24b25357396

Figure 3.4: Download MSI Installer

4)   Click "Save" the MSI Installer and then "Run".

5)   Now choose Install for all user and click Next> as shown in figure 3.5.

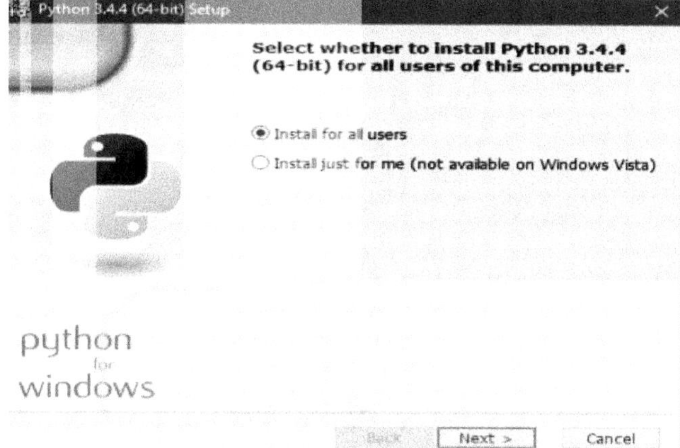

Figure 3.5: Python setup

5) Select the directory where you want to install python and click Next > as shown in the figure 3.6 and then click Next>.

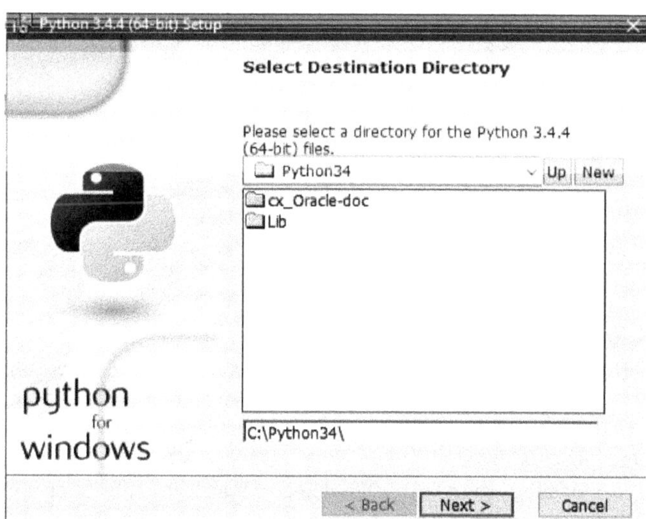

Figure 3.6: Select destination directory

Select install now to install the python with default settings or select customize installation

6) Once you select your destination directory python setup will get automatically installed in that location. The figure 3.7 shows the installation of MSI Installer.

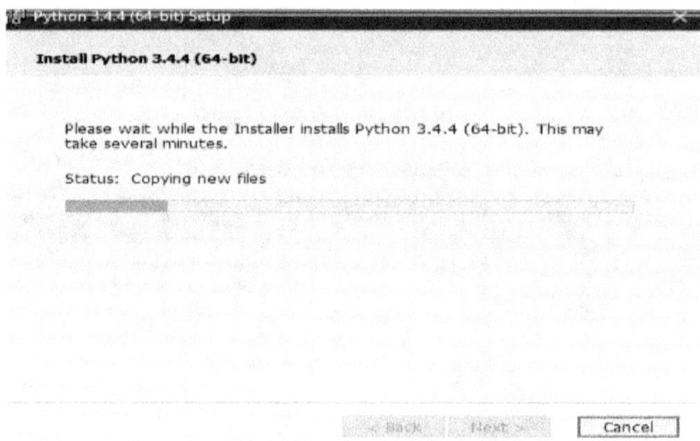

Figure 3.7: Installing python

7) When the installation finishes, you can see a screen that says the installation was successful or complete the python 3.4.4 installer. You can click "Finish" button to exit the installer as shown in figure 3.8.

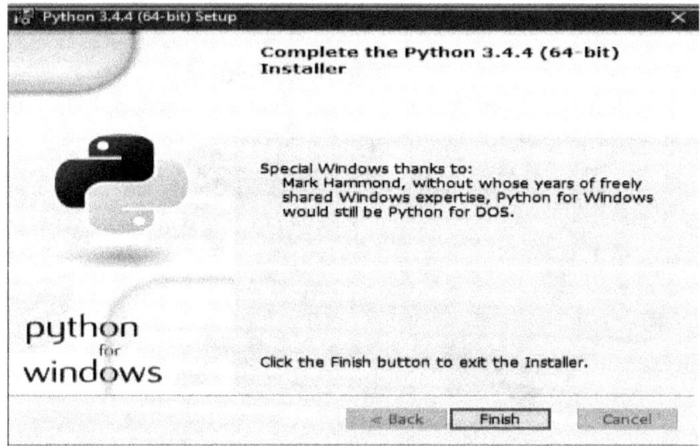

Figure 3.8: Complete the installation

3) On Mac OS X:

Python comes pre-installed with Mac OS X. If it is not in Mac OS go to https://www.python.org/downloads / and download and install the Mac Installer for your Mac OS X version from the site.

3.3.1 Executing Python

Once you install python both IDLE and command line interfaces are installed. Select IDLE from your system.

LINUX: If you're on Linux, select IDLE from Menu > Programming > IDLE
WINDOWS: For windows, select IDLE from Menu > IDLE (python GUI)
MAC: For Apple, you can find IDLE in Applications > Python

A Python shell appears indicating python version and platform as in figure 3.9. This is the Python Shell. Those three arrows (>>>) denotes the python prompt. It is also called chevrons, which means ready and waiting for expression or some calculation. Click File > new file if you want to write program in script mode.

Figure 3.9: Python shell

3.3.2 IDLE

IDLE means "Integrated Development and Learning Environment". The IDLE has python shell and python editor. It is a most popular and standard python development environment. IDLE is the standard cross platform Python development environment. It is a tool that offers a more efficient platform to write your code. It consists of text editor and language environment. IDLE is a Shell for interactive evaluation. The IDLE has a Python shell window, which gives the access to the Python interactive mode. It also has a file editor or text editor that let user to create, edit and save Python source files.

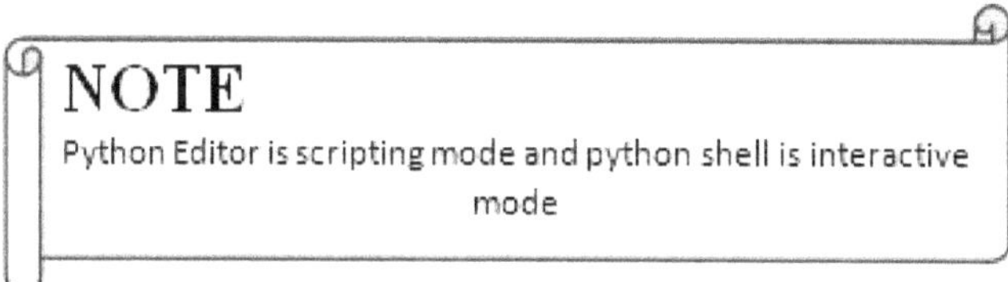

3.4 COMPILER AND INTERPRETER

A program written in high level language can be executed in any of the two ways,

    1)   By compiling the program
    2)   By passing the program through an interpreter

Compiler translates instruction written in High Level Language (HLL) into machine language. The interpreter on the other hand translates the instruction into intermediate form, which is then executed. It takes one statement a time and translates it, this process repeats until the entire program is translated. The table 3.1 shows the difference between compiler and interpreter.

No.	Compiler	Interpreter
1	It translates entire program in one time	Interpreted and executes one statement at a time
2	After translating the entire program error(s) are displayed.	Stop translating after getting one error. So, debugging is easy
3	Execution of code is faster	Since interpreter interprets line-by-line, the interpreted code runs slower than the compiled code.
4	Overall execution time is lower	Takes less time to analyze the source code but overall execution time is higher
5	Object file is generated	No object file is generated
6	Code need not be recompiled every time, it is executed	Have to be reinterpreted every time
7	It just translate the code	It translate as well as execute the code
8	Memory Requirement is More because Object Code is Generated	Memory Requirement is Less
9	Example : C Compiler	Example : PYTHON

Table 3.1: Difference between compiler and interpreter

Python use interpreter to convert the program from high level language to low level language.

3.4.1 Python Interpreter

Python is an interpreted language and python programs are executed by the interpreter. The interpreter is a program that reads and executes python code and translates it. It analyzes and executes program statements at the same time. The figure 3.10 shows the working of interpreter.

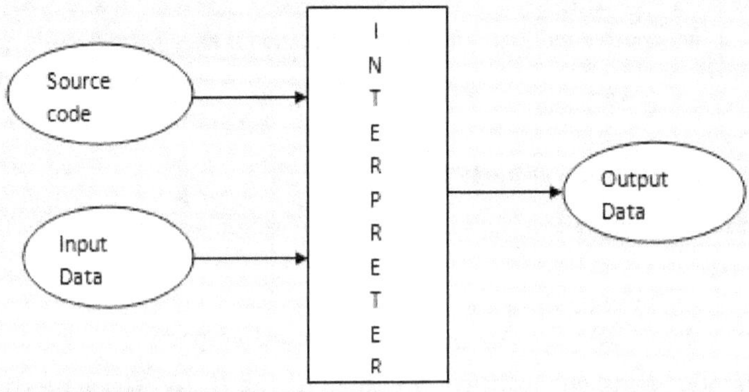

Figure 3.10: Working of interpreter

Interpreter takes less time to analyze the source code but the overall execution time is slower. The Interpreter continues translating the program until the first error is met. In case it found the error, it stops the execution and displays it. Hence debugging is easy. Python language is an interpreted language; interpreter is used to translate high level language.

3.5 INTERACTIVE MODE AND SCRIPTING MODE

Python interpreter can works on both Interactive mode and scripting mode.

3.5.1Interactive mode

Interactive Mode, allows the user to interact with the OS. When user type Python statement, interpreter displays the result(s) immediately. The window that provides this interaction is known as the Python shell. This mode is used as a calculator, except that, instead of being limited to the operations built into a calculator (addition, subtraction, etc.); it allows the entry and creation of any Python code. Typing python code in the command line will invoke the interpreter in interactive mode. '>>>' This symbol is the prompt, that indicates that the interpreter is ready for user to enter the code. Python does not display the output print( ) function is used in order to see the result. It is also known as shell window. The table 3.2 shows the difference between interactive and scripting mode.

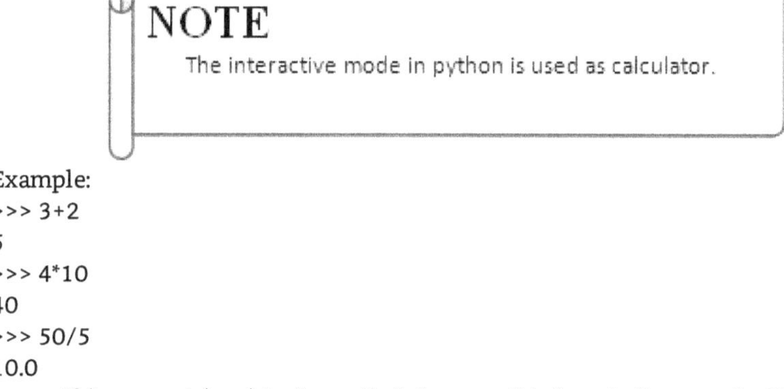

Example:
```
>>> 3+2
5
>>> 4*10
40
>>> 50/5
10.0
```
This prompt (>>>) is also called chevron, this is to indicate ready. This prompt is also used as calculator. To exit this mode type exit ( ) or quit ( ) and press enter.

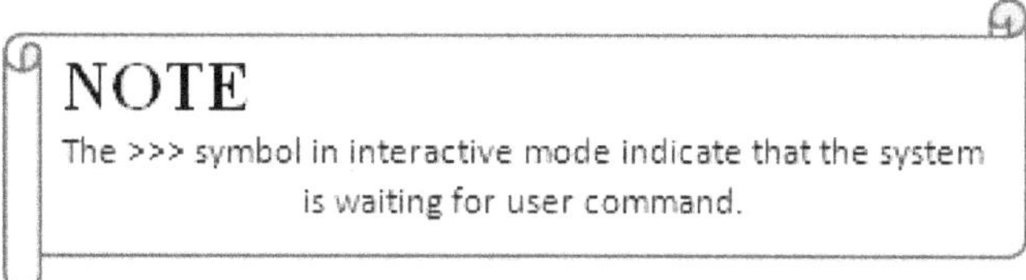

3.5.2Scripting mode

So far we have run Python in interactive mode, which means that you interact directly with the interpreter and get the result. Interactive mode is an easy to work with but to store the file for future references is not possible. The alternative way of scripting is to save code in a file called a script and then run the interpreter in script mode to execute the script. This mode is used to execute python program and save the written code in file. Such file is known as script which can be saved to disk for future use. Python scripts have the extension .py or .pyw. The figure 3.11 shows the scripting mode of python and the output will be displayed on interactive mode as in figure 3.12.

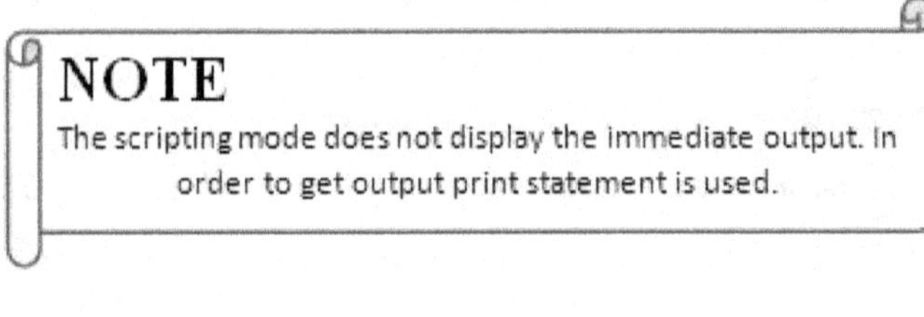

Example:
#first program

print("Hello world.........!!!")

Here, helloworld is the file name and .py is the extension.

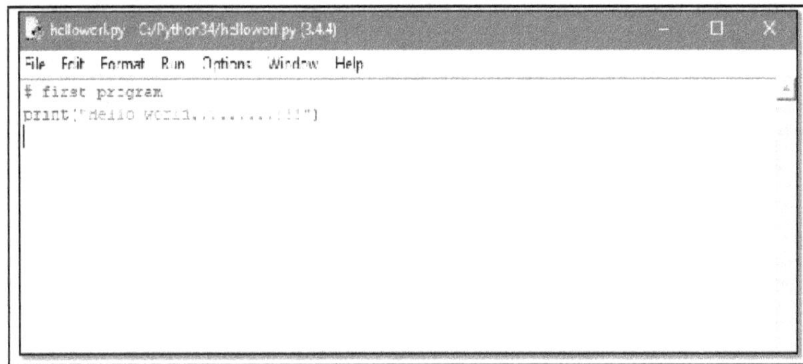

Figure 3.11: Scripting mode of python

Output:
Hello world.........!!!

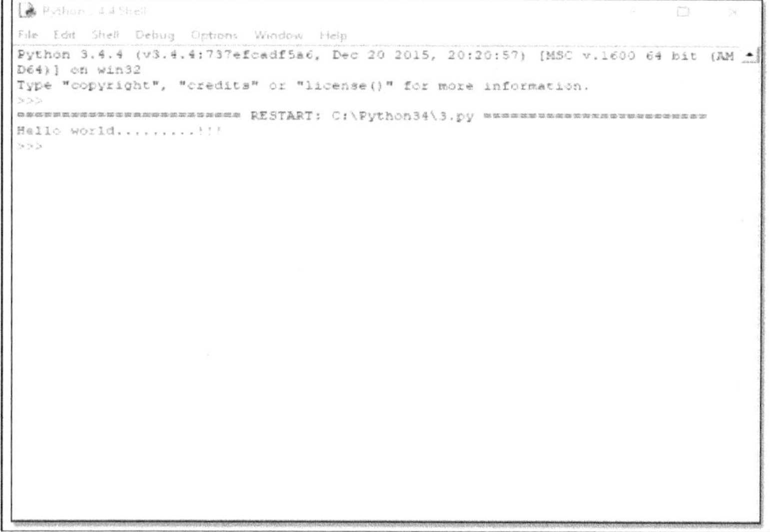

Figure 3.12: Interactive mode of python

No.	Interactive mode	Scripting mode
1	A way of typing commands and expressions at the prompt.	A way to read and execute statements in a script.
2	Can't save and edit the code	Can save and edit the code
3	User cannot save the statements for further use and we have to retype all the statements to re-run them.	User can save the statements for further use and we no need to retype all the statements to re-run them.
4	We can see the results immediately.	We can't see the code immediately.

Table 3.2: Difference between interactive mode and scripting mode

3.6 WRITING AND EXECUTING FIRST PROGRAM

The classic first program in all programming language is "Hello, World!". Type in this lines in prompt and press Enter to display the output.

>>> print("Hello world!!!")

Output:

Hello world!!!

This is an example of a print statement; it displays a result on the screen.

Steps for writing and executing python program

Step 1: Open new file from file menu by click on File> New File or click CTRL+N

Step 2: Write the program (script) in the new window

Step 3: Save the script by selecting File/Save with the filename with extension .py. If you don't save the file then the python interpreter will save that file as Untitled.py

Step 4: Run the interpreter by pressing F5 or Run>Run Module or the CTRL+F5 key

(Mac or Linux)

Step 5: Output will be displayed on the python shell

Steps in interpreting a Python program

1) The interpreter reads a Python expression or statement of the script or source code, and verifies that the code is syntactically correct or not. As soon as the interpreter encounters such an error, it halts translation with an error message.

2) If the Python expression is correct, then the interpreter translates it to low-level language called byte code.

3) This byte code is next sent to another software component, called the Python Virtual Machine (PVM), where it is executed. If another error such as exception occurs during this step, execution also halts with an error message.

The figure 3.13 shows the process takes place while the program is executed in an interpreter.

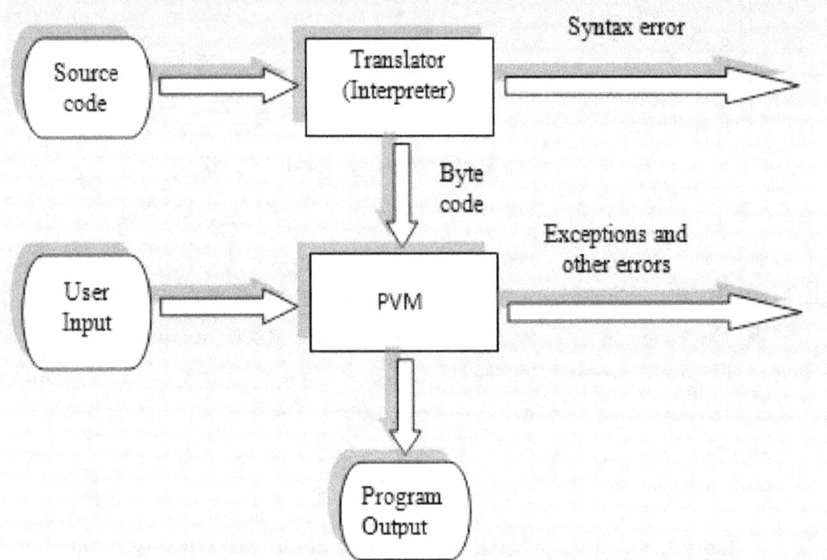

Figure 3.13: Process takes place while execution

Source code: Source code is the python code. This source code is saved with the extension .py. Translator converts this source code into byte code.

Translator: Source code is converted into byte code by the interpreter. It analyzes the source code line by line and continues translating. If any error is met the interpreter stops the process and displays the error.

Syntax error: This error is obtained because of incorrect syntax.

Byte code: Byte code is the fixed set of instructions that represents all operations which run on any operating system. Byte instructions are platform independent. The size of each byte code instructions is one byte. So it is named as byte code. This byte code is saved with an extension .pyc.

User input: User input is the input data given by the user to the PVM. If the code requests any inputs, the interpreter will pause to allow user to enter them.

PVM: PVM means Python Virtual Machine; it converts byte code into machine understandable code (0's and 1's). If there is any runtime error (Exception) then error message will be displayed otherwise this machine code is executed and results are displayed.

If the program Python executes any print functions in the code, and displays the outputs as usual in the shell window. Otherwise, program execution continues until the last line. When the interpreter has finished executing the last instruction, it quits and returns you to the shell prompt.

Executing a python program can be used in two ways,

1) Using command line and run the python interpreter directly.
2) Using GUI software that has IDLE installed with it.
1. Using command line window (Interactive mode)
>>>print 'hello'
To exit → quit ( ), exit ( ), ctrl+z
2. IDLE

Type your programs save with the extension .py and execute it.

3.7 IMPLEMENTATION OF PYTHON

The python is implemented for different programming languages such as C, Java, .NET, python etc. Some of the implementations are:

• **CPython:** It is widely used standard which is written in C programming Language. It is the default and standard implementation of python.

• **PyPy:** It is written in Python. It uses Just-in-Time (JIT) Compiler to run the code quickly and efficiently. It is the implementation of Python in Python.

• **Jython:** It is used to run python program in java platform. It is also known as JPython

• **IronPython:** It is the implementation of python for .NET Framework. It is an open source implementation which uses Dynamic Language Runtime (DLR) framework.

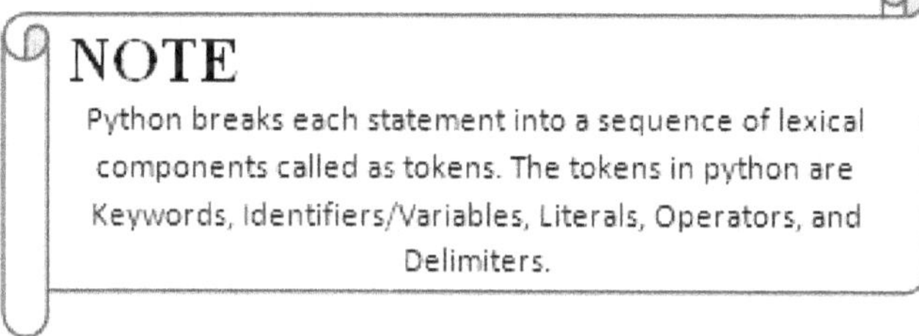

3.8 VARIABLES

Variable is a name given to the value to refer a memory location. A variable allows us to store a value, making it easy to remember and use the value later in a program. Variables are reserved memory location that stores values. A variable holds a value that may change. It can be of any length. No space is allowed in variable name. ' = ' sign is used to assign values to a variables.

Syntax:

variable_name = expression

Here, the equal sign (=) is assignment operator. The = symbol means assignment, an expression or a value is assigned to a variable. The Python interpreter first evaluates the expression on the right side of the assignment symbol and then binds the variable name on the left side to this value. Expression is any value, text or arithmetic expression. The value of the expression is stored in variable.

Example:

>>>s='hello'

>>>a=9.8

>>>n = 17

Here, 's', 'n' and 'a' are the variable names. All the Values are given a name by means of an assignment statement. The text to the left of the assignment is the name, and the text to the right is the value, the value will be remembered by its name. In the above example n is the variable name that holds the value 17 and it is remembered by using the name n.

In python initially an object is created then the variable is tagged to that object.

Example:

>>> x=10

>>> id(x)

1882245488

In the above example, value 10 is first created in the memory location 1882245488. Then the variable x is tagged to that variable.

Example:

>>> y=10

>>> id(y)

1882245488

In the above example, the variable y also has the same value s x. The variable 10 is already created in memory, so the variable y is tagged to 10. Here the variable x and y is tagged to that object. So they both refer same memory space.

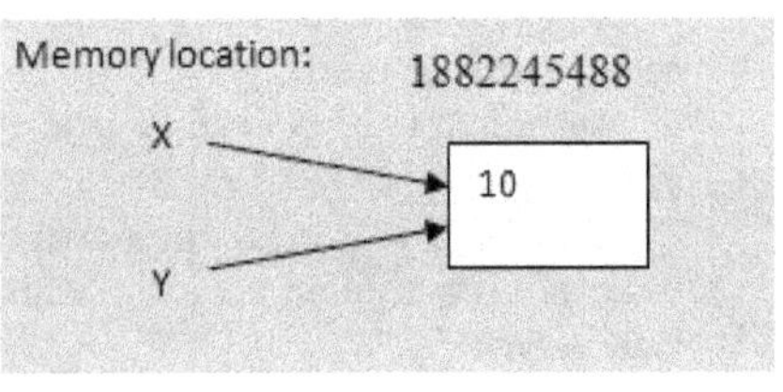

Rules for writing a variable name:

•	Variable must begin with alphabet ((a-z) or (A-Z)) or underscore (_) followed by letters, numbers or underscore.

•	Keyword or reserve words cannot be used as variable name.

•	Variable name can be as long as user like. They can contain letters and numbers.

•	Special characters such as! , @, #, %, etc., cannot be used as variable name.

•	Python variables are case sensitive (sum, Sum) both are different.

•	In Python, it is not needed to declare a variable name before using it. Just assign a value to a variable and it will exist.

Example:

>>> hai_hello=1 # valid assignment

>>> hai@hello=1 # can't assign special characters as variable name

SyntaxError: invalid syntax

>>> while=1 # can't assign reserve word as variable name

SyntaxError: invalid syntax

>>> 1haihello=1 # variable name should start with letters or underscore

SyntaxError: invalid syntax

In python, single and multiple assignments of values are possible.

Example:

```
>>>a=5 # single assignment
>>>x=y=z=2 #assigning one value to multiple variables
>>>b,c=2,3 # multiple assignment
```

In the above example value 2 is stored in b and value 3 is stored in c. And also user can assign single value to multiple variables directly.

Example:

```
>>>a,b=1,2,3
Traceback (most recent call last):
  File "<pyshell#50>", line 1, in <module>
    a,b=1,2,3
ValueError: too many values to unpack
```

Number of variable on the left side and number of values on the right side have to be same. If not, the above error will be displayed.

3.9 EXPRESSIONS

Expression are combination of literals, variable and operators that python evaluates to produce a value. An expression represents data items such as variables, constants and is interconnected with operators. Expression is evaluated using assignment operator. It usually contains combinations of operators and operands.

Syntax:

variable= expression

Expression must contain at least one operand and can have one or more operators.

Example:

```
>>> a=5
>>> x=10+a
>>> x
15
```

In the above example a=5 and x=10+a are the expressions. This expressions contains operands such as 'a' and 'x' and operators such as '+'.

3.10 STATEMENTS

The statement is an instruction that a Python interpreter can executes. A script contains sequence of statements. Each and every line in a program is known as statement. If there is more than one statement, the result appears one at a time as the statement executes. The Python programming has three basic statements, they are:

1. Assignment statement (Input statement)
2. Print statement (output statement)
3. Import statement.

First and second types of statements are used in almost all simple programs. First statement is the input or assignment statement in which value is given by user. Second statement is the output statement which displays output on the screen. Other than these three statements, there are iterative statements, looping statements, branching statements, etc,

Example:

```
>>>n=4  # Assignment statement
```

>>>print(n) # Print statement

4

First line is the input statement that assigns the value to n and Second line is the output statement that prints the value of n.

Assignment statement (Input statement)

Input is a data entered by user in the program. In python, input ( ) function is used to get input from user. The input ( ) reads a value from user and store that response as string. The assignment statement is used to assign the input value to a variable.

Example:

>>>a=input("enter a number")

Output:

enter a number3

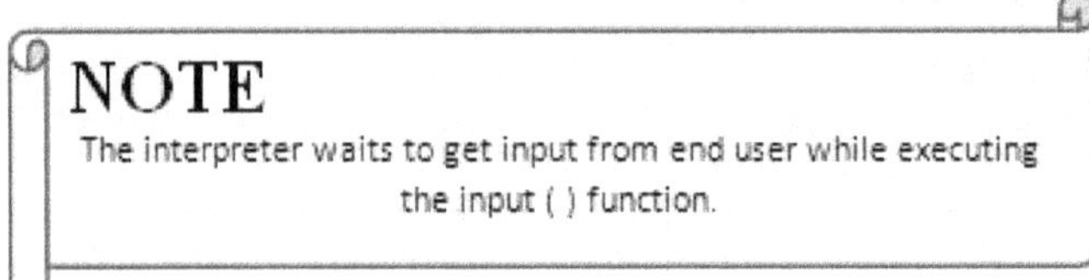

By default, the input( ) function produce only string. Even if the numeric value is entered, the python will consider as string.

Example:

a=input("Enter value of a")

print("Value of a is",a)

print("Type of a is", type(a))

Output

Enter value of a10

Value of a is 10

Type of a is <class 'str'>

Using type conversion function int( ), we can convert string into integer.

a=int(input("Enter value of a"))

print("Value of a is",a)

print("Type of a is", type(a))

Output:

Enter value of a10

Value of a is 10

Type of a is <class 'int'>

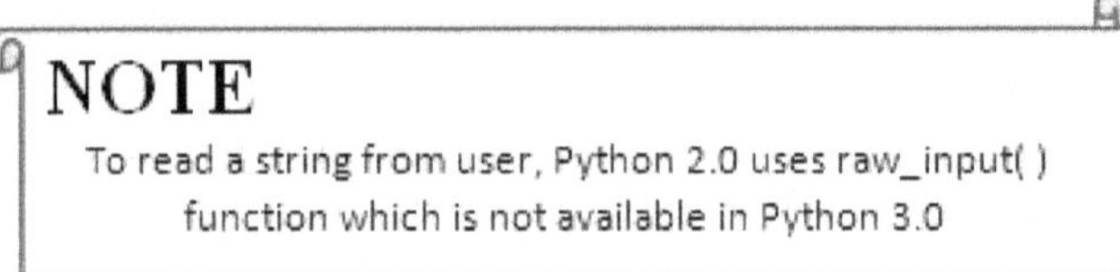

Print statement (output statement)

The Print statement is the output statement to display output to the user. The print ( ) function is used to display the output on the screen.

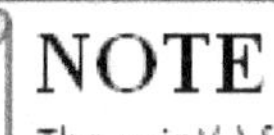

Example:
>>>print (a)
Output:
3

In general, statement does not have any values. When user type a statement the interpreter executes, this means that the interpreter do whatever the statement says. The print statement recognizes a few commands that can be used to format input. The escape characters are written as a character following a backslash. The most common escape character is the newline character '\n'. This moves the output on to a new line.
>>> print "one\ntwo\tthree"
Output:
one
two three

Import statements

The import statement is a statement to include or add package or module into the program. The module contains collection of functions.
Syntax:
import module_name
Example:
>>> import math
>>> print(math.sqrt(9))
3.0

The math is a module which contains function related mathematical calculations such as sqrt( ), pow( ), etc.

Based on the length of the statement, the python statements are divided into two types:
1. single line statements
2. multi line statements

Single line statements

The Statement ends in only one line is known s Single line statements. These types of statements are ended with newline.
Examples:
>>>a=1
>>>b=2
>>>c=a+b

Multiline statements

Python allows the user to write multi line statement using line continuation character '\'. The '\' denote that the line is not ended.
Example:
>>> print('hai\
how are you')
haihow are you

3.11 COMMENTS

As programs get bigger and complicated, they will get more difficult to read. In order to get better understanding, a text or note is added in the program. This text or note is known as comment. Comments are non-executable statements in a program, which are added to describe the meaning of the statements. The comment starts with the symbol '#' and extends to the end of the line. Everything from the # to end of the line is ignored. The comments have no effect on the execution of the program. Any text that appears after a hash symbol (#) is known as a comment.

Comments are ignored by the Python system. They are used purely to communicate information to a human reader. It is a piece of code or program text that the interpreter ignores but that provides useful documentation to programmers. Good variable names can reduce the need of comments, but long names can make complex expressions hard to read. Start comments with # and the rest of line is ignored.

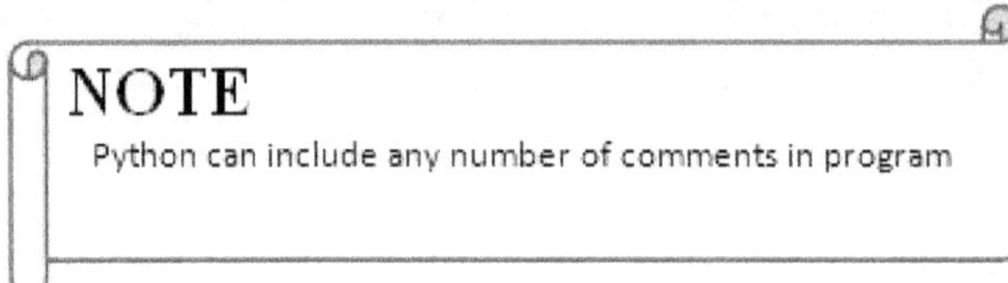

Types of comments:
1. Single line comments
2. Multi line comments

Single line comments:
The single line comment begins with hash sign (#). Anything written after that # to the end of the line is ignored by interpreter.
Example:
a= 24 # a is the variable name -> comments

Multi line comments:
Multiple line comment in python is written using triple quotes (''' and '''). Multiline comments starts and ends with a pair of triple single quotes (''') or triple double quotes ("""").
Example:
>>> '''hai
How are you !!! '''

3.12 RESERVED WORDS

In every programming language there are certain words which are reserved for some specific purpose. These words are known as reserved words or keywords in python. These words have pre-defined meanings. These keywords should not be used as variable name or function name. They are case sensitive. Python has 33 keywords, those words in python are:
>>> import keyword
>>> keyword.kwlist
['False', 'None', 'True', 'and', 'as', 'assert', 'break', 'class', 'continue', 'def', 'del', 'elif', 'else', 'except', 'finally', 'for', 'from', 'global', 'if', 'import', 'in', 'is', 'lambda', 'nonlocal', 'not', 'or', 'pass', 'raise', 'return', 'try', 'while', 'with', 'yield']

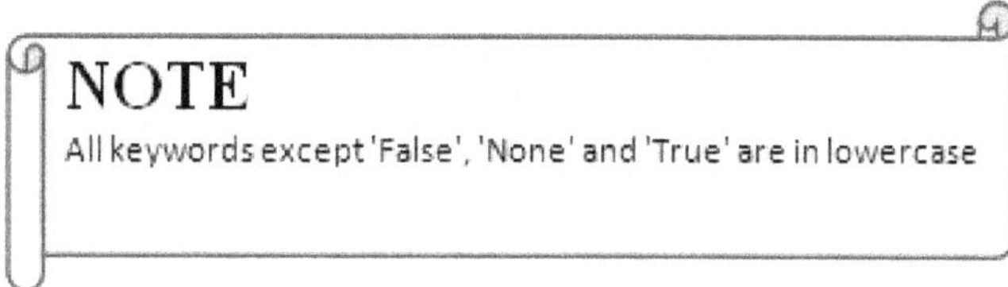

3.13 INDENTATION

The whitespace at the beginning of the line is known as indentation. User need to specify that indentation in 4 spaces or one tab. It is a space given to the flow of control, block of codes for class and function definitions. Indented group of statements is the block. All the statement inside the block must have same indentation level.

Blocks of code are denoted by line indentation. Most of the programming languages such as C, C++, Java use a pair of braces { } to define a block of code. But, python uses the concept of indentation to represent block.

Example:

```
a=3
b=1
if a>b:
   print("a is greater")
else:
   print("b is greater")
```

In the above example if statement (flow of control) i.e. fourth line is indented which is known as body of if block. This is given by pressing a tab which denotes indentation or blocks.

Example:

```
a=3
b=1
if a>b:
print("a is greater")
else:
   print("b is greater")
```

In the above example in line 4 syntax error message is produced indicating there is an error in your program: expected an indented block. In most programming language indentation has no effect on program logic. It is just to align the statement to make the code more readable. But python clearly checks the indentation level and displays the error if the indentation is not correct.

3.14 OPERATORS

Operators are special symbols that represent the computation. These operators are used to manipulate the values of operands. The basic operators in python are +,-, /,*. The table 3.3 explains the basic operators of python in detail with example.

OPERATOR	SYMBOL	DESCRIPTION	EXAMPLE	OUTPUT
Exponential	**	This is used to perform exponential calculation. Operand on the right side raises on the left of the operator.	>>> 4**2	16
Division	/	This is used to divide two numbers and returns the quotient. The operand on the left side divides the right side	>>> 4/2	2
Multiplication	*	It is used to multiplies the two operands or values	>>> 4*2	8
Addition	+	It is used to adds the operands or value	>>> 4+2	6
Subtraction	-	It is used to subtract the operands or value on the right from the operand on the left	>>> 4-2	2

Table 3.3: Basic operators in python

3.14.1 Precedence of operators

To evaluate an expression, precedence and associativity of the operators should be known. Precedence defines the priority of an operator and guides the expression to be evaluated. The order of evaluation depends on the order of operations. When an expression contains more than one operator, PEDMAS rule is applied to find the precedence of the operator.

P → Parentheses

E → Exponential   High precedence

D → Division

M → Multiplication

A → Addition

S → Subtraction   Low precedence

Example:

```
>>>2 * (3-1)
4
```

In the above example (3-1) is evaluated first because parentheses having higher precedence than multiplication. This will get evaluated first and produce 2 as result and this is multiplied with 2 and produce 4 as result. If the operators are having same precedence they are evaluated by using associativity.

3.14.2 Associativity

If the operators are having same precedence then associativity is used to decide the order in which the operators have to be executed. Associativity is of two types,

1. Left to Right
2. Right to Left

Most of the operators in python has left-to-right associativity. The table 3.4 shows the associativity of the arithmetic operators.

OPERATORS	ASSOCIATIVITY
( ) → Parentheses	Left to Right
** → Exponential	Right to Left
/, * → Division, Multiplication	Left to Right
+, - → Addition, Subtraction	Left to Right

Figure 3.4: Associativity of operators

Example:
```
>>>3*4/6
2
```

In the above example * and / have same level of precedence. So associativity of left to right takes place. First 3 is multiplied with 4 and the result is divided to 6. The chapter 4 explains the type of operators in detail.

3.15 DATATYPES AND VALUES

Value is the basic units of data like number or string that a program manipulates. Values are letters or number given to the variable. A name is given to a value by using an assignment statement, or simply an assignment.

Example:

```
>>>a=2
```

Here, 'a' is variable and 2 is the value for that variable. Each value belongs to different data types.

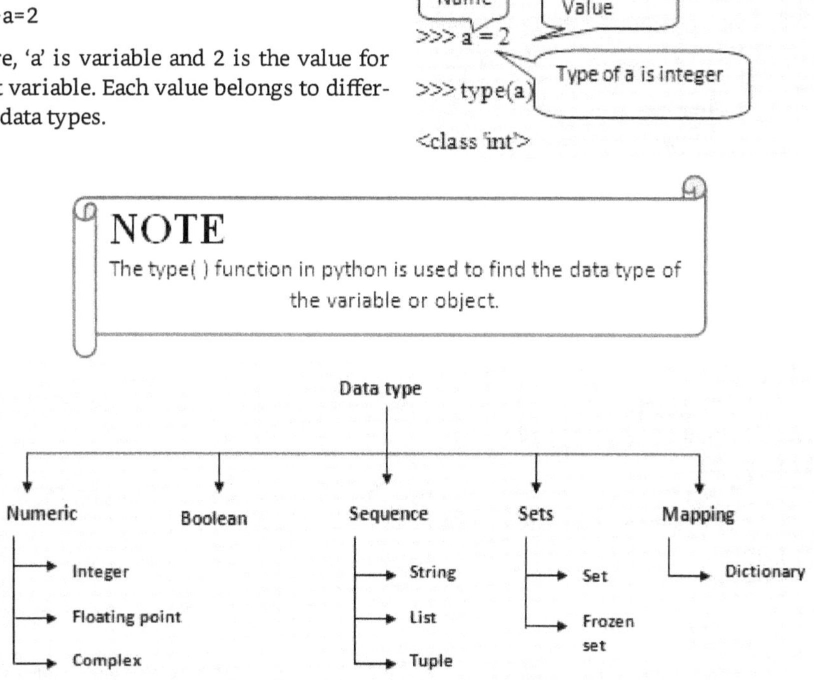

Figure 3.14 Data types of python

Datatype	Name	Example
Integer	int	a=124
Floating Point	float	B=23.12
Complex	complex	c=2+9j
Boolean	bool	z=True
String	str	s='hello'
List	list	l=[1,2,3,4]
Tuple	tuple	t=(1,2,3,4)
Set	set	s={1,'w',0}
Dictionary	dict	D={'a':1,'b':'python','c':23}

Table 3.5: Data types with example

NUMERIC

Number data type stores Numerical Values such as whole number, real number and complex number. This data type is immutable. Python supports following number types

1. Integers
2. Floating point numbers
3. Complex numbers

3.15.1 Integer (int)

Integers are whole numbers without decimal point. It contains digits from 0 to 9, they can be positive or negative. Integers have unlimited size in python. The type ( ) function is used to find the data type of the variable.

Example:

```
>>>a = -25
>>> type(a)
<class 'int'>
```

The python also support binary integer (Base 2), octal integer (Base 8) and Hexadecimal integer (Base 16).

Binary integer:

A number in the form 0 followed by 'B' or 'b' is a binary integer. The binary integer is with base 2, has only 0's and 1's.

Example:

```
>>> 0B1001
9
```

Octal integer:

A number in the form 0 followed by 'o' or 'O' is known as octal integer. The octal number is with base 8, from 0 to 7.

Example:
```
>>> Oo1236
670
```
Hexadecimal integer:

A number in the form 0 followed by 'x' or 'X' is known as hexadecimal integer. The hexadecimal number is with the base 16, from 0 to 9 and also from 'a' to 'f'.

Example:
```
>>> 0x459e
17822
```

3.15.2 Floating point (float)

It is known as real number or fractional number. It is written with decimal point. Decimal point separates the integer and fractional part. It contains both positive and negative signs.

Example:
```
>>> z=13.4
>>> type(z)
<class 'float'>
```

The floating point integer can be represent in scientific notation by using the letter "e" or "E".

Example:
```
>>> 12.5e1
125.0
>>> 12.5e5
1250000.0
```

3.15.3 Complex

Complex number is pairs of real and imaginary numbers. The real part is a number and imaginary part is a number with imaginary unit j.

Example:
```
>>> c=2+9j
>>> type(c)
<class 'complex'>
>>> d=1+2j
>>> print(c+d)
(3+11j)
```

3.15.4 BOOLEAN (bool)

It is a data type having two values usually denoted as 'True' or 'False'. It represents truth value in logic. The Boolean value is the result of conditional statements.

Example:
```
>>> x=True
>>> type(x)
<class 'bool'>
```

SEQUENCE

A sequence is an ordered collection of items. It contains both mutable and immutable data types. There are three types of sequence data type in Python, they are

1. Strings

2. Lists

3. Tuples

All three sequence types; tuples, strings, and lists; have similar syntax and functionality. The table 3.6 shows the difference of these three sequences.

No.	TUPLES	LISTS	STRINGS
1	Tuple is a sequence of items.	List is an ordered sequence of items. Values in the list are called elements / items.	String is defined as a sequence of characters.
2	Tuples are defined using parentheses ( ).	Lists are defined using square brackets [ ].	Strings are defined using quotes (", ', or """).
3	A tuple is an immutable list.	List is mutable.	Strings are immutable.
4	Example:	Example:	Example:
	>>> tu = (23, 'abc', 4.56, (2,3), 'def')	>>> li = ["abc", 34, 4.34, 23]	>>> st = "Hello World"
			>>> st = 'Hello World'

Table 3.6: Differentiate Tuple, List and String

3.15.5 STRING (str)

String is a sequence of characters. It is represented by using a pair of single or double quotation mark. String is assigned by using " " or ' '. String is a continuous set of characters which is immutable. We can use triple double-quotes for multi-line strings or strings that contain both ' and " inside of them: """a'b"c""". Individual character in a string is accessed by using its index. String performs operations such as Indexing, Slicing, Concatenation, Repetitions and Member ship.

Example:
```
>>>s='hai'
>>> type(s)
<class 'str'>
```

3.15.6 LIST (list)

List is Mutable ordered sequence of items of mixed types. List contains elements/items separated by commas, enclosed within [ ]. List also contains operations such as indexing, slicing, concatenation, repetition. List is mutable ordered sequence of items of mixed types.

Example:
```
>>> l=[12,11.3, 0.04]
>>> type(l)
<class 'list'>
```

3.15.7 TUPLE

Tuple is similar to a list, it also store sequence of items. It contains set of items separated by commas. Tuple is enclosed by ( ), items can have mixed data type. A tuple cannot be modified once created so it is known as immutable. Tuples are faster than lists. Tuples have keys in dictionaries, while lists don't. Operations on Tuples are Indexing, Slicing, Concatenation and Repetitions.

Example:
```
>>>t=(7,'eight',9.0)
>>> type(t)
```

```
<class 'tuple'>
```

SETS

Set is an unordered collection of objects which is enclosed by { }. There are two type of set. There are:

1) Set
2) Frozen set

3.15.8 Set

Set is an unordered collection of data and is enclosed by { }. Set does not contain any duplicate values or elements; each and every element in set is unique. It has a collection of immutable objects. Some of the operations performed by sets are union, intersection and symmetric difference.

Example:

```
s={'','e',1}
>>> type(s)
<class 'set'>
```

3.15.9 FROZEN SET

Frozen set is just like set but the elements of frozen set cannot be modified. Elements are frozen so it is named as frozen set. This set can be used as key in dictionary.

3.15.10 DICTIONARY (dict)

Dictionaries is an unordered set of objects. It is enclosed by { } and separated by commas. Python dictionary is unordered collection of key-value pairs. Colon ':' is used to separate key from values. Dictionaries are accessed via keys and not via their index. A dictionary has a mapping between a set of keys and its respective set of values. Keys can be any immutable type. Values can be any type and is mutable. A single dictionary can contain different types of values and keys.

Example:

```
>>> d={'a':1,'b':'python'}
>>> type(d)
<class 'dict'>
```

Here, 'a' and 'b' are keys, 1 and 'python' are values. The chapter 4 explains data type and its operations in detail.

SUMMARY

- Expression is a combination of operators and operands.
- Python is a high level general purpose, object-oriented scripting programming language which follows object oriented concept.
- Python was developed during 1985- 1990 by Guido van Rossum.
- Python got its name from a comedy series Monty Python's flying circus telecasted in BBC. Python was released in the year 1991.
- Python is derived from All Basic Code (ABC), modula-3, C, C++, Algol-68, Small talk and UNIX shell and many other scripting languages.
- Python 2.7 and Python 3.4 versions are mostly used versions of python programming.
- The three arrows (>>>) denotes the python prompt. It is also called chevrons, which means ready and waiting for expression or some calculation.
- IDLE means Integrated Development and Learning Environment. The IDLE has python shell and python editor. It is a most popular and standard python development environment.

- Interpreter takes one statement a time and translates it, this process repeats until the entire program is translated.
- The interactive mode in python is used as calculator.
- To exit from interactive mode type exit ( ) or quit ( ) and press enter.
- Variable must begin with alphabet ((a-z) or (A-Z)) or underscore (_) followed by letters, numbers or underscore.
- Operators are special symbols that represent the computation. These operators are used to manipulate the values of operands. The basic operators in python are +,-, /,*.
- If the operators are having same precedence then associativity is used to decide the order in which the operators have to be executed.

ILLUSTRATIVE PROGRAMS

1. Write a python program to find output for a^b.

```
a=int(input("Enter the value of a"))
b=int(input("Enter the value of b"))
print("power is ",a**b)
```

Output:

```
Enter the value of a3
Enter the value of b2
power is  9
```

2. Write a python to demonstrate input and output statement.

```
a=input("Enter your input ")# Input statement
print("The user input is ",a) # Output statement
```

Output:

```
Enter your input Hai
The user input is  Hai
```

3. Write a python program to demonstrate id( ) and type( )

```
a=int(input("Enter your input"))
print(id(a)) # id( ) is to identify the memory location of object
print(type(a)) # type( ) is used to find the data type of object
```

Output:

```
Enter your input10
1355794800
<class 'int'>
```

4. Write a python program to find square root of a number

```
a=int(input("Enter your input"))
print("The square root of ", a,"is",a**0.5)
```

Output:

```
Enter your input9
The square root of 9 is 3.0
```

5. Write a python program to get quotient and remainder of two numbers.

```
a=int(input("Enter your input"))
b=int(input("Enter another number"))
print("The quotient of two numbers is", int(a/b))
print("The remainder of two numbers is",a%b)
```

Output:

```
Enter your input12
Enter another number3
```

The quotient of two numbers is 4
The remainder of two numbers is 0

6. Write a python program to print Hello World.

print("Hello World")

Output:

Hello World

7. Write a python program to print Hello World using string variables.

s="Hello World"

print(s)

Output:

Hello World

8. Write a python program to find area of rectangle.

l=int(input("Enter the length of rectangle "))
b=int(input("Enter the breath of rectangle "))
area=l*b
print("Area of rectangle is ",area)

Output:

Enter the length of rectangle 4
Enter the breath of rectangle 2
Area of rectangle is 8

9. Write a python program to find GCD of two numbers using % operator.

a=int(input("Enter a number "))
b=int(input("Enter another number "))
rem=a%b
while rem!=0 :
   a=b
   b=rem
   rem=a%b
print("gcd of given numbers is ",b)

Output:

Enter a number 12
Enter another number 4
gcd of given numbers is 4

ADDITIONAL PROGRAMS

1. Write a python program to demonstrate the arithmetic operators.
2. Write a python program to convert integer to hexadecimal.
3. Write a python program to convert integer to octal.
4. Write a python program to demonstrate a block.
5. Write a python program to convert Fahrenheit to Celsius.

REVIEW QUESTIONS

1. What is python? Explain the features.
2. Give the rules for writing a variable name.
3. Explain about variable and expression.
4. Explain about statements and its type.
5. Differentiate single line and multiline statements.
6. Differentiate operand and operators.
7. What is a comment? What are its uses?

8.   Explain about precedence and associativity.
9.   Explain the basic operators in python.
10. What are data types? Explain its types.
11. What are the types of modes in python?
12. What is the use of type( ) function? Explain with example.
13. Differentiate integer and floating point number.
14. Write the advantages and disadvantage of python.
15. What are the applications of python?

MUTIPLE CHOICE QUESTIONS

1.   Python convert source code into an intermediate form known as __________.
     a. Byte code
     b. Binary code
     c. progarm code
     d. readable code

2.   The numeric of the form 3+2j is known as __________.
     a. Real numbers
     b. Integer
     c. Floating point
     d. Complex
3.   The number 5265.5E5 is a floating point number which is equal to?
     a. 526550000.0
     b. 5265.55
     c. 526555
     d. 5265550000.0
4.   What is the output for the code?
a=10;
b=a
print("sum is: ",a+b)
     a. SyntaxError
     b. LogicalError
     c. sum is: 20
     d. None of these
5.   What is the output for the program?
a=10
b=20
if a>b:
print("a is greater")
else:
   print("b is greater")
     a. SyntaxError
     b. a is greater
     c. b is greater
     d. None of these
6.   Which of the following is not a tuple?
     a. t1=(1,4,5)
     b. t2=1,4,5
     c. t3=(3)

    d. t4=(2,4,'hai',[1,3])
7.   Which of the following is a valid variable name?
    a. v_name=10
    b. pass=50
    c. v@name=20
    d. 1_vname=10
8.   Which of the following is not a string?
    a. s='hai'
    b. s1="hai"
    c. s2='''hai'''
    d. None of these
9.   What is the output for this program?

```
a=2+6j
b=8+3j
print(a-b)
```

    a. Error
    b. (-6+3j)
    c. (6+3j)
    d. (6-3j)
10. What is the octal value for the number 155265?
    a. 457201
    b. 45720
    c. 0O457201
    d. 0O45720
11. What is the data type of 'a' if the code is:

```
>>>a=10.5>5
```

    a. Integer
    b. Boolean
    c. Floating point
    d. None of these
12. What is the output for the following code?

```
a, b=9,6,5
print(a)
```

    a. 9
    b. 5
    c. 6
    d. ValueError
13. What is the output for the expression(12-2)*10/5**2
    a. 40.0
    b. 4.0
    c. 25.0
    d. Error
14. How many lines will it takes to print this output statement?

```
>>> print("red\ngreen\nblue\torange")
```

    a. 4
    b. 3
    c. 2
    d. 1
15. Which of the following is not a data type?

a. String
b. Array
c. Complex
d. Tuple

16. Which of the following is not a keyword?
a. def
b. yield
c. assert
d. local

17. Which of the following is the correct output for the code:
>>> format(65.86427,'.4f')
a.   '65.8642'
b.   '65.8643'
c.   Error
d.   'float'

18. Which of the following interprets entire high level language code during exection?
a. Compiler
b. Interpreter
c. Assembler
d. None of these

TRUE OR FALSE

1. The interpreter is relatively slower than a compiler.
2. Python is a case sensitive language.
3. In python we cannot refer more than one variable to the same object.
4. Interpreter executes on instruction at a time.
5. Tuple contains key-value pairs.
6. In python keywords can be used as variable name.
7. Python is an interpreted language.
8. Python follows both procedural oriented and object oriented approaches.
9. The output( ) function is used to display output on the screen.
10. The python programs are stored with the extension .py.
11. Value of the variable can be assigned only once.
12. Interpreter saves object code for future use.

FILL IN THE BLANKS

1. The binary form of 54 is ___________.
2. If 14_________2 = 0, fill in the blanks with an operator.
3. In python power of a number is represented by using _________ operator.
4. The data type of the variable is assigned during _________.
5. The ___________ symbol in python represents comments.
6. The block in python is marked by the level of _________.
7. The process of execution more than process of program at a time is known as ___________.
8. Python has ___________ for collecting object which is no longer referred.
9. Python follows ___________ and ___________ approaches.
10. The _________ executes one instruction at a time.

11. The ______________ converts byte code into machine understandable code.

ANSWERS

MUTIPLE CHOICE QUESTIONS

1. a	3. a	5. a	7. a	9. b	11. b	13. b	15. b	17. b
2. d	4. c	6. c	8. d	10. c	12. d	14. a	16. d	18. b

TRUE OR FALSE

1. True
2. True
3. False
4. True
5. False
6. False
7. True
8. True
9. False
10. True
11. False
12. False

FILL IN THE BLANKS

1. 0b110110
2. % (modulo operator)
3. ** (Exponent)
4. Runtime
5. #
6. indentation
7. multithreading
8. garbage collector
9. Object oriented, procedure oriented
10. Interpreter
11. Python virtual machine (PVM)

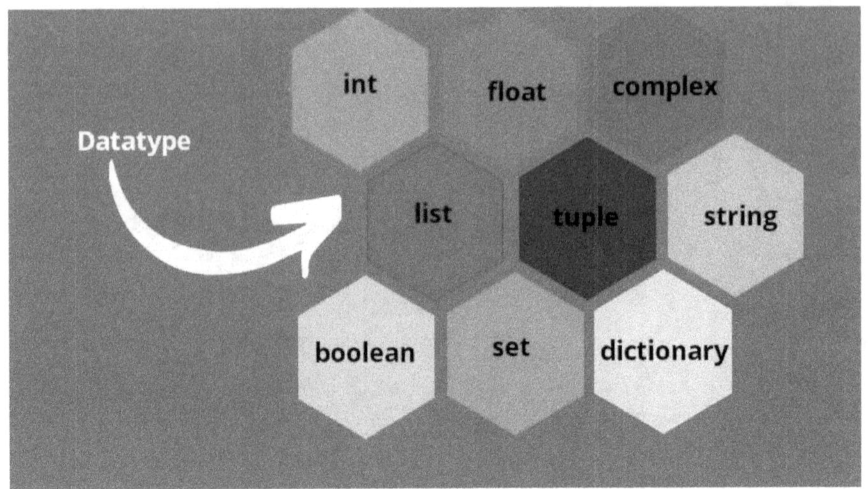

CHAPTER 4: OPERATORS AND DATA TYPE

In Chapter 4 you come across the data type and operators in the Python programming language. The data type such as integer, long, floating point, complex, list, tuple, string, set, dictionary are explained with their operations. This chapter also discuss about type conversion of various data types and comprehension of list, set and dictionary. Some of the basic operations that can be performed on a sequence are indexing, slicing, adding, multiplying, and checking memberships are also explained.

CHAPTER OUTLINE

Operators: Associativity, precedence – Type conversions – Data types: Integer, Floating point, Complex, String, List, Tuple, Set, Frozen set and Dictionary – indexing – slicing –repetition– concatenation – mutability – methods – comprehensions

OBJECTIVE

After covering the chapter, the student will be in a position:

- To know about operators and its type.
- To know about associativity and precedence of operator.
- To understand about type conversion.
- To know about data types of python.
- To know how to create a data type and how to access it.
- To know about manipulation of sequences.
- To know about indexing, slicing, repetition, concatenation.
- To known about built-in function, methods and modules of string.

- To know about compound data types.
- To known about built-in function and methods of compound data type.
- To know about comprehensions in list, set and dictionary.
- To understand the difference between equality and identity.
- To know about aliasing and need for cloning.
- To know about mutability and immutability of data type.

4.1 OPERATORS

The operator is a symbol which is used to perform some operation with one or more operand. It is the constructs used to control or manipulate the value of operands. Some of the basic operators are +, -, * and /.

Example:

```
>>> 3+4
7
```

In the above expressions 3 and 4 are the operands whereas + is operator. Based on the functionality operators are categorized into seven types.

1. Arithmetic operator
2. Comparison or relational operator
3. Assignment operator
4. Logical operator
5. Bitwise operator
6. Membership operator
7. Identity operator
8. Unary operator

4.1.1 Arithmetic operators

These operators are used to perform arithmetic operations such as addition, subtraction, multiplication and division. Table 4.1 explains the entire arithmetic operator with example. Let's take two operands x=10 and y=2.

OPERATOR	SYMBOL	DESCRIPTION	EXAMPLE	OUTPUT
Add	+	Add left and right numbers or operands	>>> x+y	12
Subtract	-	Subtract right side operand from left operand	>>> x-y	8
Multiply	*	Multiply left and right operands	>>> x*y	20
Divide	/	Divide left operand by the right operand and display the quotient.	>>> x/y	5
Exponent	**	Left operand raise to the power of right. It is used to perform exponential (power) calculation on operands.	>>> x**y	100
Floor division	//	Divide left operand by the right operand. If the result contains fractional part just cut the fractional part and display only the integer part as result. The result is the quotient in which the digits after the decimal point are removed	>>> x%y	0
Modulo	%	Divide left operand by the right operand and returns remainder.	>>> x//y	5

Table 4.1: Arithmetic operators

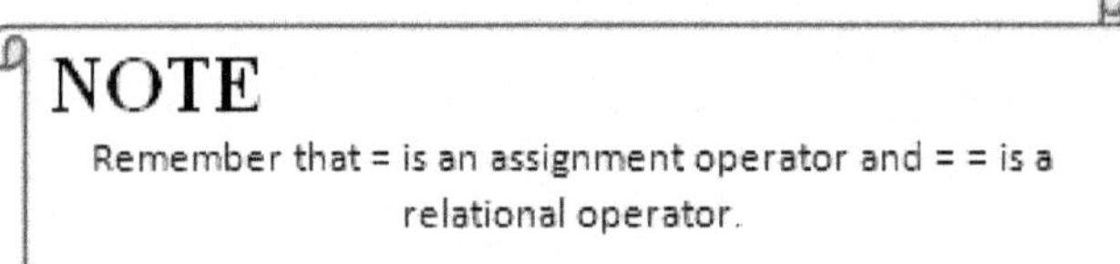

4.1.2 Comparison or Relational operators

Comparison operators are used to compare values or operands and the result of these operators is always Boolean values, that is either 'True' or 'False'. Table 4.2 explains the entire comparison operator with example. Let's take two operands x=10 and y=2.

OPERATOR	SYMBOL	DESCRIPTION	EXAMPLE	OUTPUT
Equal to	= =	Display True if both operand are equal otherwise False	>>> x==y	False
Not equal to	!=	Display True if both operand are not equal otherwise False	>>> x!=y	True
Less than	<	Display True if left operand is less than the right operand otherwise False	>>> x<y	False
Greater than	>	Display True if left operand is greater than the right operand otherwise False	>>> x>y	True
Greater than or equal to	> =	Display True if left operand is greater than or equal to the right operand otherwise False	>>> x>=y	True
Less than or equal to	< =	Display True if left operand is less than or equal to the right operand otherwise False	>>> x<=y	False

Table 4.2: Comparison operators

4.1.3 Assignment operators

This operator is used to assign value to the operand or expression. This operator is used to store right hand side operand or value to the left hand side operand. It is used to assign value to the variables. The basic assignment operator is equal (=). Table 4.3 explains the entire assignment operator with example. Lets assign value of x as 5, Always assign x=5 and perform this assignment operations.

OPERATOR	SYMBOL	DESCRIPTION	EXAMPLE	EQUIVALENT TO	RESULT OF x IS:
Assignment	=	This is the assignment operator which assigns a value to variable	x=5	x=5	5
Add AND	+=	It adds right operand to the left operand and assign the result to left operand	x+=5	x=x+5	10
Subtract AND	-=	It subtracts right operand from the left operand and assign the result to left operand	x-=5	x=x-5	0
Multiply AND	*=	It multiplies right operand with the left operand and assign the result to left operand	x*=5	x=x*5	25
Divide AND	/=	It divides left operand with the right operand and assign the result to left operand	x/=5	x=x/5	5
Modulo AND	%=	It takes modulus using two operands and assign the result to left operand	x%=5	x=x%5	0
Exponent AND	**=	Performs exponential (power) calculation on operators and assign value to the left operand	x**=5	x=x**5	3125
Floor division AND	//=	It performs floor division on operators and assign value to the left operand	x//=5	x=x//5	1
Right shift AND	>>=	It performs Right shift and assigns that value to left the operand	x>>=5	x=x>>5	0
Left shift AND	<<=	It performs left shift and assigns that value to left the operand	x<<=5	x=x<<5	160

Table 4.3: Assignment operators

NOTE

The operators such as +=, -=, *=, /=, %=, //=, **=, >>= and <<= are called as in-place operators or shortcut operators.

4.1.4 Bitwise operators

These are the operators performs bit level operation on operands. It operates bit by bit. The table 4.4 explains the Truth table for entire bitwise operator and table 4.5 explains the entire bitwise operator with example.

X	Y	X&Y	X|Y	X^Y	~X	~Y
0	0	0	0	0	1	1
0	1	0	1	1	1	0
1	0	0	1	1	0	1
1	1	1	1	0	0	0

Table 4.4: Truth table of bitwise operators

Let's take two operands X=10 and Y=12. Conversion of this number to binary number can be written as:

X=10	➜	1010
Y=12	➜	1100
X & Y = 8	➜	1000

OPERATOR	SYMBOL	DESCRIPTION	EXAMPLE	OUTPUT
Bitwise AND	&	If both operand True then output will also be True else False	>>> x&y	8
Bitwise OR	|	If any one of the operand True then output will also be True else False	>>> x|y	14
Bitwise NOT	~	It is the inverse of the operand. If the operand is True then result will be False. It is also known as one complement.	>>> ~x	-11
Bitwise XOR	^	True if True is present in only one operand otherwise False	>>> x^y	6
Bitwise Left shift	<<	It shift the bit towards the left	>>>x<<2	40
Bitwise Right shift	>>	It shift the bit towards the right	>>>x>>2	2

Table 4.5: Bitwise operators

Bitwise NOT:

This operator performs one's complement of the number. The given number is converted into binary and then one's complement is done. This operator will return the decimal value as output.

Example:

```
>>> x=10
>>> ~x
-11
```

The above example is explained here:

```
x   = 1010
~x = ~(1010)
    = -(1010+1)
    =- (1011)
```

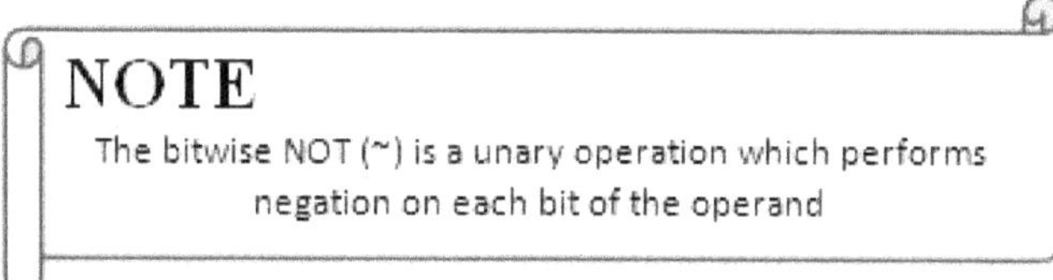

Left Shift:

Left shift means shifting the bit toward the left. Here Figure 4.1 explains the working of left shift.

```
>>>x=8
```

```
>>>x<<2
```
Example:

Here, left shift 2 means shift two bit towards left.

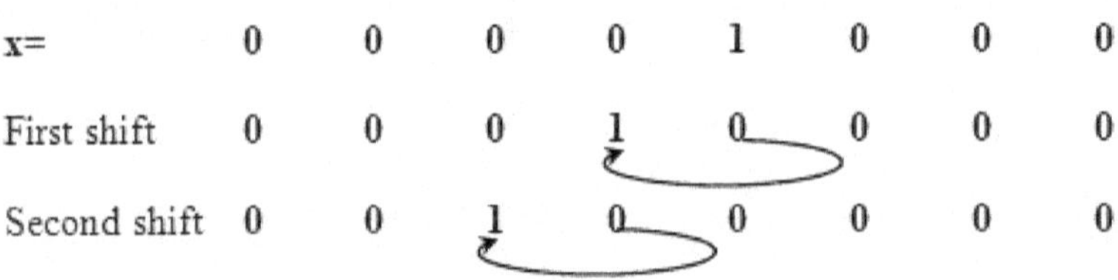

Figure 4.1: Left shifting

4.1.5 Logical operators

Logical operator is used to check and compare two or more conditions and the resultant is Boolean values. The table 4.6 explains the Truth table for entire logical operators and table 4.7 explains the entire logical operators with example.

X	Y	AND	OR	Not X	Not Y
0	0	0	0	1	1
0	1	0	1	1	0
1	0	0	1	0	1
1	1	1	1	0	0

Table 4.6: Truth table for logical operators

Let's consider x=True and y=False

OPERATOR	SYMBOL	DESCRIPTION	EXAMPLE	OUTPUT
Logical AND	And	Return True if both the operands are True otherwise False	>>>x and y	False
Logical OR	Or	Return True if any of the operands is True otherwise False	>>> x or y	True
Logical NOT	not	Return True is the operand is False and vice versa	>>> not x	False

Table 4.7: Logical operators

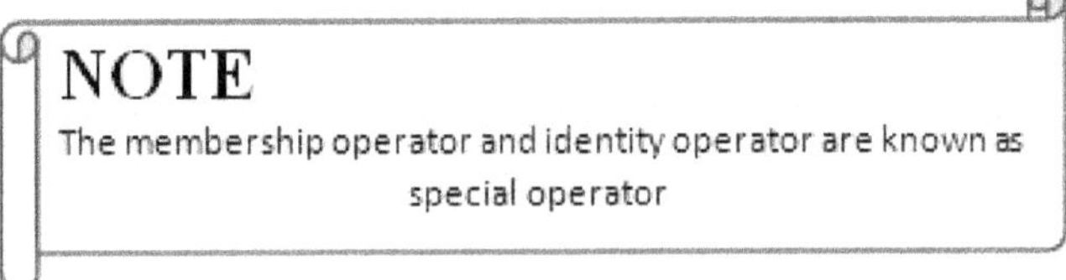

4.1.6 Membership operators

These operators are used to check an item or an element that is part of a sequence or not. The sequence such as string, list, set or a tuple. This operator reduces the effort of searching an element in sequence. This operator is used to check whether the sequence such as list, string or tuple contains that value or not. The table 4.8 explains about the membership operators with example. Let's consider a sequence of character (string) s='python'

OPERATOR	SYMBOL	DESCRIPTION	EXAMPLE	OUTPUT
IN	in	Return True, if item is in the sequence otherwise False	>>> 't' in s	True
NOT IN	not in	Return True, if item is not in the sequence otherwise False	>>> 'p' not in s	False

Table 4.8: Membership operators

Example:
>>> x=[2,71,6]
>>> 7 not in x
True
>>> 2 not in x
False
>>> 2 in x
True

4.1.7 Identity operators

These operators are used to check whether both operands are same or not. This operator compares the memory location of two objects. It returns True, if both objects are same else return False. The table 4.9 explains identity operator with example. Let's consider two values x=10 and y =10

OPERATOR	SYMBOL	DESCRIPTION	EXAMPLE	OUTPUT
IS	is	Return True if the operands are identical otherwise False	>>> x is y	True
IS NOT	is not	Return True if the operands are not identical otherwise False	>>> x is not y	False

Table 4.9: Identity operators

Example: Demonstrate identity operator
>>> x=10
>>> y=10
>>> x is y
True
>>> id(x)
1591134576
>>> id(y)
1591134576

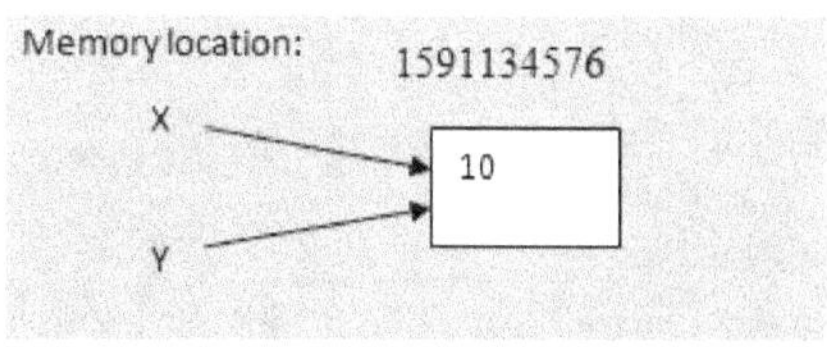

From the above example it is clear that x and y refers the same memory location 1591134576. So the output for " x is y " is True. In python initially an object is created then the variable is tagged to that object. In the above example, first 10 is created in the memory location 1591134576, If any other variable is assigned with the same value 10, then that variable is tagged to it. Here the variable x and y is tagged to that object.

So they both refer same memory space.

4.1.8 Unary Operator

Unary operator is an operator which has only one operand. The table 4.10 shows the unary operators with example. Let's consider two values x=10

OPERATOR	SYMBOL	DESCRIPTION	EXAMPLE	OUTPUT
Unary PLUS	-	Return the negation of the numeric value.	>>> -(x)	-10
Unary MINUS	+	Return the numeric value itself.	>>> +(x)	10
Unary NOT	~	It is the inverse of the operand. It is also known as one complement or Bitwise NOT.	>>> ~x	-11

Table 4.10 Unary Operators

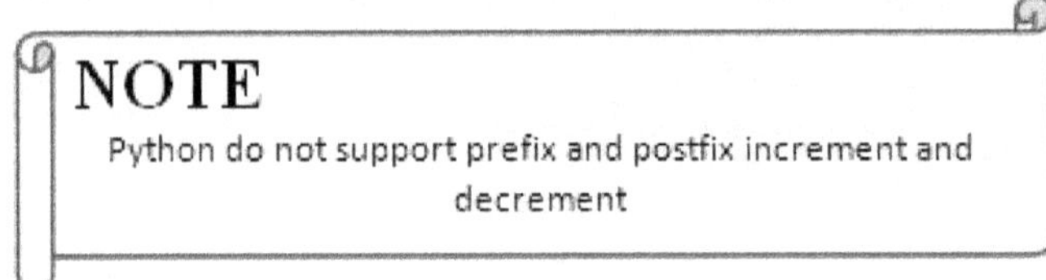

4.1.9 Precedence

Precedence defines the priority of an operator and guides the expression to be evaluated. This means which operator gets a change to evaluate first. When an expression contains more than one operator, the order of evaluation depends on the order of precedence and associativity. The table 4.11 shows the precedence of operators.

OPERATORS	SYMBOLS	PRECEDENCE
Parentheses	( )	HIGH PRECEDENCE
Exponential	**	
Unary	~, +, -	
Arithmetic operators	*, /, %, //	
Addition and subtraction	+, -	
Left shift, Right shift	<<, >>	
Bitwise AND	&	
Bitwise XOR	^	
Bitwise OR	|	
Relational operators	<=, <, >=, >	
Equal to, Not Equal to	==, !=	
Assignment operators	=, %=, /=, //=, -=, +=, *=, **=	
Identity operator	is, is not	
Membership operator	in, not in	
Logical not	Not	
Logical and	And	LOW PRECEDENCE
Logical or	Or	

Table 4.11: Precedence of operators

Example:
```
>>> 10+12/6*3-6
10
```

The above expression is 10+12/6*3-6 which contains more the one operators. The order of precedence in which the operators executes is:

```
= 10+12/6*3-6
= 10+2*3-6
= 10+6-6
= 16-6
= 10
```

If the operators are having same precedence they are evaluated by using associativity.

4.1.9 Associativity

If the operators are having same precedence then associativity decides the order in which the operator executes. It is of two types:

- Left to Right
- Right to Left

Most of the operators in python have left-to-right associativity. The table 4.11

shows the associativity of operators.

OPERATORS	ASSOCIATIVITY
( ) → Parentheses	Left to Right
** → Exponential	Right to Left
/, * → Division, Multiplication	Left to Right
+, - → Addition, Subtraction	Left to Right

Table 4.11: Associativity of operators

Example:
>>> (10+14)/6*3-6
6

The order of evaluation is:

= (10+14)/6*3-6
= 24/6*3-6
= 4*3-6
= 12-6
= 6

In the above example operators such as +, /, *, - are used. Parentheses is given higher precedence so the sub expression (10+12) will get evaluated first then * and / have same level of precedence. Here, associativity of left to right takes place. First division takes place and the result is multiplied with 3 and that result is subtracted by 6, finally 6 is obtained as result.

4.2 TYPE CONVERSION

The type conversion is a process of converting one data type into another. Python contain many built-in functions for this conversion. This function will return the converted value. The data type conversion is done in two ways:
- Explicit conversion
- Implicit conversion

4.2.1 Implicit conversion

The implicit conversion is known as type coercion, this type of conversion takes place automatically.

Example:
>>> a=12.0
>>> b=2
>>> c=a+b
>>> c
14.0

In the above example, the data type of b is not converted into floating point to perform the process. This conversion was done by interpreter implicitly such type of conversion is known as implicit conversion.

4.2.2 Explicit conversion

Explicit conversion is also known as type casting, in this conversion user explicitly convert one data type to another.

Example:
a='Python'
b=2.7
print(a+b)

In such case error will be displayed. This is because we cannot add string and floating point number together.
Traceback (most recent call last):
  File "C:\Python27\4.py", line 3, in <module>
    print(a+b)
TypeError: Can't convert 'float' object to str implicitly

For this cases user has to convert the floating point data type into string, in order to concatenate the string.

Example:
a='Python'
b=str(2.7) #explicit conversion
print(a+b)
print(type(b))
Output:
Python2.7
<class 'str'>

NOTE

In python explicit type conversion is known as **type casting** and implicit type conversion is known as **type coercion**

The built-in functions of python to convert one data type into another are explained with example in Table 4.12.

FUNCTION NAME	DESCRIPTION	EXAMPLE	OUTPUT
int(x)	It convert x into a integer. The int(x) truncate the fractional part if the x is a floating pint number.	>>> x=12.5 >>> int(x)	12
float(x)	It convert x into floating point number.	>>> x=10 >>> float(x)	10.0
str(x)	It convert x into a string	>>> x=10 >>> str(x)	'10'
tuple(x)	It convert x into a tuple	>>> x=[1,2,'hai'] >>> tuple(x)	(1, 2, 'hai')
list(x)	It convert x into a list	>>> x=(1, 2, 'hai') >>> list(x)	[1, 2, 'hai']
set(x)	It convert x into set	>>> x=(1, 2, 'hai') >>> set(x)	{1, 2, 'hai'}
dict(x)	It convert x into dictionary if x has key-value pairs.		

Table 4.12: Type conversion function

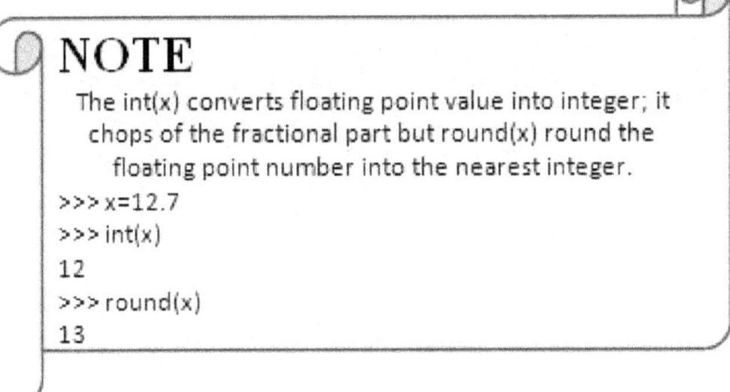

Other than this, there are some other conversions such as converting octal to hexadecimal values and vice versa.

4.3 DATATYPES

The object in python has value which is of different types commonly known as data type. Variables are type less. Python supports dynamic typing and the variable type is decided at runtime. Python has five standard data types. They are, Numeric, Boolean, sequence, sets and mapping. The figure 4.2 shows various data types which python supports.

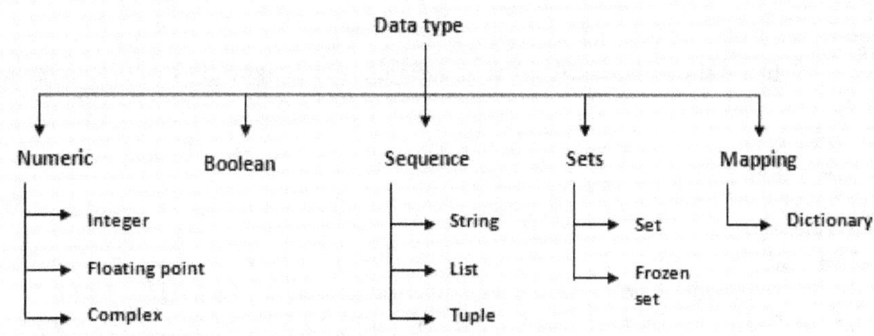

Figure 4.2: Data types

Python has five standard data types:

1) NUMBERS

Number data type stores Numerical Value such as whole number, real number and complex number. This data type is immutable which means the values/items cannot be changed. Python supports following number data types:

1. Integers
2. Floating point numbers
3. Complex numbers

2) BOOLEAN (bool):

It is a data type having two values usually denoted as 'True' or 'False'. It represents truth value in logic. The Boolean value is the result of conditional statements.

3) SEQUENCE

A sequence is an ordered collection of items which is indexed by positive integers. The some sequence datatype are immutable (values cannot be changed) and some are mutable (value can be changed) data types. Python has three types of sequence data, they are:

1. String
2. List
3. Tuple

4) SETS

Set is an unordered collection of objects which is enclosed by { }. There are two type of set. There are:

1. Set
2. Frozen set

5) MAPPING

Mappings are collections of objects that store objects by key instead of its position. The mapping object maps immutable value to object. Dictionary is the only one data type that supports mapping. This dictionary contains key-value pairs; any key of the dictionary is mapped to a value. Lets discus each datatypes of python in detail.

4.4 INTEGER

Integers are whole numbers without decimal point. They can be positive or negative. Integers have unlimited size in python.

Example:

```
>>>a=10 # Giving integer number in compile time
```

```
>>> print a
10
```

    In the above example, value of variable 'a' is assigned in compile time of the program.

Example:

```
>>> b=input('enter a value')
enter a value7
>>> type(b)
<class 'int'>
```

    In the above example, input( ) function is used to get value from user during runtime. This function will take a value which may be number or string or any other type. In python data type of a variable can be assigned during runtime. The type( ) function is used to find the data type of the variable.

```
>>> c=int(input('enter value'))
enter value78
```

    In the above example, int( ) unction is used in order to convert the given input into integer value.

Example:

```
>>> d=int(input('enter value'))
enter value7.907
>>> type(d)
<class 'int'>
>>> print d
7
```

    In the above example, value passed by the user is a floating point value. The int( ) function converts the entered floating point value into integer value. Here, the data type conversion is done; the interpreter will take only the whole number.

Example:

```
>>> integer_value=89
>>> float_value=float(integer_value)
>>> print float_value
89.0
```

    In the above example, float( ) function converts integer into floating point values. This process is known as type conversion.

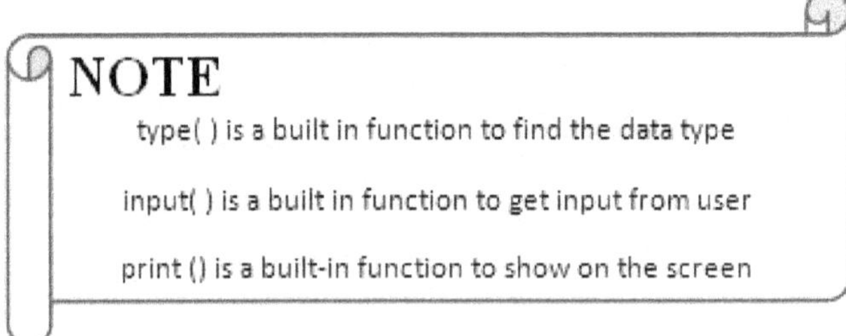

4.5   FLOATING POINT

    It is known as real number or fractional number. It is written with decimal point. It has decimal part and fractional part. Decimal point separates the integer and fractional parts.

Example:
>>>a=3.15
>>> b=float(input('enter a value'))
enter a value7.89
>>> type(b)
<class 'float'>
Example:
>>> int(b)
7

In above example, int( ) function is used to convert floating point number into integer. This process is known as type conversion.

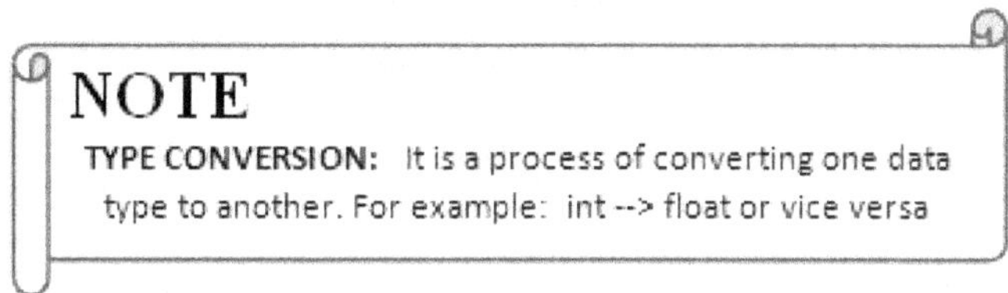

4.6 COMPLEX

Complex number is a combination of real and imaginary part. It is in the form a+bi, whereas 'a' carries real part and 'bi' has imaginary part.
Example:
>>> c=2+9j
>>> type(c)
<class 'complex'>

4.7 BOOLEAN (BOOL)

It is a data type having two values known as 'True' or 'False'. It represents truth value in logic. It is the primary result of conditional statements. Boolean data type have two values either it can take 0 or 1. The value 0 means False and 1 means True. In python, True and False are keyword.
Example:
>>> x=True
>>> type(x)
<class 'bool'>
Example:
>>> 10==20
False
>>> 'python'=="python"
True
>>> 2.00==2
True
>>> 6>=7
False

The output of relational operator, logical operator, membership operator and Identity operator are Boolean values. In the above example relational operator are used to check whether the output is True or False. Section 4.2 explained the detailed concepts of operator with example.

NOTE

The data types such as numeric (integer, floating point, and complex) and Boolean are called **scalar data types**. These are the elementary forms of data

4.8 STRING

String is defined as a sequence or set of characters represented in quotation marks. The characters may be number, letters, whitespace character, other symbols or combination of these. A pair of single quotes (' ') , double quotes (' ' ' ') or triple quotes (' ' ' ' ' ') can be used to denote a string. An individual character in a string is accessed using a subscript also known as index. The subscript should always be an integer this may be either positive or negative integer. A subscript or index of string starts from 0 to n-1. The contents of the string cannot be changed after it is created which means it is immutable.

NOTE

Python does not support character data type. A string of size 1 can be treated as characters.

Example:
```
>>>s='hai'
>>> type(s)
<class 'str'>
```
The type( ) function is used to identify what data type it is. In python string is an object of str class.

Quotation marks in python are:

    1. Single quotes ('   ')

Example:
```
a='hai'
```
    2. Double quotes ("   ")

Example:
```
a=" hai"
```
    3. Triple quotes (''' ''')

Example:
```
>>> '''hai ..................
how are you'''
'hai ..................\nhow are you'
```
Here, \n represents newlines.

Example:
```
>>> s='hai'
>>> print s
hai
```

Any this inside the quotation mark is considered as string. We can also print a string without using print function.

Example:

```
>>> s='hai'
>>> s
'hai'
```

Or simply type the string in quotation mark and then press enter.

```
>>> 'hai'
'hai'
```

> **NOTE**
>
> Python does not support character data type. The single quotes(' ') and Double quotes(" ") are exactly same but triple quotes(''' ''') are used to specify multi-line statements.

Like on numbers, we can also manipulate strings by performing operation on them such as +,*, slicing, etc. Whitespace and other special characters are also the part of string and it has its own index number. Individual character in a string is accessed by using its index. String performs operations such as:

- Indexing
- Slicing
- Concatenation
- Repetitions
- Membership

4.8.1 Indexing

In order to access the individual character string indexing is used. The indexing operator is represented in square bracket [ ], it is also known as subscript. Index values start at zero, and extend upwards to the number of characters in the string minus one (n-1). There are two types of indexing:

- Forward indexing
- Backward indexing

The Positive indexing is for accessing the string from the beginning. Negative indexing is for accessing the string from the end. Below figure 4.3 represents the index of a string, s= 'PYTHON'

FORWARD INDEXING	0	1	2	3	4	5
STRING	P	Y	T	H	O	N
BACKWARD INDEXING	-6	-5	-4	-3	-2	-1

Figure 4.3: Indexing of string

Syntax:

```
string_name[index_number]
```

The expression in the bracket is called index. The index indicates which character in the sequence you want to access.

Example:
>>> s[0]
'P'

It is clear that the indexing starts from 0, In order to access that value use s[0]. Here s is the name of the string and 0 is the index.
Example:
>>> s[3]
'H'
Example:
>>> s[-1]
'N'

In the above example, the index number -1 represents negative indexing. Here the indexing starts from the end.

4.8.2 Slicing

Slice operator is used to slice or to extract the subsets of string. A segment of a string or substring of a string is called a slice, [:] is the operator used to slice the string. You have to specify the index of the string that you want to slice. Index of first character is 0 and last character is n-1 whereas, n is the total number of characters in a string.
Syntax:
string_name[start_index:finish_index]
Example:
>>> a='sequence'
>>> len(a)
8

In the above example len( ) function is used to find the length of the string. String contains set of character starting from the index 0 to n-1.In the above example length of the string is 8 and index ranges from 0 to 7.

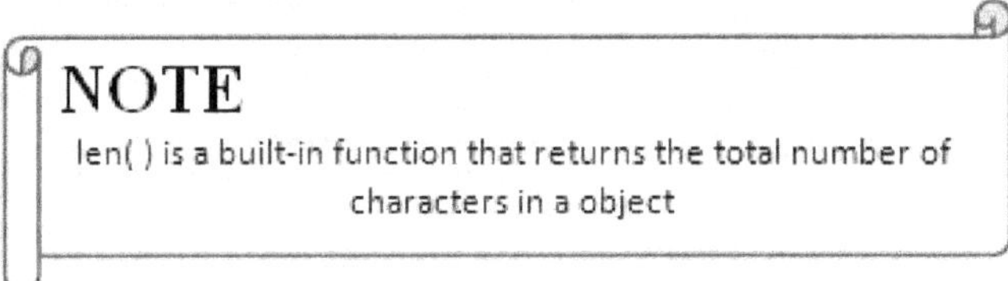

Example:
>>> a[:]
'sequence'
>>> a[0]
's'
>>> a[5]
'n'
>>> a[0:3]
'seq'

If the starting and ending indexing is not mentioned entire string will get displayed. If you omit the first index or starting index i.e. the index before the colon, the slice starts at the beginning of the string. If you omit the second index or ending index, the slice goes to the end of the string:
Example:

```
>>> a[:5]
'seque'
```

This will display the value from 0 to 4. If the starting index is not mentioned value from the starting index is taken.

Example:

```
>>> a[-6]
'q'
```

Negative indexing is also used to access the string.   Here, -6 denote backward indexing.

Example:

```
>>> a[9]
Traceback (most recent call last):
  File "<pyshell#12>", line 1, in <module>
    a[9]
IndexError: string index out of range
```

In above example the last index of 'a' is 7 if you try to access value out of this limit then IndexError is raised. This indicates that the string index is out of range.

Example:

```
>>> a[::-1]
'ecneuqes'
```

In the above example -1 denotes reverse; this will reverse the entire string.

Example:

```
>>> a[4:4]
''
>>> a[6:4]
''
```

If the first index is greater than or equal to the second index then the result is empty string represented by a pair of quotation marks (''). An empty string do not contains any characters and has length 0.

4.8.3 Concatenation

The process of adding or combining two strings in python is known as concatenation. The + operator is used for this purpose. The + operator joins the string on both sides of the operator.

Syntax:

```
'string_1' + 'string_2'
```

Example:

```
>>> a='python'
>>> b='programming'
>>> a+b
'pythonprogramming'
```

In the above example + sign join both the string together.

Example:

```
>>> '12'+'90'
'1290'
```

This + operator add or join whatever thing which is given inside the quotes. This means if you use a number within quotes then it is considered as string, for that number concatenation is done. Here the output is numbers that are represented as string.

Example:

```
>>> a='string'+1
Traceback (most recent call last):
 File "<pyshell#16>", line 1, in <module>
   a='string'+1
TypeError: cannot concatenate 'str' and 'int' objects
```

From the above example it is clear that concatenation is only possible between strings not between string and integer object.

4.8.4 Repetitions

You cannot add a string and a number but you can multiply a string and an integer. This operation is known as repetition, replication or string multiplication. The * operator is used for repetition. The * operator repeats the string on the left hand side times the value on right hand side and vice versa. The repetition is only done with a string and an integer, not with other data type.

Syntax:

'string_1' * n

Where n is the integer, here n number of time the repetition of string is done.

Example:

```
>>> print ('hello'*3)
hellohellohello
```

Example:

```
>>> print (5*'hai\n')
hai
hai
hai
hai
hai
```

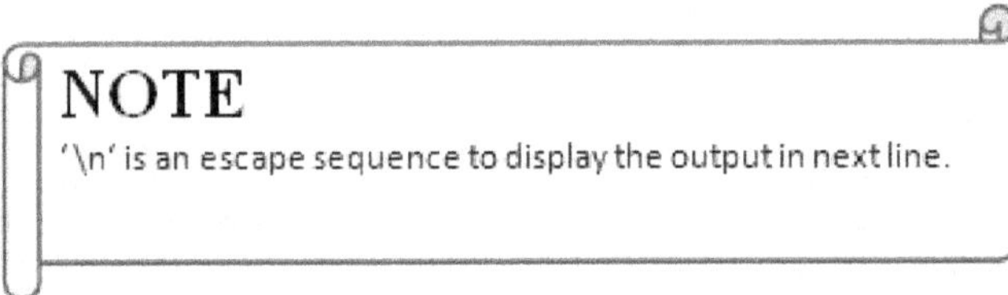

4.8.5 Membership

The membership operators are used to check a particular character is in string or not. It Returns True if that character is the member of string otherwise return False. In some case it is used to determine whether a string is present in another string.

Example:

```
>>> b='how are you'
>>> 'y' in b
True
>>> 'g' in b
False
```

From the above example, it is clear about the operation of membership operator.

4.8.6 String Immutability

Strings are immutable; you cannot change or modify the string once it is created. Therefore [ ] operator cannot be used on the left side of an assignment. We cannot change or delete an element of a string. If you want to change the element of a string, you have to assign a new string.

Example:

```
>>> a='hello'
>>> a[0]='b'
Traceback (most recent call last):
  File "<pyshell#31>", line 1, in <module>
    a[0]='b'
TypeError: 'str' object does not support item assignment
```

From the above example it is clear that string object is immutable. That means string does not support character assignment. String is immutable, meaning they cannot be changed once assigned. Instead of that, a new string is constructed out of an existing string, using slicing commands.

```
>>> a='hello'
>>> b='b'+a[1:]
>>> b
'bello'
```

This has no effect on original string. You had created a new string by concatenating and slicing the original one.

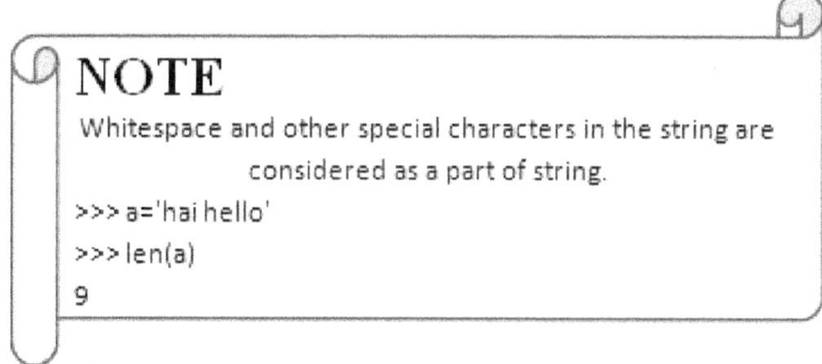

4.8.7 String Functions and Methods

String contains many built-in function and methods to manipulate the string. Function contains codes to perform some related tasks or actions. The method is similar to function which takes arguments and returns a value, but the syntax of method and function are different.

Syntax:

object.<method _name>(argument(s))

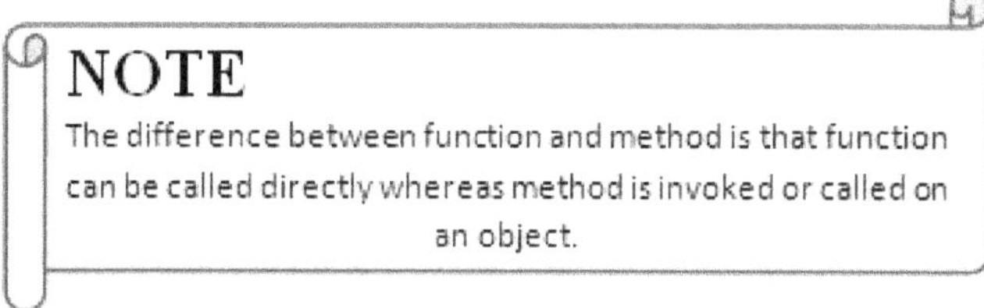

Example:

Dot notation specifies the name of the method (upper) and name of the string(a) to apply the method. The method calling is called invocation. Here upper() is invoked on 'a'. There are a number of useful operations that can be performed with string. Among these are the following:

Example:

>>> a='hello'

FUNCTION	METHODS
>>>a='hello'	>>>a='hello'
>>>print upper(a)	>>>b=a.upper()
'HELLO'	>>>b
	'HELLO'

Take the string a='hello' and perform all the function of string. The table 4.13 explains some of the functions and methods of string in detail with example.

FUNCTION	DESCRIPTION	EXAMPLE	OUTPUT
capitalize()	Returns a copy of the string with the first character of the string capitalized	>>> a.capitalize()	'Hello'
find()	It will display the lower index where the value is found otherwise return -1	>>> a.find('e')	1
index()	This function indicates in which index the item is present	>>> a.index('l')	2
rfind()	It is same as find() but it will display the rightmost index or last index where the value is found otherwise return -1	>>> a.rfind('l')	3
rindex()	It is same as index() but it will display the rightmost index or last index of the value	>>> a.rindex('l')	3
isalnum()	Returns True if string contains alphabets or numbers.	>>> a.isalnum()	True
isdigit()	Returns True if string contains digits.	>>> a.isdigit()	False
isalpha()	Returns True if string contains alphabet.	>>> a isalpha()	True
islower()	Tests if all characters of the string are in lowercase and returns True if string is in lower case.	>>> a islower()	True
isupper()	Tests if all characters of the string are in uppercase and returns True if string is in upper case.	>>> a.isupper()	False
len()	Display the length of the string	>>> len(a)	5
lower()	Returns a copy of string in which all characters are converted to lowercase.	>>> a.lower()	'hello'
upper()	Returns a copy of string in which all characters are converted to uppercase.	>>> a.upper()	'HELLO'

Table 4.13: Common string methods

4.8.8 String Module

A String module is a file containing Python definitions, constants, classes, functions, statements and instructions. These functions of this module are used to manipulate the strings. To use these modules in a program, programmer needs to import the module first. Once a module is imported, we can use any of its functions, methods or constants in our code.

```
>>> import string
>>> dir(string)
['ChainMap', 'Formatter', 'Template', '_TemplateMetaclass', '__builtins__', '__cached__', '__doc__', '__file__', '__loader__', '__name__', '__package__', '__spec__', '_re', '_string', 'ascii_letters', 'ascii_lowercase', 'ascii_uppercase', 'capwords', 'digits', 'hexdigits', 'octdigits', 'printable', 'punctuation', 'whitespace']
```

The functions, constants present in the string module are shown in this example. The dir( ) function is used to see the contents in this module.

Example:

```
import string
a='how are you'
print(string.capwords(a))
print("The digits are:\t",string.digits)
print("The ASCII letters are:\t",string.ascii_letters)
print("The punctuations are:\t",string.punctuation)
```

Output:
How Are You
The digits are: 0123456789
The ASCII letters are: abcdefghijklmnopqrstuvwxyzABCDEFGHIJKLMNOPQRSTU-VWXYZ
The punctuations are: !"#$%&'()*+,-./:;<=>?@[\]^_`{|}~
      In the above example, string.capwords(a)) capitalize all the words of the string 'a'. The string.digits displays all the digits present and string.ascii_letters returns all the ASCII letters. The string.punctuation returns all the punctuations present in string module.

4.8.9 String iteration or traversal

      Iterating through the string is called string traversal or iterating string. This traversal is done by using for loop or while loop. . You can access one character of a string at a time. Iteration starts at the beginning, select a character, do some process to it, and continue until the end. This type of processing is called a traversal.

Using While loop:
Example:
```
a=input("Enter a string for traversing\n")
index = 0
print ('string \t index')
while index < len(a):
   string = a[index]
   print(string,'\t',index)
   index = index + 1
```
Output:
Enter a string for traversing
python
string   index
p   0
y   1
t   2
h   3
o   4
n   5

      The above example shows loop traverses the string and displays each letter of the string and its index.

Using For Loop:
      Traversing can also be done by using for loop to display the values and its respective index.
Example:
```
a='python'
print('index \t value')
for index in range(len(a)):
    print(index,'\t',a[index])
```
Output:
index   value
0   p
1   y
2   t

3 h
4 o
5 n

   In the above example, for loop is used to traversal the string and display index and value. From the above example it is clear that the index always starts from 0 and end in n-1 where n is the length of the string.

4.8.10 Escape sequence

   Escape sequence is a combination of characters that is represented in back-slash notation within single or double quotes. The escape sequence controls the display of output. The table 4.14 shows the escape sequence in python.

ESCAPE SEQUENCE	DESCRIPTION	EXAMPLE	OUTPUT
\n	To print a new line	>>> print("HAI \n HELLO")	HAI HELLO
\t	To print a TAB space	>>> print("HAI \t HELLO")	HAI HELLO
\\	To print backslash	>>> print("HAI\\ HELLO")	HAI\ HELLO
\'	To print single quotes	>>> print("let\'s learn")	let's learn
\"	To print double quotes	>>> print("learn \"python\" now")	learn "python" now
\	It represent that the string is continued in next line.	>>> print("learn \ now")	learn now

Table 4.14: Escape sequence in python

4.8.11 Formatting string

   The format( ) function is built-in function which is used to format the text, it uses many symbols to format the text. The table 4.15 explains about the format symbol in detail with example.

Syntax:

format(values[,format_specifier])

Symbol	Description	Example	Output
<	The string is left aligned within the available space.	>>> format('python','<10')	'python '
>	The string is right aligned within the available space.	>>> format('python','>10')	' python'
^	The string is center within the available space.	>>> format('python','^10')	' python '

Table 4.15: Symbols of format functions

   The format( ) functions is also used to format integer also.

Example:

```
>>> format(5678,',')
'5,678'
```

   This function is used to insert comma in the string.

Example:
```
>>> format(66.66666666666666,'.4f')
'66.6667'
```
> This function is used to round of the integer up to 4 decimal places.

4.8.12 Unicode String

> The Unicode text is the way of writing the text in any native language. This code is a standard way of writing the international text. To uses this Unicode, we need to have Unicode enabled text editor. The text with 'U' or 'u' in the prefix represents Unicode text. This contains text written in language other than English.

Example:
```
U"Unicode strings"
```

4.8.13 Encoding, Decoding and Bytes

> Encoding is a process of storing the data in the encrypted form so that others may not be able to understand or interpret it. To encode the string there is a built-in function in python known as encode( ). This function will return the encoded version of a string based on the encoding scheme. The resultant output of encode( ) function is bytes.

Example:
```
>>> s="exchange the code to the doctor".encode('utf16')
>>> s
b'\xff\xfee\x00x\x00c\x00h\x00a\x00n\x00g\x00e\x00   \x00t\x00h\x00e\x00
\x00c\x00o\x00d\x00e\x00  \x00t\x00o\x00  \x00t\x00h\x00e\x00  \x00d\x00o
\x00c\x00t\x00o\x00r\x00'
```

> The encoding schemes in python are utf32 and utf16 which encode the message.

```
>>> s="exchange the code to the doctor".encode('utf32')
>>> s
b'\xff\xfe\x00\x00e\x00\x00\x00x\x00\x00\x00c\x00\x00\x00h\x00\x00\x00a
\x00\x00\x00n\x00\x00\x00g\x00\x00\x00e\x00\x00\x00        \x00\x00\x00t
\x00\x00\x00h\x00\x00\x00e\x00\x00\x00                \x00\x00\x00c
\x00\x00\x00o\x00\x00\x00d\x00\x00\x00e\x00\x00\x00              \x00\x00\x00t
\x00\x00\x00o\x00\x00\x00            \x00\x00\x00t\x00\x00\x00h\x00\x00\x00e
\x00\x00\x00          \x00\x00\x00d\x00\x00\x00o\x00\x00\x00c\x00\x00\x00t
\x00\x00\x00o\x00\x00\x00r\x00\x00\x00'
```

> From the above example, it is clear that the output of the encode( ) function is the byte code which is the encrypted form. Decoding is the process of decrypting the data. In order to decode or decrypt the string the built-in function decode( ) with decode scheme is used. This function will return the decoded string. Similarly decoding also has the decoding schemes such as utf32 and utf16 to retrieve the original message.

Example:
```
>>> s.decode('utf32')
'exchange the code to the doctor'
```
> The original string is retrieved back correctly by using decode( ) function.

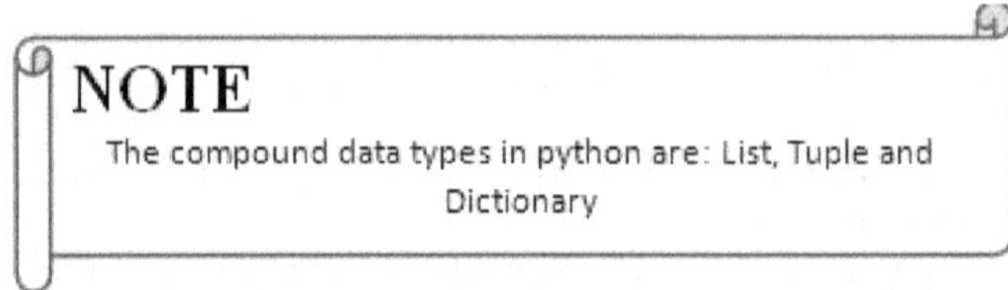

4.9 LISTS

List is an ordered sequence of values. Values in the list are known as elements or items. The list can be written as a list of items (values) separated by comma in square brackets [ ]. Items in the lists can be of any numberic datatype and may be of different data types. There is no requirement that a list contain elements of the same type. Unlike a string, a list is mutable which means that the elements in a list can be changed after it is created. This can be done by using an index as assignment.

4.9.1 Create a list

A pair of square brackets is used to create the empty list. Often lists are grown by using the append operator. The syntax for creating list is:

variable_name=[ ]

Example:

a=[] # Empty list

b=[1,2,8] #list with integer data type

c=[2, 'hai',9.1] # list with mixed data type

d=['hai',[2,1],34.6] #Nested list

Example:

>>> l=[1,2,3,9]

>>> type(l)

<type 'list'>

In this way we can create a list at compile time. The list in python also supports nested indexing.

4.9.2 Indexing

Accessing the items of the list is known as indexing. Accessing of an item is done by using bracket operator in the left side of assignment. Index is an integer which holds the value or subsequence of the list this may be positive or negative. The figure 4.4 shows the positive and negative indexing of a list. The indexing in the list is of three type, they are:

- Positive indexing
- Negative indexing
- Nested indexing

Syntax:

list_name[index]

Example:

>>> l=[1,12,3,9,20]

>>> type(l)

<type 'list'>

FORWARD INDEX	0	1	2	3	4
LIST	1	12	3	9	20
BACKWARD INDEX	-5	-4	-3	-2	-1

Figure 4.4: Indexing of list

Example:
```
>>> l=[1,12,3,9,20]
>>> l[0] # Accessing item in index 0
1
>>> l[-2] # Accessing item using negative indexing
9
```
Example:
```
>>> l[7]
Traceback (most recent call last):
 File "<pyshell#12>", line 1, in <module>
   l[7]
IndexError: list index out of range
```
   If you access an item which is not in that index it will display index error. In the above example list don't contain index 7 so it displayed list index out of range.

Example:
```
>>> a=[1,2,[2,7],6]
>>> a[2][0]
2
```
   We can also access element of the nested list by using nested indexing.

4.9.3 Slicing

   We can make a slice of list from an existing list using a technique known as slicing. A list slice is an expression of the form:

Syntax:
list_name[start_index : end_index]

   Where, list_name is the name of the list, start_index is the starting index of the list which access the first element in the list and end_index is the ending index of the list which access the last element in the list.

Example:
```
>>> l=[1,12,3,9,20]
>>> l[0:4]
[1, 12, 3, 9]
```
   In the above example slicing of list take place, here [0:4] represents the index of the list. Slicing of values from index range 0 to 3 will be displayed; last index value will not be included for slicing.

Example:
```
>>> l[0:]
[1, 12, 3, 9, 20]
```
   If the ending index is not mentioned all the items from start_index to the end of the list will be displayed.

Example:
```
>>> l[:]
```

[1, 12, 3, 9, 20]

       If there is no start_index and end_index all the values of the list will display.

Example:

>>> l[:3]

[1, 12, 3]

       All the items from index 0 to end_index – 1 will be displayed.

Example:

>>> l[3:3]

[]

       If starting index and ending list are same it will create an empty list.

4.9.4 Concatenation

       The process of joining two lists is known as concatenation of list. Concatenation means joining or adding to list together. ' + ' operator is used to perform concatenation of list.

Example:

>>> a=[1,3,7]

>>> b=[2,3,1]

>>> a+b

[1, 3, 7, 2, 3, 1]

       In the above example joining of list ' a ' and list ' b ' takes place by using + operator.

4.9.5 Repetition

       The process of repeating the list n times is known as repetition of list. Here ' * ' operator is used to perform this process.

Example:

>>> a=[1,3,7]

>>> a*2

[1, 3, 7, 1, 3, 7]

       It creates or multiplies the list n number of times. In the above example, same list ' a ' is multiplied 2 times this process is known as repetition.

4.9.6 Membership

       Membership operator is used to test whether the element is in the list or not. If the element is in the list it return True otherwise False is return. The membership operators are in and not in.

Example:

>>> x=[2,5,3,7]

>>> 2 in x

True

>>> 9 in x

False

       From the above example, it is clear that the working of membership operators.

4.9.7 List Mutability

       List is mutable that means the values or items in the list can be changed. The Syntax for accessing the values of a list is same as that of accessing the characters of a string. Here [ ] operator is used to access the value of the list. We can update a list, insert a list, delete or remove element in the list because list is mutable.

- **Updating the list**

```
>>> a=[1,3,7]
>>> a[2]=700
>>> a
[1, 3, 700]
```

Now the value of the index 2 is updated from 7 to 700. Updating of list is done by using its index value.

- **Inserting an element**

Syntax:

```
L.insert(index, object)
```

Here, L is the name of the list, insert( ) is the method used to insert an element in the list. The first parameter index indicates the index or position of the list where you want to insert and object is the value which you want to insert in that list L.

Example:

```
>>> a.insert(2,9)
>>> a
[1, 3, 9, 700]
```

In the above example, inserting value 9 in 2nd position is done.

- **Removing an element**

Syntax:

```
List_name.remove(object)
```

Here, L is the name of the list, remove( ) is the method used to remove the element from the list, and object is the value which you want to remove from list L.

Example:

```
>>> a=[1, 3, 9, 700]
>>> a.remove(3)
>>> a
[1, 9, 700]
```

Value 3 is removed from the list.

- **Deleting the list**

The del statement can be used to delete an element from a list. If you want to delete the entire list completely use del operation.

Example:

```
>>> a=[1, 9, 700]
>>> del a[1]
>>> a
[1, 700]
```

This del statement deleted the value in the index 1 from the list.

Example:

```
>>> a=[1, 700]
>>> del a
>>> a
Traceback (most recent call last):
 File "<pyshell#19>", line 1, in <module>
   a
NameError: name 'a' is not defined
```

In the above example it is clear that the del will delete the entire list.

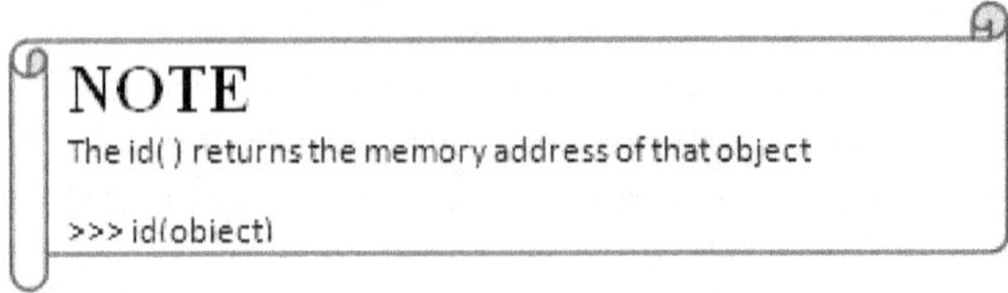

4.9.8 List Traversal

In order to perform looping in list 'for' loop is used. In addition to for loop, range function is used to produce a list of values. In for loop elements are checked one by one and it is assigned to loop variable.

Syntax:

    for loop_variable in sequence:
        statement(s)

Example:
>>> a=[4,2,5]
>>> for i in a:
    print i

Output:

4

2

5

This is the simple example to show all the elements in the list. This for loop traverses all the elements in the list from left to right.

Example:

Program to print all the even numbers in the range using for loop

num=input("Enter the range")
for i in range(0,num):
   if i%2==0:
     print i

Output:

Enter the range10

0

2

4

6

8

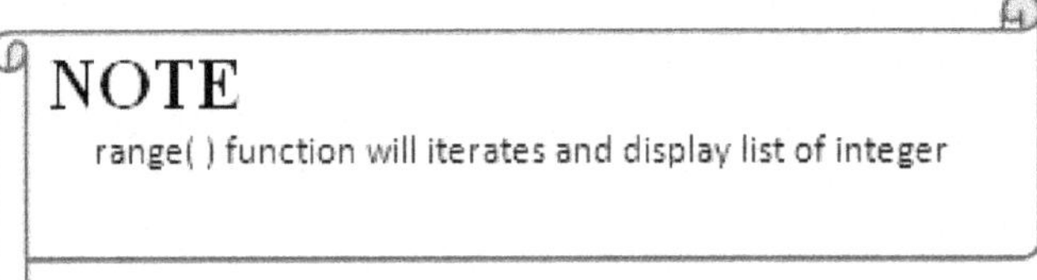

4.9.9 Equality

Two lists are equal if they are the same length and their corresponding elements are equal. Here, == operator is used to checks the equality. There are two cases to analyze whether two list are equal.

Case 1: Checks two lists are of same length

Case 2: Checks both lists contains same items

If both the cases are 'True' then only the two lists are said to be equality

Example:

```
>>> a=[7,8,9]
>>> b=[7,8,9]
>>> a==b
True
```

The == operator first check the length of both list ' a ' and list ' b ' are equal or not. If it is equal it will check the elements in both the list are equal or not. If both the condition is ' True ' then the two lists are equal.

4.9.10 Identity

Two lists are identical if they are exactly the same object. Membership operator ' is ' is used to check the identity of two lists. It not only checks the values of the list are same but also checks whether the references area also same. There are three cases to analyze whether two list are identical.

Case 1: Checks two lists are of same length

Case 2: Checks both lists contains same items

Case 3: Checks whether both lists refers the same memory location

If all the three cases are ' True ' then only the list is said to be Identity.

Example:

```
>>> a=[7,8,9]
>>> b=[7,8,9]
>>> a is b
False
```

From the above example it is clear that list a and list b are not identity.

Example:

```
>>> id(a)
95269952
>>> id(b)
95267776
```

' is ' operator checks whether the references of two variable are same or not. From the above example by using id(object) it is clear that variable a and b have different references.

4.9.11 Aliasing

Assigning two variables for one list in memory location is known as aliasing. The assignment (=) operator is used to perform aliasing. A list has two different names for same values. When one list is assigned to another list using assignment operator a new copy of list is made. Whenever 1 variable's value is assigned to another variable aliasing happens. In order to say two lists are aliasing it has to satisfy two cases.

Case 1: Conditions for equality (= =) should be True

Case 2: Conditions for identity (is) should be True

If both cases are True then it is said to be aliasing. It should satisfy ' = = ' and ' is ' operations. Create a list and assign it to a variable named l1 and then assign the variable l1 to another variable l2. This is known as aliasing.

Example:

```
l1=[1,2,3]
l2=l1
```

print l2
[1,2,3]

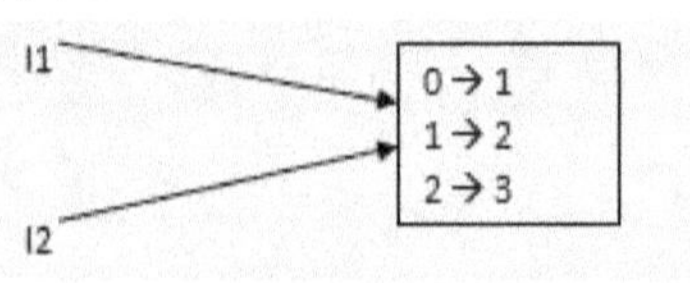

Figure 4.5: Aliasing in list

Above example shows aliasing of list. The figure 4.5 shows the aliasing in list for the above example. Here, two variables l1 and l2 point one list in memory location. This is known as aliasing a list.
Example:

```
>>> l1==l2
True
>>> l1 is l2
True
```

Both identity and equality are True from this it is clear that aliasing is done. Here whatever changes made in l1 will affect l2 and vice versa. This is because both variables refer same object in memory location.

Example:

```
>>> l2[1]=400
>>> l1
[1, 400, 3]
>>> l2
[1, 400, 3]
```

In the above example variable name l1 refer to same value in the memory as l2. So the change made from anyone of the variable will change the value stored in memory. This is known as reference assignment. Here list uses a same memory location but are known by two different names, which means that the two lists are aliased. Since list is mutable, change made with on alias affect the other. It is safe to avoid aliasing with mutable objects; changes in one list will affect another list. To prevent aliasing, a new object has to create and copy the values of the original list, this is called cloning.

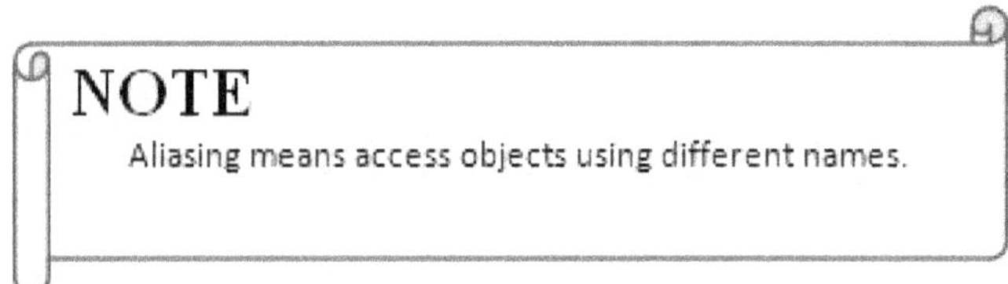

4.9.12 Cloning

In order to avoid the disadvantages of aliasing we are using cloning. It creates a copy of a same list of elements with two different memory locations is called cloning. Changes in one list will not affect locations of another list. If you want to modify a list and also keep a copy of original list, then create a separate copy of the list not just the reference. This process is called cloning. Slice operation is used to clone a list. It has to satisfy two cases:

Case 1: Conditions for equality should be True

Case 2: Both should not refer same memory location

If both cases are satisfied then it is cloning.

Example:

```
>>> l1=[1,2,3,4]
>>> l2=l1[:]
```

```
>>> print l2
[1, 2, 3, 4]
```
Here copy of l1 is taken to l2 by using slice operator.

Example:
```
>>> l1==l2
True
>>> l1 is l2
False
```
From the above example it is clear that l1 is equal to l2 but won't refer the same memory location.

Example:
```
>>> l2[2]=900
>>> l2
[1, 2, 900, 4]
>>> l1
[1, 2, 3, 4]
```
The above example shows that whatever changes made in one list will not affect other. We can make changes without worrying about other list. But if the list is nested one this method wont works.

Example:
```
>>> a=[9,8,[1,2]]
>>> b=a[:]
>>> print b
[9, 8, [1, 2]]
```
The above example shows nested list that means a list inside a list. Here we are cloning a nested list.

Example:
```
>>> b[2][1]=1000
>>> b
[9, 909, [1, 1000]]
>>> a
[9, 8, [1, 1000]]
```
If it is a nested list change in list b affects list a. In order to overcome this issues a module known as copy is used. To use this module we have to import it first. In this copy module there are two operations:

1. Shallow copy
2. Deep copy

Shallow copy

Shallow copy construct a new compound objects and then insert reference into the objects found in the original. This copy will not take the copy of the nested object, here only the values of nested list will get changed.

Syntax:
```
copy.copy(x)
```
Return a shallow copy of x

Example:
```
import copy
a=[9,8,[1,2]]
b=copy.copy(a)
print a==b
```

```
print a is b
b[1]=98
b[2][1]=1000
print 'list a is', a
print 'list b is', b
```
Output:
```
True
False
list a is [9, 8, [1, 1000]]
list b is [9, 98, [1, 1000]]
```
From the above example it is clear that whatever changes made in nested list of b will change the value of nested list of a.

Deep copy

Deep copy constructs a new compound object and then recursively insert copies into it of the objet found in the original. This copy even creates of the list including the copies of the nested objects.

Syntax:
```
copy.deepcopy(x)
```
Return a deep copy of x

Example:
```
import copy
a=[9,8,[1,2]]
b=copy.deepcopy(a)
print a==b
print a is b
b[1]=98
b[2][1]=1000
print 'list a is', a
print 'list b is', b
```
Output:
```
True
False
list a is [9, 8, [1, 2]]
list b is [9, 98, [1, 1000]]
```
The slice makes a copy of the value. Now a change to one will not alter the other.

4.9.13 Built-in functions

The List in python has many built-in functions to manipulate the list. The table 4.16 illustrates the use of some of these operations with example.

Example:
```
>>> l=[3,4,5]
```

OPERATION	DESCRIPTION	EXAMPLE	OUTPUT
len( )	Return the total length of the list	>>> len(l)	3
In	Return True if the value is in the list otherwise False	>>> 3 in l	True
not in	Return True if the value is not in the list otherwise False	>>> 3 not in l	False

+	The + operator is used to join or concatenate two list.	>>> l=[3,4,5]
		>>>
		l2=['pen','pencil']
		>>> l+l2
			[3, 4, 5, 'pen', 'pencil']

*	The * operator is used to perform repetition of list.	>>> l2*2	['pen', 'pencil', 'pen', 'pencil']
max( )	Return maximum value of the list	>>> max(l)	5
min( )	Return minimum value of the list	>>> min(l)	3
sum( )	Add all the numbers in the list	>>> sum(l)	12
all( )	Returns True if all elements of the list are True else False	>>> all(l)	True
any( )	Returns true if any element of the list are True else False	>>> any(l)	True
sorted( )	Return the sorted list	>>>l=[3,9,5,1] >>> sorted(l)	[1, 3, 5, 9]
list( )	Convert other data type (tuple, string, set, dictionary) to a list	>>> z=(1,2,3) >>> list(z)	[1, 2, 3]
del(list)	It will delete the entire list. Again if you try to print that list error will displayed.	>>> del(z) >>> z	Traceback (most recent call last): File "<pyshell#26>", line 1, in <module> z NameError: name 'z' is not defined

Table 4.16: Common operations of list

4.9.14 List Methods

Lists also provide a number of operations written using dot notation. Here the list being modified is followed by a dot, then the name of the operation and an argument list. Methods are used in lists to manipulate the data quickly. Since list is mutable the values of the list can be changed, added, or deleted. The table 4.17 summarizes the methods that are used in list with example:

Syntax:

list_name.method_name(element)

Example:

>>> z=[1,2,3,9,0]

METHOD	DESCRIPTION	EXAMPLE	OUTPUT

list.append (object)	Add or insert the object to the end of the list	>>>z=[1,2,3,9,0]
		>>> z.append(20)
		>>> z
			[1, 2, 3, 9, 0, 20]

list.extend (list)	Appends (extends) one list with other list	>>>[1, 2, 3, 9, 0, 20]
		>>>a=[1,2]
		>>> z.extend(a)
		>>> z
			[1, 2, 3, 9, 0, 20, 1, 2]

list.count(object)	Return the total count of occurrences of that value in that list	>>> [1, 2, 3, 9, 0, 20, 1, 2] >>>z.count(2)	2
list.index(object)	Returns the first index of the list. If the value is not present excection is rised or out of range	>>> [1, 2, 3, 9, 0, 20, 1, 2] >>> z.index(20)	5
list.pop( )	Remove last element of the list and display the list element. If the list is out of range gives exception	>>> [1, 2, 3, 9, 0, 20, 1, 2] >>> z.pop()	2

list.remove (value)	Searches the value and removes it from the list. Raise exception if the value is not present.	>>> z=[1, 2, 3, 9, 0, 20, 1]
		>>>z.remove(0)
		>>> z
			[1, 2, 3, 9, 20, 1]

list.reverse (value)	Reverse elements of list in place	>>> [1, 2, 3, 9, 20, 1]
		>>> z.reverse()
		>>> z
			[1, 20, 9, 3, 2, 1]

list.sort()	Sort elements of list in ascending order	>>> z=[1, 20, 9, 3, 2, 1]
		>>>z.sort()
		>>> z
			[1, 1, 2, 3, 9, 20]

list.pop(index)	Removes the element of that index from list and return the value of the index.	>>> z=[1, 1, 2, 3, 9, 20] >>>z.pop(4)	9
list.insert(index, object)	Inserts and return the object in the index mentioned.	>>>z=[1, 1, 2, 3, 20] >>>z.insert(2,100) >>> z	[1, 1, 100, 2, 3, 20]

List.clear( )	This method is used to clear all the elements from the list.	>>> z=[1, 1, 2, 3, 20]
		>>> z.clear()
		>>> z
			[ ]

del(list)	It will delete the entire list. Again if you try to print that list error will displayed.	>>>z=[ ]
		>>> del(z)
		>>> z
			Traceback(mostrecentcalllast):
			File "<pyshell#26>", line 1, in
			<module> z
			NameError: name 'z' is not defined

Table 4.17: List methods

4.9.15 List Comprehensions

List comprehension gives a shortened way for creating new list. List comprehensions are short and easy way to read, with minimal line. The bracket operators indicate that we are constructing a new list. The expression inside the brackets specifies the elements of the list, and the for statement indicates what sequence we are traversing.

Syntax:

[expression for item in list if condition]

For example, this function takes a list of strings, maps the string method capitalize to the elements, and returns a new list of strings.

Example:

Write a program to print the uppercase string of a list.

```
def only_upper(t):
  res = []
  for s in t:
    if s.isupper():
        res.append(s)
        return res
```

We can rewrite it using a list comprehension, the means shorthand notation for the above program.

```
def only_upper(t):
    return [s for s in t if s.isupper()]
```

Output:

```
>>>t=['Pen','PENCIL',]
>>>print(only_upper(t))
['PENCIL']
```

Example:

This program is display all the even number within the range.

```
num=[]
for i in range(11):
  if i%2==0:
    num.append(i)
print (num)
```

The shorthand notation for creating s list of even numbers is

```
num=[i for i in range(11) if i%2==0]
print (num)
```

Output:

```
[0, 1, 2, 3, 4, 5, 6, 7, 8, 9, 10]
```

4.9.16 List as Array

Array is similar to list but it is a collection of similar data items. Python does not support array data type.

Example:

```
a=[1,9,6]
for i in a:
  print(i,end='\t')
```

Output:

```
1    9    6
```

4.10 TUPLE

A tuple is same as list, except that the elements in the tuple are enclosed in parentheses instead of square brackets. A tuple is an immutable which means once a tuple has been created; you can't add elements to a tuple or remove elements from the tuple. All other operations in tuple are as like list. A list can be changed into a tuple, and vice versa.

Benefit of Tuple:

- Tuples are faster than lists.
- If the user wants to protect the data from accidental changes, tuple can be used.
- Tuples can be used as keys in dictionaries because it is immutable, while lists

can't be used as key in dictionaries.
- It is used to store value of different types.
- Best for storing data which is write protected.
- Tuple can return multiple values from a function.
- Multiple value can be assigned at a same time.

4.10.1 Creating a tuple

In tuple elements are separated by commas and enclosed by parentheses, we can create the tuple with elements of different data types. The tuple is a read only list.
Example:
```
>>> t=() # empty tuple
>>> t1=('a',1,'hai',3.2) # tuple with multiple data type
>>> t2=('hai',2.3,(2,9)) # Nested tuple
>>> type(t2)
<class 'tuple'>
```

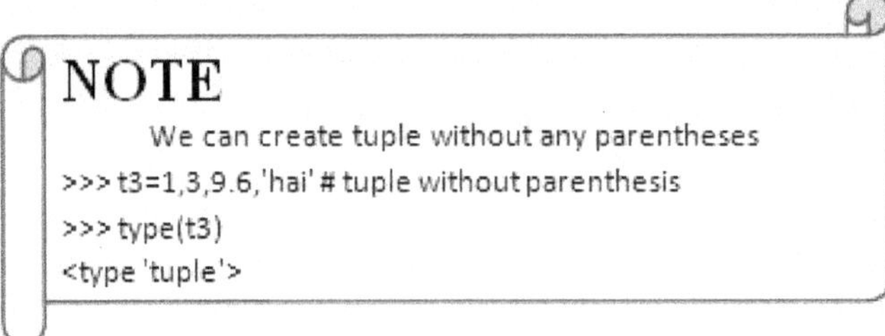

4.10.2 Indexing

Accessing the item in tuple is known as indexing, this is done by using the bracket operator and index of the tuple. In tuple there are two types of indexing, they are:
- Positive indexing
- Negative indexing

FORWARD INDEX	0	1	2	3
TUPLE	'a'	1	'hai'	3.2
BACKWARD INDEX	-5	-4	-3	-2

Figure 4.6: Indexing of tuple

The figure 4.6 shows the forward and backward index of the tuple.
Syntax:
```
tuple_name=[index]
```
Example:
```
>>> t1=('a',1,'hai',3.2)
>> t1[2] # Accessing the item in the index 0
'hai'
>>> t1[3] # Accessing the item in the index 3
3.2
>>> t1[-1]
3.2
```

Negative indexing is also possible in tuple.

Example:
>>> t1[5]
Traceback (most recent call last):
 File "<pyshell#6>", line 1, in <module>
   t1[5]
IndexError: tuple index out of range
   If you try to access the item whose index is not in tuple then it will produce index error.

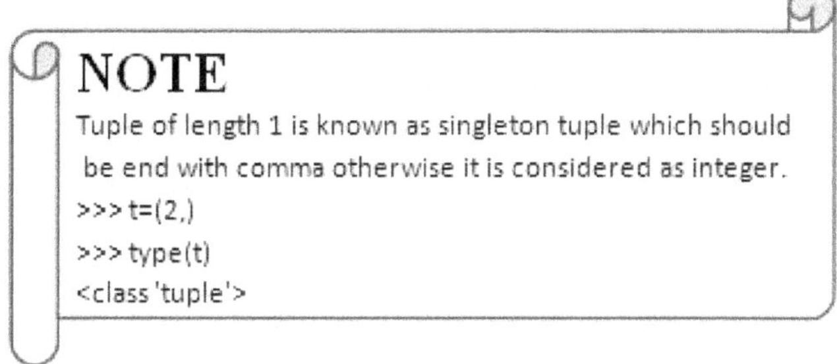

4.10.3 Slicing
   Cutting or segmenting the tuple is known as slicing, this is done by using bracket operator [:].
Syntax:
tuple_name[start:end]
Example:
>>> t1 =('a',1,'hai',3.2)
>>> t1[:]
('a', 1, 'hai', 3.2)
   If starting and ending index is not mention entire tuple will displayed.
Example:
>>> t1[0:2]
('a', 1)
   Here, values from position 0 and 1 will be displayed. Slice operator will skip the element in last index.
Example:

4.10.4 Concatenation
   Adding or joining tuple elements at the end of other tuple elements.
Example:
>>>t1 =('a',1,'hai',3.2)
>>> a=(1,3)
>>> t1+a
('a', 1, 'hai', 3.2, 1, 3)

4.10.5 Repetition
   It is the process of repeating the tuple in n no of times, where n is the integer. The repetition is done by using * operator.
Example:
>>> a=(1,3)
>>> a*4
(1, 3, 1, 3, 1, 3, 1, 3)

4.10.6 Membership

Membership operators are used to check whether the value is in the tuple or not. 'in' and 'not in' operator is used for this purpose. If the value is present in the tuple, it will display True else False.
Example:
>>> a=(2,5,9,7)
>>> 5 in a
True

4.10.7 Tuple Immutability

Tuple is immutable which means the values in the tuple cannot be change. If we want to change the value of tuple, we have to create a new tuple.
Example:
>>> a=(1,3)
>> a[0]=1000
Traceback (most recent call last):
  File "<pyshell#15>", line 1, in <module>
    a[0]=1000
TypeError: 'tuple' object does not support item assignment
In the above example value of index 0 is tried to change which lead to type error.

4.10.8 Tuple returns multiple values

A common use for tuples is the need to return two or more values from a function. The following function, for example, takes two integers to compute addition and subtraction and display the output at the same time. This is done by using tuple as return multiple values.
Example:
```
def AddandSub(a,b):
    add=a+b
    sub=a-b
    return (add,sub)
x=input('Enter x value')
y=input('Enter y value')
print (AddandSub(x,y))
```
Output:
Enter x value6
Enter y value4
(10, 2)
From the above example it is clear that tuple can return multiple value. (10,2) is a tuple of two value obtained as a result of performing addition and subtraction. We can also compute two integers to get maximum, minimum and sum of elements of the tuple.
Example:
>>> def min_max_sum(tup):
        return max(tup),min(tup),sum(tup)
>>> t=(2,5,6,7,57,8)
>>> min_max_sum(t)
(57, 2, 85)
In the above example we get tuple with three values. Here, min, max, sum are the inbuilt functions are used to return the minimum, maximum and sum total of the

elements of the tuple.

4.10.9 Tuple Assignment

Tuple assignment allows variables on the left of an assignment operator and values of tuple on the right of the assignment operator. In tuple assignment number of variable is the left side should be equal to the number of value in the right side. Tuple assignment is one of the powerful features in python. In tuple assignment first the expression or values in right side is evaluated and that is assigned to the left side.

Syntax:

```
 x, y = y, x
```

Example:

```
>>> x,y=10,9
>>> print 'x is', x,'\n','y is',y
x is 10
y is 9
```

Tuple assignment is often useful to swap the values of two variables.

Example:

```
a=input('enter first value')
b=input('enter second value')
print 'after swapping'
temp=a
a=b
b=temp
print 'a is',a
print 'b is',b
```

Output:

```
enter first value7
enter second value9
after swapping
a is 9
b is 7
```

Usually, swapping is done taking a temporary variable to store the value and then swapping is done. But tuple assignment makes this process simple.

```
temp=a

a=b                          =              a,b=b,a

b=temp
```

Both are equivalent this tuple assignment makes the job simpler and easier.

Example:

```
a=input('enter first value')
b=input('enter second value')
print 'after swapping'
a,b=b,a
print 'a is',a
print 'b is',b
```

Output:
enter first value7
enter second value9
after swapping
a is 9
b is 7
Multiple assignments:
      We can perform multiple assignments using tuple assignment.
Example:
```
>>> a,b,c=1,7,5
>>> a
1
```
      In tuple assignment number of variables in left side and values or expressions in right side should be equal. If not it will produce error.
Example:
```
>>> a,b=1,3,4
Traceback (most recent call last):
  File "<pyshell#18>", line 1, in <module>
    a,b=1,3,4
ValueError: too many values to unpack
```
      Tuple assignment also works inside of lists.
Example:
```
>>> [x,y,z] = [3,'hai',9]
>>> print 'x ix',x,'\n','y is',y,'\n','z is',z
x ix 3
y is hai
z is 9
```
      The above example x and y assigns the values 3 and 9 respectively.

4.10.10 Functions and Methods of tuple

      The python has many built-in functions to manipulate tuple. Some of the built-in functions are explained in table 4.18 with example.
Example:
```
>>> t=(1,9)
```

OPERATION	DESCRIPTION	EXAMPLE	OUTPUT
t.index(value)	Return the index of the value	>>> t.index(9)	1
t.count(value)	Return the total number of occurrences of value	>>> t.count(9)	1
len( )	Return the length of the tuple	>>> len(t)	2
max( )	Return the maximum element of the tuple	>>> max(t)	9
min( )	Return the minimum element of the tuple	>>> min(t)	1
sorted( )	This function sorts the elements of the tuple and returns the sorted element in the form of list.	>>> a=(2,4,1) >>> sorted(a)	[1, 2, 4]
sum( )	Return the sum of elements in the tuple.	>>>a=[1, 2, 4] >>> sum(a)	7
del()	Delete the entire tuple	>>> del t >>> d	Traceback (most recent call last): File "<pyshell#22>", line 1, in <module> d NameError: name 'd' is not defined

Table 4.18: Functions/methods of tuple

4.11 SETS

Set is an unordered collection of values of any data type. Sets are list without duplicate entries. In set every element is unique and it is mutable. Elements are separated by, enclosed with { }. Sets can hold mixed data type but it should not be nested. Removing and adding element in set is easy.

Creating a set

variable_name={value1,value2,...}

Example:

```
>>> s={1,6,4,8,9} # integer data type
>>> s3={2,'h',5} # mixed data type
>>> type(s)
<class'set'>
```

Example:

```
>>> b={3,7,{2,9}}
Traceback (most recent call last):
 File "<pyshell#15>", line 1, in <module>
  b={3,7,{2,9}}
TypeError: unhashable type: 'set'
```

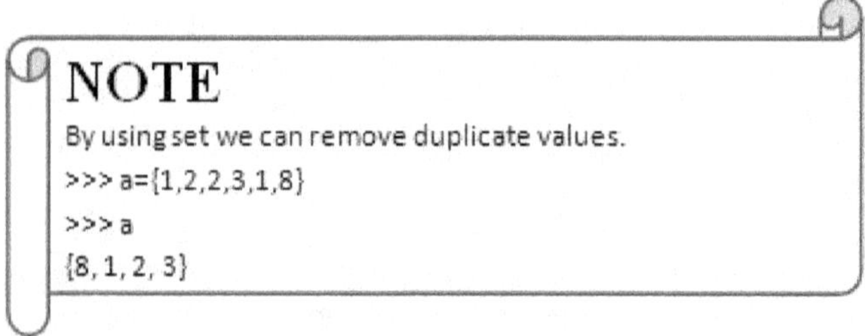

Sets support several set operations, such as:

- Union
- Intersection
- Difference
- Symmetric_difference
- Copy
- Subset (<=) and Superset(>=)

4.11.1 Union

Return the combination of elements of two sets without any duplicate entries.

Example:
```
>>> a={1,2,3}
>>> b={4,6,3}
>>> a|b
set([1, 2, 3, 4, 6]
```

4.11.2 Intersection

Return the common elements of two or more set as a new set.

Example:
```
>>> a&b
set([3])
```

4.11.3 Difference

Return the difference of two or more set as a new set.

Example:
```
>>> a-b
set([1, 2])
>>> b-a
set([4, 6])
```

4.11.4 Indexing

Set is unordered, so it does not support indexing. We can't access value in the set because set is unordered collections of values.

Example:
```
>>> a[0]
Traceback (most recent call last):
 File "<pyshell#12>", line 1, in <module>
   a[0]
TypeError: 'set' object does not support indexing
```

Other operations in set are symmetric_difference, copy, subset and superset.

Example:

```
a={1,2,3}
b={2,3,9}
print("The union is:\t",a.union(b))
print("The intersection is:\t",a.intersection(b))
print("The Symmetric_difference is:\t",a.symmetric_difference(b))
print("The difference is:\t",a.difference(b))
print("The copy is:\t",a.copy())
print("To check it is subset or not:\t",a.issubset(b))
Output:
The union is:      {1, 2, 3, 9}
The intersection is:   {2, 3}
The Symmetric_difference is:      {9, 1}
The difference is:      {1}
The copy is:  {1, 2, 3}
To check it is subset or not:    False
```

> **NOTE**
> The set does not support indexing, slicing, concatenation and repetition because it is unordered

4.11.5 Operations of Set

The Set contains many built-in function, methods and operations. The table 4.19 shows the operations with example.

```
>>> s={4,9,3,1}
```

OPERATION	DESCRIPTION	EXAMPLE	OUTPUT
s.update()	Update a set with the union of itself and others.	>>> s.update({2}) >>> s	set([9, 2, 3, 4, 1])
s.add()	Add an element to a set	>>> s.add(7) >>> s	set([1, 2, 3, 4, 7, 9])
len(s)	Return the length of the set	>>> len(s)	6
s.remove()	Remove an element of the set which is the member of the set	>>> s.remove(2) >>> s	set([1, 3, 4, 7, 9])
s.pop()	Remove and return the value which is removed. Raise error if the set is empty	>>> s.pop()	1
x is s	Return True if the x is the set otherwise False	>>> 3 is s	False
x in s	Return True if the value is in the set else False	>>> 3 in s	True

s.issubset(a) (s<=a)	Return True if another subset contain this set	s={3, 4, 9, 7}
		>>> a={4,7}
		>>> s<=a
			False

s.issuperset(a)(s>=a)	Retun True if this set contains another set	>>> s>=a	True
s.union(a) (|)	Return the union of set as a new set	>>> s.union(a)	set([3, 4, 7, 9])
s.intersection(a)(&)	Return the intersection of two or more set	>>> s.intersection(a)	set([4, 7])
s.difference(a) (-)	Return the difference of two or more set	>>> s.difference(a)	set([9, 3])
s.copy()	Return the shallow copy of the set	>>> s.copy()	set([9, 3, 4, 7])
all(s)	Return True if all the elements in the set is non zero	>>> all(s)	True
any(s)	Returns True if any one of the element in the list is non zero	>>> any(s)	True
max(s)	Return the maximum element of the set	>>> max(s)	9
Min	Return the maximum element of the set	>>> min(s)	3
Sum	Add all the elements in the list and return it	>>> sum(s)	23

Table4.19:   Operations of set

4.11.6 Set iterating

The iterating through the set is also known as traversal through the set. It is done by using for loop or while loop.

Example:

```
s={4,9,3,1}
for i in s:
    print(i,end='\t')
```

Output:

```
1   9   3   4
```

4.11.7 Set comprehension

The set comprehension is short and easy way to write code. It is a shortened way of creating a set, it contains expression and for statement in curly bracket { } with elements separated by comma.

Syntax:

```
{expression for item in list}
```

Example:

```
cubes={}
cubes={i**3 for i in range(5)}
print (cubes)
```

Output:
{0, 1, 8, 27, 64}

4.12 FROZEN SET

A Frozen set is a set, the difference between set and frozen set is that set is mutable where as frozen set is immuatable.
Syntax:
variable_name={value1,value2,…}
Example:
>>> a={1,2,3}
>>> b=frozenset(a)
>>> b
frozenset({1, 2, 3})
>>> type(b)
<class 'frozenset'>
   Similar to set, the frozen set has operations such as union( ), intersection( ), difference( ), symmentic_difference( ), issubset( ), isdisjoint( ), issuperset( ) and copy( ) method.
Example:
Demonstrate the operations of frozen set.
a=frozenset({1,2,3})
b=frozenset({2,3,9})
print("The union is:\t",a.union(b))
print("The intersection is:\t",a.intersection(b))
print("The Symmetric_difference is:\t",a.symmetric_difference(b))
print("The difference is:\t",a.difference(b))
print("The copy is:\t",a.copy())
print("To check it is subset or not:\t",a.issubset(b))
Output:
The union is: frozenset({1, 2, 3, 9})
The intersection is: frozenset({2, 3})
The Symmetric_difference is: frozenset({9, 1})
The difference is: frozenset({1})
The copy is: frozenset({1, 2, 3})
To check it is subset or not: False
   The above example demonstrates the operations of frozen set.

4.13 DICTIONARIES

   Dictionaries are unordered sets; it has key-value pairs. The dictionary is represented by using curly brackets, i.e. { }. The dictionary contains key – value pairs, the items are accessed via keys and not via their position. A dictionary is an associative array. The values of a dictionary can be of any Python data type. Dictionaries don't support the sequence operation of the sequence data types like strings, lists and tuples. In a dictionary the indices are not positions, but values. Values are stored as a pair of key and value. Dictionaries are also known as key-value pairs, maps, hashes or associative arrays. Some of the real time examples for dictionary are menus, phonebook, etc.

4.13.1 Creating a dictionary

   Dictionary is created by using curly brackets { } and each value in the dictionary should be separated by using comma. It should contain key value pair, this keys and values are separated by using colon (:).

Syntax:

dictionary_name={key : value }

Example:

>>> d={} # empty dictionary

>>> d1={1:'a',2:'p',3:'p',4:'l',5:'e'}

>>> type(d)

<type 'dict'>

We can create the dictionary with elements of different data types.

4.13.2 Indexing

Accessing an element of dictionary is not done by using its index but by using its key.

Example:

>>> d={1:'a',2:'p',3:'p',4:'l',5:'e'}

>>> d[1]

'a'

Here, 1 is the key and the value of the key is 'a'

Example:

If we try to the value who key is not in the dictionary keyerror will be displayed.

>>> d={1:'a',2:'p',3:'p',4:'l',5:'e'}

>>> d[0]

Traceback (most recent call last):

 File "<pyshell#62>", line 1, in <module>

 d[0]

KeyError: 0

4.13.3 Mutability in dictionary

Dictionaries are accessed by key, not by its index. The dictionary is mutable. The values of the dictionary are mutable but the key is immutable.

Example:

>>> d={1:'a',2:'p',3:'p',4:'l',5:'e'}

>>> d[1]='A'

>>> d

{1: 'A', 2: 'p', 3: 'p', 4: 'l', 5: 'e'}

The index expression is termed a key, while the element stored in association with the key is termed a value. Just as individual elements in a list can be accessed by indexing, values are returned from a dictionary using the indexing operation.

Example:

To remove a key-value pair from a dictionary pop(key) is used and return the deleted key.

>>> d.pop(2)

'p'

>>> d

{1: 'a', 3: 'p', 4: 'l', 5: 'e'}

4.13.4 Functions and Methods in dictionary

The dictionary contains many built-in function and methods to manipulate the elements of dictionary. The table 4.20 explains many built-in functions with

example.
```
>>> d1={1:'A',2:'p',3:'p',4:'l',5:'e'}
>>> d2={'a':'How','b':'are','c':'you'}
>>> cmp(d1,d2)
1
```

OPERATION	DESCRIPTION	EXAMPLE	OUTPUT
Cmp	It will compare two dictionary	>>> cmp(d1,d2)	1
Len	Number of elements in dictionary	>>> len(d1)	5
str(dict)	Return the entire dictionary into string	>>> str(d1)	"{1: 'A', 2: 'p', 3: 'p', 4: 'l', 5: 'e'}"
d.copy( )	Make a shallow copy of dictionary	>>> d1.copy()	{1: 'A', 2: 'p', 3: 'p', 4: 'l', 5: 'e'}
d.get(key)	Return the value of key if it is present otherwise it won't return anything	>>> d1.get(2)	'p'
d.has_key(key)	Return True if dictionary has key k, 0 otherwise	>>> d1.has_key(2)	True
d.items()	Return a list of (key, value) pairs	>>> d1.items()	[(1, 'A'), (2, 'p'), (3, 'p'), (4, 'l'), (5, 'e')]
d.keys()	Return a list of keys in dictionary	>>> d1.keys()	[1, 2, 3, 4, 5]
d1.update(d2)	It update the value of d2 to d1	>>> d1.update(d2) >>> d1	{'a': 'How', 1: 'A', 2: 'p', 3: 'p', 4: 'l', 5: 'e', 'c': 'you', 'b': 'are'}
d.values()	Return a list of values in dictionary d	>>> d1.values()	['How', 'A', 'p', 'p', 'l', 'e', 'you', 'are']
in	Return True if the index is in dictionary	>>> 1 in d1	True
not in	Return True if the index is not in dict.	>>> 5 not in d1	False
d[k]	Return the value of key if it is present in the dictionary	>>> d1[3]	'p'
del d[k]	Delete key-value pair of k from dictionary d.	>>> del d1['a'] >>> d1	{1: 'A', 2: 'p', 3: 'p', 4: 'l', 5: 'e', 'c': 'you', 'b': 'are'}
d.clear()	Remove all items from dictionary d	>>> d1.clear() >>> d1	{}
sorted(d)	Return the index in sorted order	>>> sorted(d2)	['a', 'b', 'c']
all(d)	Return True if all the keys of the dictionary are True or empty	>>> all(d1)	True

Table 4.20: Operations of dictionaries

4.13.5 Traversal the dictionary

Just as a for statement can be used to loop over the elements in a list, a for can also be used to cycle through the values in a dictionary. If you simply use the dictionary as the target of the for statement, the values returned are the keys for the collection:

Example:
```
>>> d={1:'A',2:'p',3:'p',4:'l',5:'e'}
>>> for i in d:
    print i,d[i]
```
Output:
1 A

2 p
3 p
4 l
5 e

4.13.6 Dictionary Comprehension

The dictionary comprehension is a shortened way of creating a new dictionary. The dictionary comprehension is the short and easy way of creating dictionary. It contains key-value expression and for statement in curly bracket { } with key-value pairs separated by commas.

Example:

```
square={}
square={i:i**2 for i in range(6)}
print (square)
```

Output:
{0: 0, 1: 1, 2: 4, 3: 9, 4: 16, 5: 25}

In this the keys and values pairs are separated by using colon.

SUMMARY

- The expression is the combination of operands and operators.
- The operator is a symbol which is used to perform some operation with one or more operand. It is the constructs used to control or manipulate the value of operands. Some of the basic operators are +, -, * and /.
- An individual character in a sequence is accessed using an index. The index is also known as subscript. The subscript should always be positive integer or negative integer.
- To extract subsets of strings by using the slice operator [:] is used. This operator returns a segment of string as slice.
- The process of adding or joining two sequences in python is known as concatenation. For concatenating two sequences + operator is used.
- The process of repeating the sequence n number of times is known as repetition. Here the * operator is used to multiply a sequence and number.
- Membership operator is used to check whether the value is belongs to the sequence or not. Output for this membership operator is either True or False. The membership operators are in and not in.
- Left shift is to shift the bit towards left and right shift is used to shift the bits towards the right.
- Sequence is an ordered collection of values. The sequences in python are string, list and tuple.
- The relationship in which each element of one set corresponds to an element of another set is known as mapping.
- Comprehension gives shortened way for creating lists, sets and dictionaries.
- Numeric data type stores Numerical Value such as whole number, real number and complex number. This data type is immutable which means the values/items cannot be changed. The numeric data types in python are Integers, Floating point and Complex numbers.
- A sequence is an ordered collection of items which is indexed by positive integers. It may be immutable (values cannot be changed) or mutable (value can be changed). There are three types of sequence data type available in Python; they are

string, list and tuple.
•   An individual character in a string is accessed using a subscript also known as index. The subscript should always be an integer this may be either positive or negative integer. The indexing operator is represented in square bracket [ ], it is also known as subscript.
•   Slice operator is used to slice or to extract the subsets of string. A segment of a string or substring of a string is called a slice, [:] is the operator used to slice string.
•   The process of adding or combining two strings in python is known as concatenation. The + operator is used for this purpose. The + operator joins the string on both sides of the operator.
•   The process of repeating the string n times is known as repetition. This operation is known as repetition, replication or string multiplication, * operator is used for this purpose.
•   Escape sequence is a combination of characters that is represented in backslash notation within single or double quotes. The escape sequence controls the display of output.
•   Mappings are collections of objects that store objects by key instead of its position. The mapping object maps immutable value to object. Dictionary is the only one data type that supports mapping.

ILLUSTRATIVE PROGRAMS

1.   Write a python program to get quotient and remainder of two numbers.

```
a=int(input("Enter a number"))
b=int(input("Enter another number"))
remainder=a%b
quotient=a//b
print("Quotient= ",quotient)
print("Remainder= ",remainder)
```
Output:

```
Enter a number10
Enter another number5
Quotient= 2
Remainder= 0
```
2.   Write a python program to find distance between two points.

The formula for finding distance between two points is:
$\sqrt{((x2-x1)2+(y2-y1)2)}$
```
x1=int(input("enter x1"))
y1=int(input("enter y1"))
x2=int(input("enter x2"))
y2=int(input("enter y2"))
a=(x2-x1)**2
b=(y2-y1)**2
distance=(a+b)**0.5
print(distance)
```

Output:

enter x112
enter y14
enter x26
enter y22
6.324555320336759

3. Demonstrate + and * operator in string and integer.

print(" + in integer is ",10+2) #10 and 2 are integer + will add these two integers
print(" + in string is ",'10'+'2')#10 and 2 are string + will join these two strings
print(" * in integer is ",10*2)#10 and 2 are integer * will multiply these two integers
print(" * in integer is ",'10'*2)#10 is integer and 2 is string * will repeat 10 twice
Output:

+ in integer is 12
 + in string is 102
* in integer is 20
* in integer is 1010

4. Write a program to swap two numbers using tuple assignment.

a=int(input("Value of a "))
b=int(input("Value of b "))
a,b=b,a
print("After swapping ....")
print("Value of a is ",a)
print("Value of b is ",b)
Output:

Value of a 5
Value of b 10
After swapping ....
Value of a is 10
Value of b is 5

5. Write a python program to find whether the character is in the string.

a=input("Enter a value ")
e=input("Character to be search ")
str=a.count(e)
if str>0:
   print("The character is in the string")
else:
   print("The character is not in the string")
Output:

Enter a value hello
Character to be search e
The character is in the string

6. Write a python program to count number of vowels in the string.

```python
a=input("Enter a string")
vowel=('a','e','i','o','u','A','E','I','O','U')
b=0
for i in a:
  if i in ('a', 'e', 'i', 'o', 'u'):
    b=a.count(i)
if b>0:
  print("The string has vowel." )
  print("The total number of vowel in the string is ",b)
else:
  print("No vowel in the string")
```
Output:

Enter a stringheep
The string has vowel.
The total number of vowel in the string is 2

7. Write a python program to count number of times the character is in the string.

```python
a=input("Enter the string")
e=input("Character to be search ")
str=a.count(e)
print("Count= ",str)
```
Output:

Enter the string heep
Character to be search e
Count= 2

8. Write a python program to change the case of the string.

```python
a=input("Enter the string ")
b=a.swapcase()
print(b)
```
Output:

Enter the string Hello
hELLO

9. Write a python program to Getting a 2D matrix and display it.

```
r1 = int(input('Number of Rows in First Matrix : '))
c1 = int(input('Number of Columns in First Matrix : '))
r2 = int(input('Number of Rows in Second Matrix : '))
c2 = int(input('Number of Columns in Second Matrix : '))
matrix1 = []
matrix2 = []
print('Enter the element of First Matrix:')
for i in range(0,r1):
   matrix1.append([])
   for j in range(0,c1):
     matrix1[i].append(int(input()))
print('Enter the element of Second Matrix :')
for i in range(0,r2):
   matrix2.append([])
   for j in range(0,c2):
     matrix2[i].append(int(input()))
print('First Matrix is : ')
for i in range(0,r1):
   print(matrix1[i])
print('Second Matrix is : ')
for i in range(0,r2):
   print(matrix2[i])
```

Output:

```
Number of Rows in First Matrix : 2
Number of Columns in First Matrix : 2
Number of Rows in Second Matrix : 2
Number of Columns in Second Matrix : 2
Enter the element of First Matrix:
1
2
1
7
Enter the element of Second Matrix :
2
5
1
3
First Matrix is :
[1, 2]
[1, 7]
Second Matrix is :
[2, 5]
[1, 3]
```

10. Write a python program to add two matrix

```
a=[[1,2],[1,2]]
b=[[2,1],[2,1]]
c=[[0,0],[0,0]]
print("Addition of two matrix is")
for i in range(len(a)):
   for j in range(len(b)):
      c[i][j]=a[i][j]+b[i][j]
for i in c:
   print(i)
```
Output:

```
Addition of two matrix is
[3, 3]
[3, 3]
```
11. Write a python program to transpose two matrixes.

```
a=[[1,2],[1,2]]
c=[[0,0],[0,0]]
print("Transpose of matrix:")
for i in range(len(a)):
   for j in range(len(a)):
      c[i][j]=a[j][i]
for i in c:
   print(i)
```
Output:

```
Transpose of matrix:
[1, 1]
[2, 2]
```
12. Write a python program to get a list of n numbers and display it.

```
l=[]
n=int(input("Enter total number of elements/items in the list"))
for i in range(0,n):
   a=input("Enter the value")
   l.append(a)
print(l)
```
Output:

```
Enter total number of elements/items in the list5
Enter the value1
Enter the value'hai'
Enter the value67
Enter the value9.6
```

Enter the value[2,3]
['1', "'hai'", '67', '9.6', '[2,3]']

13. Write a python program to find minimum element in a list.

```
l=[]
n=int(input("Enter total number of elements/items in the list"))
for i in range(0,n):
   a=int(input("Enter the value"))
   l.append(a)
print(l)
min=l[0]
for i in range(1,n):
   if min>l[i]:
     min=l[i]
print("The minimum element in the list is ",min)
```
Output:

```
Enter total number of elements/items in the list4
Enter the value12
Enter the value4
Enter the value1
Enter the value7
[12, 4, 1, 7]
The minimum element in the list is  1
```

14. Write a python program to Remove duplicate from the list

```
l=[]
n=int(input("Enter total number of elements/items in the list"))
for i in range(0,n):
   a=int(input("Enter the value"))
   l.append(a)
print(l)
s=set(l)
print(list(s))
```
Output:

```
Enter total number of elements/items in the list5
Enter the value12
Enter the value3
Enter the value12
Enter the value1
Enter the value6
[12, 3, 12, 1, 6]
[1, 3, 12, 6]
```

15. Write a python program to sort the elements in the list.

```
l=[]
n=int(input("Enter total number of elements/items in the list"))
for i in range(0,n):
    a=int(input("Enter the value"))
    l.append(a)
print(l)
print("The sorted list is",sorted(l))
```
Output:

```
Enter total number of elements/items in the list4
Enter the value12
Enter the value5
Enter the value6
Enter the value2
[12, 5, 6, 2]
The sorted list is [2, 5, 6, 12]
```

16. Write a program to create histogram.

```
def histogram(a):
    for i in a:
        sum = ''
        while(i>0):
            sum=sum+'@'
            i=i-1
        print(sum)
a=[1,2,3,4,5]
histogram(a)
```
Output:

```
@
@@
@@@
@@@@
@@@@@
```

17. Write a program to create a valid the username and password.

Conditions to create Username and password are, username should be in uppercase and password should contain both alphabets and numbers.

```
u_name=input("Enter username ")
if u_name.isupper():
    print("Enter password")
    p_word=input()
    if p_word.isalnum():
        print("Successfully Registered")
        print("Your username is ",u_name," and password is ",p_word)
```

```
  else:
     print("Enter valid password")
else:
   print("Enter valid username")
```
Output:

```
Enter username gentry
Enter valid username
>>>
Enter username GENTRY
Enter password
gen123
Successfully Registered
Your username is  GENTRY  and password is  gen123
```
18. Write a python program to get a string and count the occurrences of fist letter of the string.

```
str=input("Enter a string ")
first=str[0]
l=len(str)
count=0
for i in str:
   if i==first:
      count=count+1
print("occurrences of ",first," in string is ", count," times")
```
 Output:

```
Enter a string people
occurrences of  p  in string is  2  times
```
19. Write a python program to find first number is greater than the other number in one single statement.

```
a=input("Enter value of a")
b=input("Enter value of b")
c=input("Enter value of c")
print("a>b>c is: ",a>b>c)
print("a<b<c is: ", a<b<c)
```
Output:

```
Enter value of a10
Enter value of b20
Enter value of c30
a>b>c is:  False
a<b<c is:  True
```
20. Write a python program to convert all the vowels into uppercase.

```python
def upper(w):
  x=''
  for i in w:
    if(i=='a'or i=='e'or i=='i' or i=='o' or i=='u'):
      x=x+i.upper()
    else:
      x=x+i
  return x
w=str(input("Enter a string :"))
print(upper(w))
```
Output:

Enter a string :eat apple
EAt ApplE

21. Write a python program to remove all the consonants from the given words.


```python
def remove_consonant(w):
  x=''
  for i in w:
    if(i=='a'or i=='e'or i=='i' or i=='o' or i=='u'):
      x=x+i
  return x
w=str(input("Enter a string :"))
print(remove_consonant(w))
```
Output:

Enter a string :python programming
ooai

22. Write a python program to reverse the content of the list.


```python
def reversing(l):
  l.reverse()
  return l
l=[]
n=int(input("Enter number of elemements in list"))
for i in range(0,n):
  l.append(input())
print("Before reversing :", l)
print("After reversing :",reversing(l))
```
Output:

Enter number of elemements in list5
2
45

12

8

51

Before reversing : ['2', '45', '12', '8', '51']

After reversing : ['51', '8', '12', '45', '2']

ADDITIONAL PROGRAMS

1. Write a python program to count number of characters in the string.
2. Write a python program to subtract two Matrix
3. Write a python program to hexadecimal value into octal.
4. Demonstrate a python program to differentiate equality and identity.
5. Write a python program to find the longest string
6. Write a python program to find length of longest string.
7. Write a python program to reverse the string.
8. Write a python program to combine list of character into string.
9. Write a python program to demonstrate tuple and related function.
10. Write a python program to find the string is palindrome or not.
11. Demonstrate aliasing and cloning.
12. Write a python program to check the number of time occurrence of the substring in sequence.
13. Write a python program to demonstrate list and related function.
14. Write a python program to compute the frequency of words from the input
15. Write a python program to get sequence of word and print the sequence of word alphabetically.

REVIEW QUESTIONS

1. What is operator and operand? Explain with example.
2. What are the types of operators in python?
3. What is data type? Explain with example.
4. What are the types of data type present in python?
5. Explain about type conversion.
6. Define indexing and slicing with example.
7. Demonstrate + and * operator in string and integer.
8. Explain about precedence and associativity of operators.
9. What are the types of special operators?
10. What are compound data types?
11. Define string
12. Differentiate concatenation in string and integer.
13. What is the purpose of escape sequence in python?
14. Explain about string module with example.
15. Explain any three string function with example.
16. Differentiate mutability and immutability. List down which data type comes under mutability.
17. Write the difference between list and dictionary.
18. Write the advantage of tuple over list.
19. Differentiate between cloning and aliasing.
20. Explain about key-value pair in dictionary.

MUTIPLE CHOICE QUESTIONS

1. The modulo % operator is used to find:
   a. Quotient
   b. Remainder
   c. Divisor
   d. Percentage
2. Find of output for the following code:
```
a=(1,2,['h','a','i'])
a[2][1]=0
print(a)
```
   a. (1, 2, ['h', 0, 'i'])
   b. (1,2,['h','a','i'])
   c. Error
   d. (1,2,[0])
3. Find the output for the following code:
```
a=(1, 2, ('h', 'a', 'i'))
a=(9,0,1)
print(a)
```
   a. Error, cannot change tuple
   b. (1, 2, ('h', 'a', 'i'))
   c. (9,0,1)
   d. None of these
4. Write the output for the following code:
```
>>> a='12'
>>> b='2'
>>> a+b
```
   a. '122'
   b. '14'
   c. Error, not possible to add two string
   d. '12'
5. Write the output for the following code:
```
a=(9,0,1)
b=(1,4,5,0)
c=set(a+b)
print(c)
```
   a. {9,0,1,1,4,5,0}
   b. {0, 9, 1, 4, 5}
   c. (9,0,1,1,4,5,0)
   d. Error
6. Which of the following is not a data type?
   a. integer
   b. dictionary
   c. floating point
   d. array
7. Which operator is used to access single character of string?
   a. [ ]
   b. [:]
   c. slice( )

    d. index( )

8. What is the output of the following code?

```
>>> a={2,1,4,2,6,5,5}
>>> len(a)
```

    a. 5
    b. 7
    c. 6
    d. 8

9. Find the data type of the below code:

```
>>> a=(5)
>>> type(a)
```

    a. <class 'tuple'>
    b. <class 'dict'>
    c. <class 'list'>
    d. <class 'int'>

10. Which of the following data types is a mutable?

    a. strings
    b. lists
    c. tuples
    d. None of these

11. What is the output for the following code?

```
l=['hai',1,12.4,9]
l.sort()
print(l[1])
```

    a. 'hai'
    b. 1
    c. 9
    d. TypeError

TRUE OR FALSE

1. The single quotes and double quotes string are same.
2. The string is a sequence of one or more character.
3. The string of length one is treated as character in python.
4. The chr( ) function is used to get the character of the ASCII code.
5. We can change or modify the string which is already created.
6. In python it is must to put space before and after each operator.
7. The default starting index of sequence is 0.
8. We can modify the tuple whenever necessary.
9. In dictionary keys are immutable where as values are mutable.
10. The floor division (//) operator divides two number and chops off the fractional part.
11. The + is both unary and binary operator.

FILL IN THE BLANKS

1. To find power of a number ____________ operator is used.
2. The character in the string is accessed by using ____________ operator.
3. The 'r' or 'R' in the prefix of the string represents ____________.
4. The ____________ error is obtained if the list index is out of range.

5. Fill the blank to get 'python' as output

s = ['p', 'y', 't', 'h','o','n'].

print____________

6. Segment of string is known as ____________

7. Individual character in the string can be accessed by using ____________

8. ____________ Function is used to get string input from user.

9. The string with prefix U is known as ____________.

10. The default starting index of sequence is ____________ and ending index is ____________.

11. The ____________ and ____________ are the two special operators in python.

12. Output for 5%12 is ____________ .

ANSWERS

CHOOSE THE CORRECT ANSWER

1) b
2) a
3) c
4) a
5) b
6) d
7) b
8) a
9) d
10) b
11) d

TRUE OR FALSE

1) True

2) True
3) False
4) True
5) False
6) False
7) True
8) False
9) True
10) True
11) True

FILL IN THE BLANKS

1) Exponential
2) Subscript
3) Rawstring
4) IndexError
5) (''.join(s))
6) Slice
7) Subscript

8)   input( )
9)   Unicode string
10) 0, n-1
11) Membership, Identity
12) 5

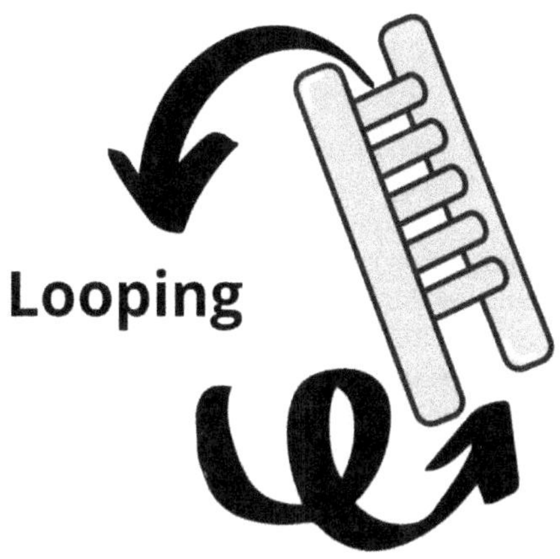

CHAPTER 5: DECISION CONTROL AND LOOPING

The control flow is a statement that determines the order in which the instructions or statements executed. This chapter discusses about different types of control statement such as sequential, selection and iteration. It also provides detailed explanations about branching control statements such as continue, break and pass.

CHAPTER OUTLINE

Control flow – Sequential control – Selection control: if, if...else, if...elif...else, inline if...else – Iterative control: for, while – Looping control statements: break, continue, pass

OBJECTIVE

After completing this chapter we will be able to:
- To know about flow control statements
- To understand the difference between sequence, selection and iterative statements.
- To implement decision making statements such as if, if...else, if...elif...else statements
- To know about different types of loops
- To make use of range( ) function in 'for' loop
- Nested if statements and nested looping
- Using else with for and while loop
- To write Boolean expressions using comparison operators and logical operators
- To implement program control statements such as break and continue

- To know about infinite loop

5. 1 CONTROL FLOW

Control flow is a statement that determines the order of flow of a set of instructions or statements. Set of instructions and the control statements which control the program execution is called a control structure. Flow of control instruction of the program is determined by using Boolean expression. The operators such as relational operators or logical operators are used in the control statement. The output obtained as the result of these operators will always be a Boolean value which is either True or False. Based on the Boolean values the flow of execution of the program happens. Every Loops in python has some structure, these structure has 2 Parts. They are:

- Control Statement.
- Body of the Loop.

(i) Control Statement: This statement has condition; it tests the condition and then directs the control to the body of the loop if and only if the condition is true.

(ii) Body of the Loop: These are the statements which get executed repeatedly until the condition is true.

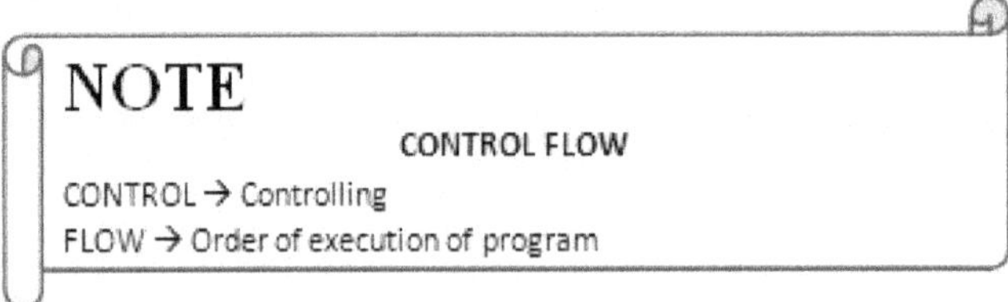

Syntax:
if (condition is true):

     do this # body of if

Here, the condition may be relational operators or logical operators and the output is Boolean expression.

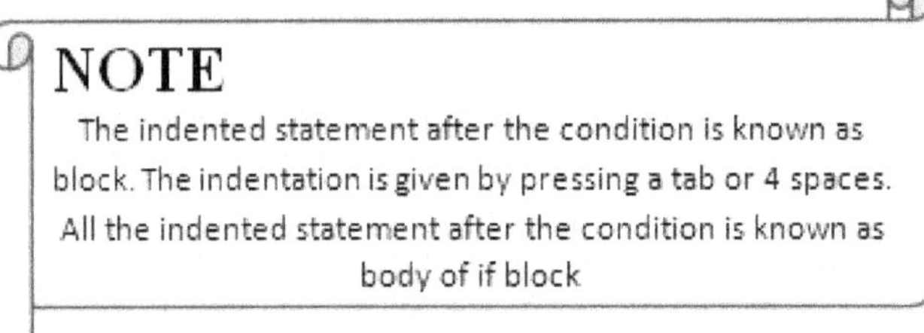

Example:

     Write a program to find whether the number is odd or even.

```python
n=int(input('enter a number'))
if n%2==0:
    print ('even number')
else:
    print ('odd number')
```

The flow of instruction can be controlled using condition. The Boolean expression after 'if' is called condition. If the condition is true, the indented statement runs. If not, the control goes to else block. Inside the body there can have any number of the number of statements, but there should be at least one statement.

In the above example if statement is used and Boolean expression is n%2. In this program relational operator (==) is used, if n% 2 is equal 0 then the condition will be True then if block will get executed otherwise else block will get executed.
Output:
enter a number 20
even number

Here, the user input is n=20. Here, 20%2 == 0 the condition is True so if block is executed and print the statement 'even number'.

There are three fundamental forms of control flow in python programming, they are:

- Sequential   control
- Selection   control
- Iterative   control

In order to determine the flow of execution, we have to know about Boolean expression, relational operator and logical operators

5.1.1 Boolean Expression

The statement that prints True or False is known as Boolean expression. In python the Boolean data type contains two Boolean values, such as True and False. A Boolean expression is an expression that evaluates to a Boolean value which is either True or False. Boolean expressions are used to denote the conditions for the conditional statements such as selection and iterative. Refer 4.3.4 to know more about Boolean data type.
Example:
>>> 2==2
True
>>> True and True
True
>>> True and False
False

Above examples uses the operator = = (comparison operator), which compares two operands and produces True if they are equal and False otherwise. In second and third examples logical operator (and) is used to find the truth value. If both conditions are True, result is True otherwise False. From the above example it is clear that the output is always Boolean values (either True or False). These operators are not only used to compare two operands but also used in control flow instructions to determine the flow of control of the program.

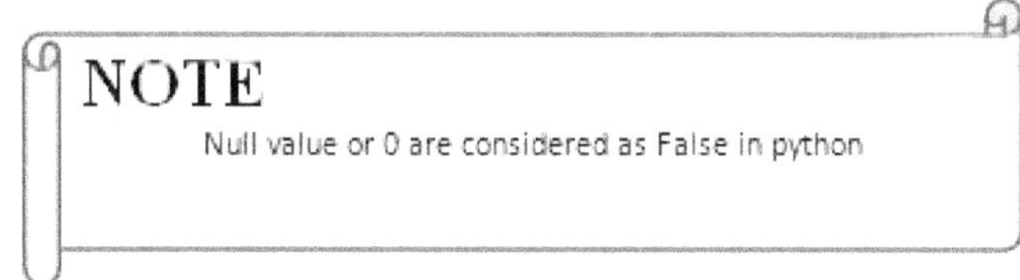

5.1.2 Comparison Operators

The comparison operator is also known as relational operators. This operators includes = =, !=, <, >, <=, >=. This operator is used to compare two operands and the result will always be Boolean value (True or False). The Chapter 4 explains about comparison operators in detail.

NOTE

Remember that there is no symbols like =< or = >. There is <= or >= symbols in relational operators.

No.	Operators	Description
1	x == y	x is equal to y
2	x != y	x is not equal to y
3	x > y	x is greater than y
4	x < y	x is less than y
5	x >= y	x is greater than or equal to y
6	x <= y	x is less than or equal to y

Example:

Write a program to find greatest among two numbers

```
a=int(input("Enter value of a"))
b=int(input("Enter value of b"))
if a>b:
   print("a is greater")
else:
   print("b is greater")
```

In the above example comparison operator is used to compare and find greatest among two numbers. The value of a and b is obtained from user, > symbol compare a and b. If a is greater than b is True then if block will get executed otherwise else block will get executed.

Output:

Enter value of a26

Enter value of b4

a is greater

In this example, value of a is 26 and value of b is 4. Here, a is greater than b so the condition is true so the if block will get executed and display the print statement a is greater.

5.1.3 Logical Operators

There are three logical operators, they are: and, or, and not. The Chapter 4 explains the detail concepts of logical operators.

No.	Operator	Description
1	and	Returns true only when both expression is true
2	or	Returns true if any one expression is true
3	not	Return negates of a Boolean expression

Example:

Write a program to find whether the given number is divisible by 6

```
i=int(input("Enter a number"))
if(i%3==0 and i%2==0):
   print ('Divisible by 6')
else:
   print ('Not divisible by 6')
```

In the above example, divisibility by 6 is checked. A number is divisible by 6 if and only if it is divisible by 3 and 2. So in the above program the given number is divided by 3 and 2, if obtained remainder is equal to 0 for both cases then the number is said to be divisible by 6. Here logical operator and is used, which check whether both condition (i%3==0, i%2==0) is True. If both conditions are True then body of if will get executed otherwise else block will get executed.

Output:
```
Enter a number12
Divisible by 6
```

The user input is i=12, 12%3==0 result True, 12%2==0 result is True. The result of True and True is True. Here if block is True so the body of if will get executed.

5.2 SEQUENTIAL CONTROL

Sequential control is an implicit form of control in which instructions are executed in the exact order that is written. This type of program is known as a "straight-line program." The Chapter 2 explains the algorithm, pseudocode and flow chart for straight-line programs. Steps are executed in sequence that follow top to bottom or left to right approach.

instruction 1
instruction 2
instruction 3
:
:
:

This follows a sequential flow, one instruction after another in straight line. The flow of this program starts from first statement and continues till the end of the program.

Example:
Python program for basic calculator to demonstrate sequential flow
```
a=int(input("Enter value of a"))
b=int(input("Enter value of b"))
c=a+b
d=a-b
e=a*b
f=a/b
print("addition of two numbers is",c)
print("subtraction of two numbers is",d)
print("multiplication of two numbers is",e)
print("division of two numbers is",f)
```

This program follows a sequential flow, each and every line come in order as it is written. This type of execution of program is known as sequential execution in python.
Output:

Enter value of a8
Enter value of b4
addition of two numbers is 12
subtraction of two numbers is 4
multiplication of two numbers is 32
division of two numbers is 2.0

From this output it is clear that the program executes in the order it is written. So this type of flow of control is known as sequential flow.

Example:

Python program to convert Celsius into Fahrenheit

```
Celsius=int(input("Enter the temperature in Celsius:"))
Fahrenheit=(Celsius*1.8)+32
print("Temperature in Fahrenheit is:",Fahrenheit)
```

Output:

Enter the temperature in Celsius:5
Temperature in Fahrenheit is: 41.0

This example also follows sequential flow which means one statement after the other.

5.3 SELECTION CONTROL

A selection control is a decision making process where decision has to be made. In selection control there are number of alterative among that only one alternative steps is executed based on the condition. This is also known as condition control, if- else construct is mostly used for these type of control flow. Once the condition is evaluated, the control flows into one of two paths. Selection structures are also called case selection structures there are two or more alternatives from that one is chosen. This control will selectively execute instructions so it is known as selection control. This selection control is of four types in python programming:

- Conditional execution (if)
- Alternative condition (if-else)
- Chained condition (if-elif-else)
- Nested condition (if inside a if)
- Inline if…else condition (inline if..else)

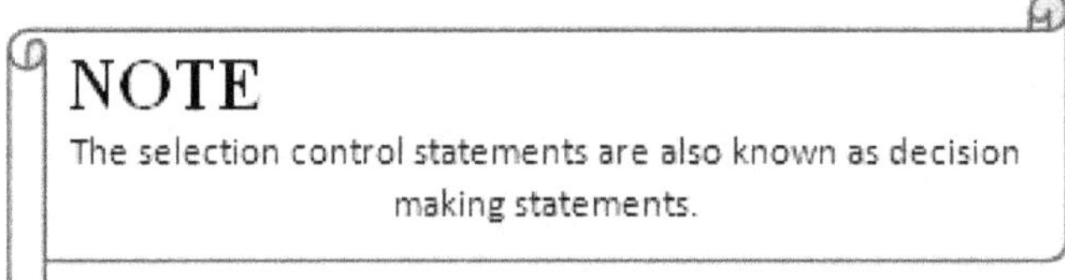

Let's now discuss about types of selection statements in detail.

5.3.1 Conditional execution

The conditional execution has condition which is generally comparisons and arithmetic expression with variables. This is evaluated to the Boolean values (True or False). The action taken by the conditional statement is entirely depending on the value of the condition. It is also called a one-way selection statement, which is the simplest form of selection. Here, there is one condition and a single sequence of statements. If the condition is True, then the sequence of statements is executed. The figure

5.1 represents the order of execution of condition execution.

Syntax:

if (condition):

    statement(s) 1

Here, if the condition is True if block (instruction(s) 1) will get executed.

Flow of execution:

- Check whether the condition is True or False.
- If the condition is true, executes the body of if statement. Otherwise, do nothing.

Example: Python program to check whether the number is positive using conditional execution.

n=int(input('enter a number'))

if n>0:

    print ('n is positive number')

In the above example, if the value of n is greater than 0 then if block or body of if will get executed.

Output:

enter a number5

n is positive number

Here, the value of n is 5, 5>0 the condition is True so if block got executed and print 'n is positive number'.

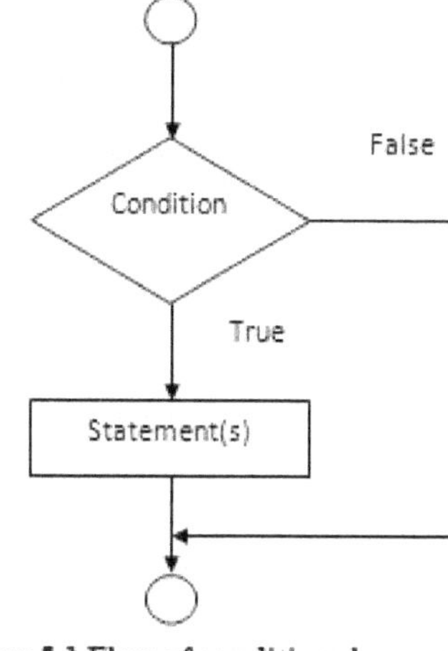

Figure 5.1 Flow of conditional execution

5.3.2 Alternative execution

Alternative execution is the second type of selection statement, it is another form of if statement. It is also known as "alternative execution" or "two way branching" or "two-way selection statement". In alternative execution there are two possibilities, if the condition is True body of if block will get executed otherwise body of else block will get executed. This is also known as if-else statement. This alternative execution contains two blocks, if block and else block. Figure 5.2 shows the flow of execution of alternative execution.

Syntax:

if condition:

    statement(s) 1   #execute this block if the condition is True

else:

    statement(s) 2   #execute this block if the condition is False

Flowchart:

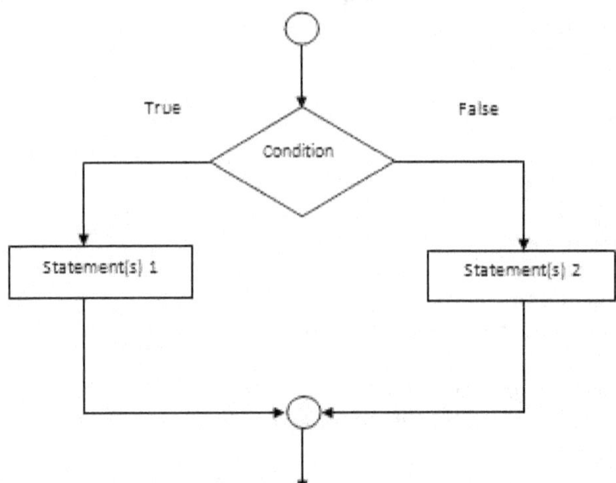

Figure 5.2 Flow of alternative execution

Flow of execution:
- Check whether the condition is True or False.
- If the condition is true, executes the body of if statement. Otherwise, execute the body of else statement.

Example:

Write a program to find whether the given year is a leap year or not

```
year=int(input("Enter a year "))
if(year%4==0 and year%100!=0 or year%400==0):
  print("LEAP YEAR!")
else:
  print("not a LEAP YEAR!")
```

This program is to find whether the given year is leap year or not. In the above example, if the Boolean expression is True then if block will get executed. This Boolean expression includes relational operators such as ==, != are used and logical operators such as and, or is used to find whether the given year is leap year or not. There are three conditions required to check whether the year is leap year or not.
- Check if the given year is divisible by 4 (year%4==0). If it is divisible go to step 2 else that year is not a leap year.
- If the number is divisible by 400 it is definitely a leap year (year%400==0) or check if it is not divisible by 100 (year%100!=0).Then that is year is a leap year.
- If that year is divisible by 100 then that year is not a leap year

Earth completes its orbit every 365.242375 days around the sun. But according to calendar we consider 365 days a year. The left 0.242375 is added as a day every fourth year. That day is 29th February which is a leap year. But after every 100 years there comes one extra day. So we have to take a day every 100 years (year%100!=0). But after every 400 year we have one day less, so add a day for every 400 year.

Output:
Enter a year 2016
LEAP YEAR!

Here, year=2016 which satisfies the condition and is True so the if block got executed and print LEAP YEAR!.

Some of the examples of this alternative execution are:
- odd or even number
- positive or negative number
- leap year or not
- greatest of two numbers
- eligibility for vote

5.3.3 Chained execution

In chained condition there are more than two choices. In some program there is necessity for more than two possibilities and we need more than two branches, in certain cases we uses chained condition. Chained condition is also known as if…elif…else condition or multipath decision statement or multi-way selection statement. In chained execution, if the condition of 'if statement' is True then the body of if block get executed. If that condition is False, body of elif block got executed. If all the conditions are False then body of else block will get executed. Figure 5.3 shows the flow of execution of chained execution.

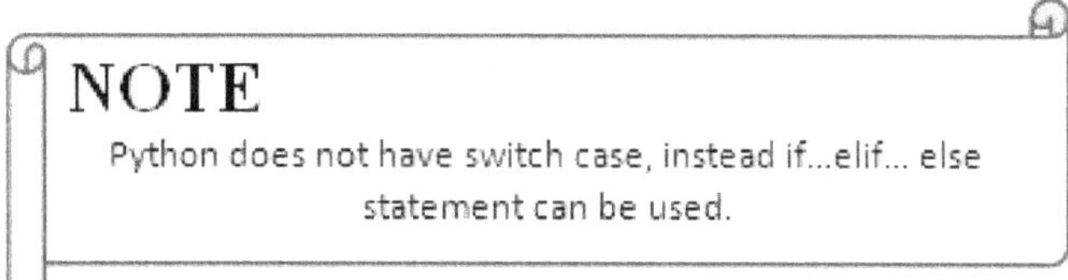

Python does not have switch case, instead if…elif… else statement can be used.

Syntax:
```
if condition:
    statement(s) 1    #execute this block if the condition is True
elif condition:
    statement(s) 2    #execute this block if the condition is True
else:
    statement(s) 3    #execute this block if the condition is False
```

Flowchart:

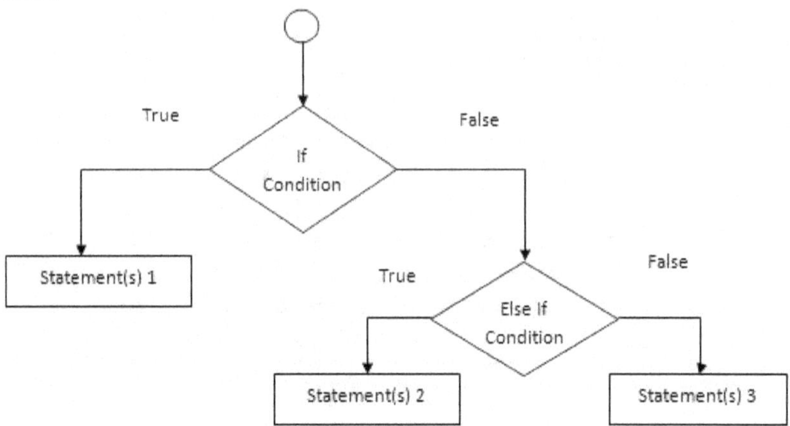

Figure 5.3 Flow of chained execution

Flow of execution:
- Check whether the condition is True or False.
- If the condition is true, executes the body of if statement. Otherwise, go to elif statement and check that condition.
- If the elif condition is True execute the body of elif otherwise executes the else statement.

Example:

Write a program to find greatest among three numbers.

```
a=int(input("Enter value of a"))
b=int(input("Enter value of b"))
c=int(input("Enter value of c"))
if a>b and a>c:
   print("a is greater")
elif b>c:
   print("b is greater")
else:
   print("c is greater")
```

In the above example, in if condition both relational operator (>) and logical operator (and) are used. Here, both condition (a>b, a>c) should be True then only if block will get executed. Otherwise the control goes to elif and check if b>c, if the condition is True then elif block will get executed otherwise the control goes to else block.

Output:

```
Enter value of a5
Enter value of b7
Enter value of c4
b is greater
```

In this example value of a is 5, b is 7 and c is 4. In if statement 5>7 and 5>4 (False and True), False and True is False. So if block will not get executed. Now the control goes to elif condition and check 7>4, It is True so elif block gets executed and display b is greater.

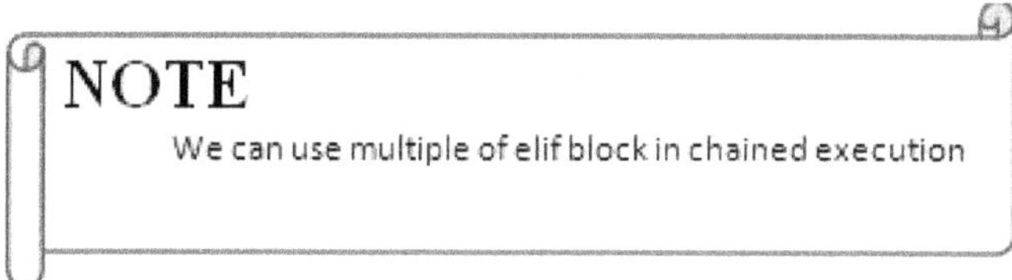

5.3.4 Nested execution

One conditional can also be written (nested) within another condition, this type of condition is known as nested condition. We can place multiple numbers of nested conditions inside one condition. One statement is nested inside another statement is known as nested statement or nested condition. Figure 5.4 represents the flow of nested if statement.

Syntax for nested if statement:

if condition
    if condition # This is nested if
        statement(s) 1
    else
        statement(s) 2
else
    statement(s) 3

Flowchart:

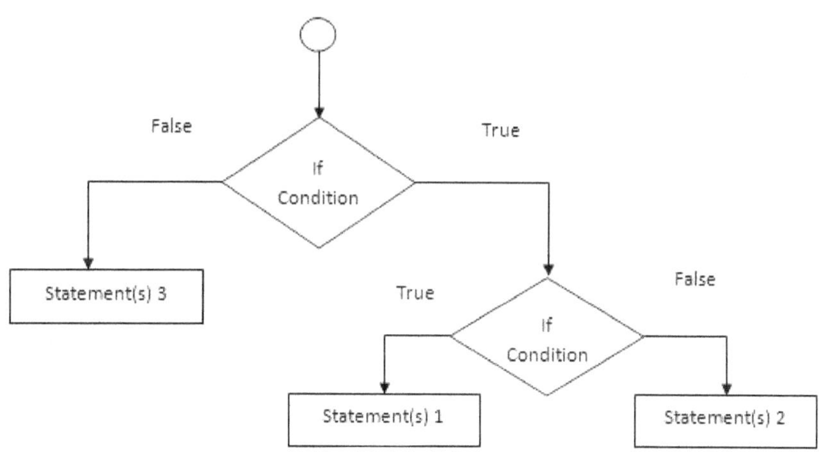

Figure 5.4: Flow of nested if statement

Flow of execution:

- Check whether the condition is True or False.
- If the condition is true, executes the body of if statement. Otherwise, go to elif statement and check that condition.
- If the elif condition is True execute the body of elif otherwise executes the else statement.
- If there is any nested loop if loop repeat the same procedure again.

Example:

Write a program to get mark of a student and display the grade of the grade using nested condition.

```python
mark=int(input("Enter mark"))
if mark>=50:
   if mark>=80 and mark<=100:
     print ("Pass with Distinction")
   elif mark>=60 and mark<80:
     print ("Pass with First class")
   else:
     print ("Pass with Second class")
else:
  print ("Fail")
```

From the above program it is clear that we can place if conditional inside another one if conditionals.

Output:

Enter mark95

Pass with Distinction

5.3.5 Inline if...else

The 'inline if...else' is the easiest and conventional form of if...else condition in python. It is mostly used to perform simple task.

Syntax:

Condition if True task_A else task_B

Example:

Inline if... else to print whether the condition is True or False

```python
>>> a=10
>>> a<=20 if a else 0
True
>>> a>=20 if a else 0
False
```

In the above example, if the condition is True then True will display and if the condition is False then False will displayed.

Example:

Inline if...else to assign values to the variable

```python
>>> x=True
>>> y='Hai' if x else False
>>> y
'Hai'
>>> z='Hai' if not x else False
>>> z
False
```

5.4 ITERATIVE   CONTROL

Repeated execution of set of instructions is known as iteration. Iterative control is provided by an iterative control statement that repeatedly executes instructions again and again. In programming there may have some situations that a block of code needs to be executed for several numbers of times in that case we have to use iterative statement. Iteration is also known as looping or repetition statements. There are two types of looping statements in python:

- while loop

- for loop

5.4.1 WHILE Loop

The WHILE is a conditional iteration which requires that a condition be tested within the loop to determine whether the loop should continue to execute or not. Such type of condition is called the loop's continuation condition. If the continuation condition is False, then the loop ends. If the continuation condition is true, then the statements within the loop are executed again. It tests the condition each time before executing the body of while loop. If the condition is True repeats a statement or block of statement. Figure 5.5 explains the flow of execution of while loop.

Syntax:

while (condition):

    statement(s) 1 # body of while

statement(s)2

Flowchart:

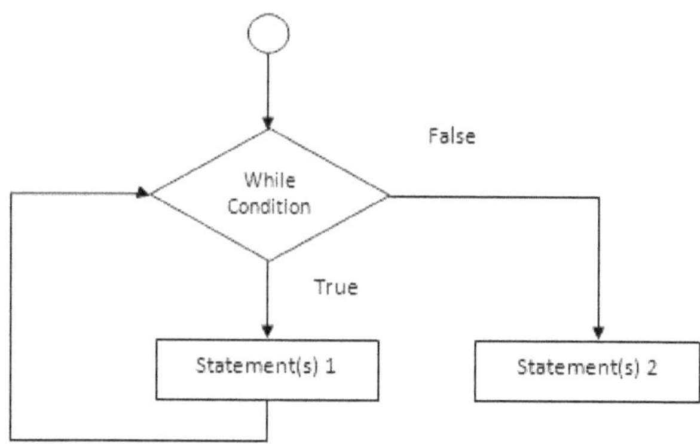

Figure 5.5: Flow of while loop

This is the syntax for while loop, the condition may be anything whose result is a Boolean value (True or False). If the condition is True the body of while loop will get executed otherwise the control won't enter into the while loop. The loop must update the variable inside the body of the loop. The condition should be set in such a way that, there must have a case that will let the condition become False and terminate from the loop. If there is no condition to terminate and a loop variable to update, then the loop will result in infinite loop.

Flow of execution:

Step 1: Check whether the condition is True or False.

Step 2: If the condition is False, exit the while statement and continue execution at the next statement.

Step 3: If the condition is True, executes the body of while and then goes back to while loop (step 1).

This type of flow is called a looping, here Step 3 loops back to Step 1 and repeat the process.

Example:

Write a python program to display even number from 1 to 10 using while loop.

a=1

print ("EVEN numbers are:")

```
while(a<=10):
  if a%2==0:
    print (a)
  a=a+1
```

In the above example, a<=10 is the condition and a=a+1 is the update statement. This program is to display even numbers from 1 to 10 using while loop, initially value of a is assigned as 1. By using while loop, the condition (a<=20) is set, if the condition is True body of while loop will get executed. In first iteration value of a is 1, the condition (1<=10) is True. So body of while loop will get executed and check a is divisible by 2 if this is True, value of a is printed. Now the value of a is updated (a=a+1), value of a become 2. Now the control goes to while loop and checks whether the condition (2<=10) is True, if so this process will get repeated otherwise it will terminate from the loop. In this way loop gets executed by increment the value and performs next iteration.

Output:

EVEN numbers are:

2

4

6

8

10

This loop executes 10 times and display the value of a if it is even.

NOTE

The while loop must contain an update statement otherwise it will not terminate which leads to infinite loop.

5.4.1.1 Infinite loop:

An infinite loop is an iterative control structure that will not terminate. This type of loop may terminate when some system error is obtained. The body of the loop should contain at least one update variable to change the value of one or more variables so that the condition becomes False and let the loop terminates. If there is no update variable the loop will not terminate, this will let steps repeats over and over again. This is known as infinite loop.

Example:

```
a=int(input("Enter a value"))
while(a>=0):
  print (a)
```

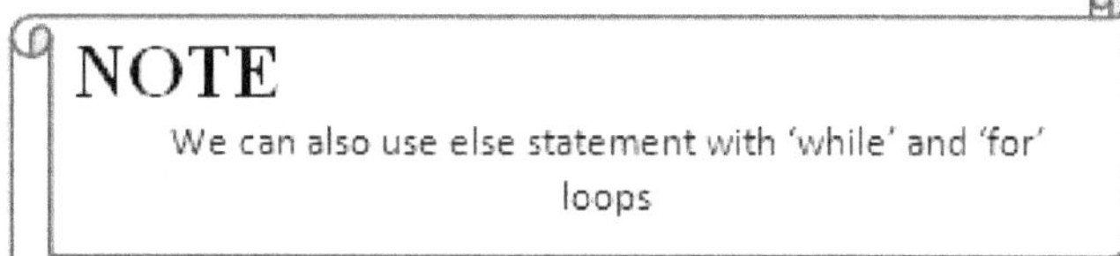

Output:
Enter a value10
10
10
10
10
Traceback (most recent call last):
  File "C:/Python27/5.py", line 3, in <module>
    print (a)
  File "C:\Python34\lib\idlelib\PyShell.py", line 1344, in write
    return self.shell.write(s, self.tags)
KeyboardInterrupt

In the above program there is no update variable so the condition of while loop will not become False. If you execute this program you will see that this loop will not get terminate leading to infinite loop.

5.4.1.2 while loop with else statement

Python supports else statement inside the while loop. The else statement gets executed when the while condition becomes False.

Example:

Python program to print sum of n numbers using while loop and else

```
n=int(input("Enter a value"))
sum=0
i=0
while i<n:
    sum=sum+i
    i=i+1
else:
    print( 'sum is:',sum)
```

Output:
Enter a value11
sum is: 55

5.4.2 FOR Loop

The for loop is another iterative statement, it iterates over a range of values such as list, tuple, string or other iterable objects. It executes the block of statement for a fixed number of times mentioned. In for loop statement for updating a variable is not necessary. Iterating over a sequence of items is called traversal. Figure 5.6 explains the flow of execution of for loop.

Syntax:

for loop_variable in sequence:

      statement(s)

      Here, loop_variable may be name given to the for loop. Sequence is any sequential data type such as string, list, tuple.

Example:

n=[1,3,4,8]

for i in n:

   print (i)

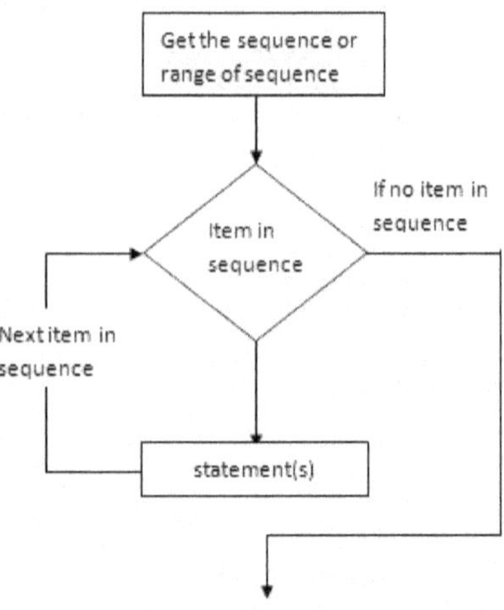

Figure 5.6: Flow of for loop

      In the above example i is variable and n is a list. This program is to iterate over the loop and display the value of the list one by one.While iterating 'i' will take values of the list 'n'. Here, iteration of this loop is done four times as the total number of elements in list 'n' is four.

Output:

1

3

4

8

      We can use range of function to simplify the performance of for loop.

5.4.2.1 Using range( ) function

      The range( ) is used to generate the sequence of numbers. We can use the range( ) function in three different ways.

- range (n) # generates numbers from 0 to n-1
- range (m,n) # generates numbers for m to n-1
- range(m,n, x) # generates numbers from m up to n-1 with skip counting of

x

Example:

```
>>> print(list(range(3)))
[0, 1, 2]
```

This prints the values of range 0 to 2 in list

```
>>> print(list(range(3,7)))
[3, 4, 5, 6]
```

This prints the value from the range 3 to 6 in list

```
>>> print(list(range(0,10,3)))
[0, 3, 6, 9]
```

This prints counting of 3 from 0 to 10 and the range is incremented by 3.

```
>>> print(list(range(7,0,-1)))
[7, 6, 5, 4, 3, 2, 1]
```

      This statement prints the inverse of the items in the list. That is the range is decremented by 1. In this example -1 is the step which is the difference between the consecutive numbers or each number in sequence.

Syntax for using range( ) function for creating a list:

for loop_variable in range(begin, end,step):

 statement(s) 1

 Here, begin is the first value in the range, by default begin value is 0 and end is one past the last value in the range. That is, end value is end-1th value. These begin and end should be an integer value, other numeric data type is not allowed. The step is the difference between each number in sequence. Generally begin and end are the two parameters which are mostly used in for loop.

Example:

 Write a python program to print sum of n number using for loop

```python
n=int(input("Enter a value"))
sum=0
for i in range(0,n):
  sum=sum+i
print( 'sum is:',sum)
```

 In for loop end range is not taken, that means the for loop executes n-1times starting from beginning range (0).

Output:

Enter a value11

sum is: 55

 The for loop executes from 0 to n-1 times excluding the last value (11). That means summing the value from 0 to 10 we get 55.

5.4.2.2 For loop using else statement

 Python supports else statement inside the for loop. The else statement gets executed when the for condition becomes False.

Example:

Program to print sum of n numbers using for loop and else

```python
n=int(input("Enter a value"))
sum=0
for i in range(0,n):
  sum=sum+i
else:
  print( 'sum is:',sum)
```

Output:

Enter a value11

sum is: 55

5.4.3 Nested Loops

 Nested Loops means placing a loop inside other loop. Python also supports nested for loop and nested while loop. The loop should be properly indented to identify the statement within the loop. The nested for loops are commonly used than nested while loops.

Example:

Program to demonstrate nested for loops.

```python
n=int(input("Enter a value"))
for i in range(n):
  print()
  for j in range(i):
    print( '*',end=' ')
```

Output:
Enter a value5
```
*
* *
* * *
* * * *
```

5.5 LOOPING CONTROL STATEMENTS

Looping control statements is used to change the execution from its normal sequence. It is also known as unconditional statement or jumping statement. It control or changes the flow of the program to get the expected result. The looping control statements supported by Python is shown in the below table.

No.	CONTROL STATEMENT	DESCRIPTION
1	Break	The break statement is used to terminate or breaks the loop statement and transfers flow of execution to the statement immediately following the loop.
2	Continue	The continue statement is used to skip the rest of its body and immediately retest its condition before reiterating.
3	Pass	The pass statement is used when a statement is syntactically required but there isn't any command or code to execute.

Table 5.2: Control statements

5.5.1 Break

In order to break out of the loop we have to use break statement. This means terminating or exiting from the actual loop. Python includes a break statement that will allow us to make this change in the program. This break statement can be used anywhere inside for and while loop.

Syntax:

break

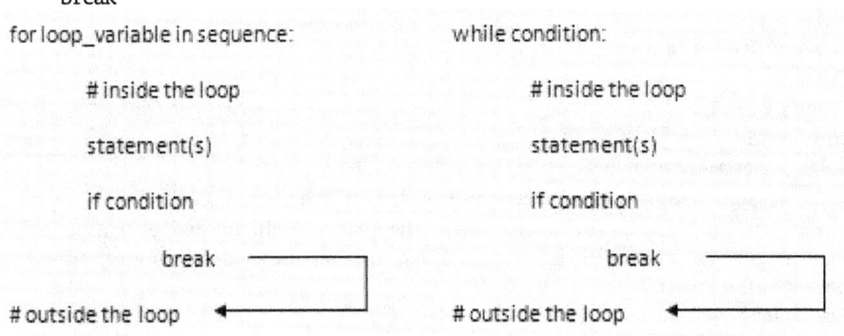

Flow of control:
- Executes the statements of the loop
- When the break statement is reaches the control automatically terminates from the loop. That means control goes outside of the loop and executes the next statement.

Example:
```
s="Learn Python"
for i in s:
   print (i)
```
Output:
```
L
e
a
r
n

P
y
t
h
o
n
```
If we use break statement in above program, the output will be.
Example:
```
s="Learn Python"
for i in s:
   if i=='P':
     break
   print (i)
```
      In the above program break statement is used. When if condition (i=='n') becomes True the body of if got executed. Once the control reaches the break statement, it terminates from for loop.
Output:
```
L
e
a
r
n
```
      So, the output of this program will be string from L to blank space is printed and when i=='P', break got executed and terminate from the loop.

5.5.2 Continue

      If we want to skip the current statement use continue statement inside the loop. This statement will skip the remaining statements and goes to the beginning of the loop.
Syntax:
```
continue
```

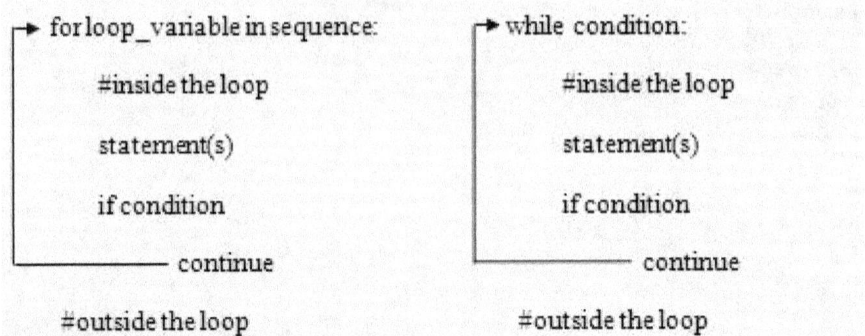

Flow of control:
- Executes statements of the loop
- When the continue statement is reach, the control skip the remaining statements in the loop and go to the beginning of the loop.

Example:
```
s="Learn Python"
for i in s:
    if i=='P':
        continue
    print (i)
```
In the above example, when if condition become True continue statement got executed. It skips the print statement and goes to the beginning of the loop.

Output:
```
L
e
a
r
n

y
t
h
o
n
```
In this example it is clear that the continue statement will skip the remaining statements after it and goes to the beginning of the loop. So in above output all string except 'P' got displayed because continue skipped the print statement and goes to for loop again.

Example:

Program to print all odd numbers from 1 to 10 using continue
```
for i in range(1,10):
    if i%2==0:
        continue
    print(i)
```
Output:
```
1
3
```

5
7
9

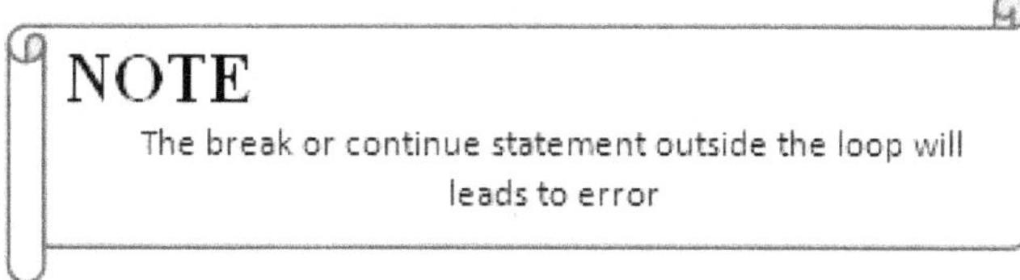

5.5.3 Pass

Pass means null statement in python, nothing happens when pass is executed. Interpreter executes the pass statement and does nothing, this will results in no operation. It is also known as NOP. It is used when a statement is required syntactically but no comment or code has to be executed. It is mostly used in body with no statements. This statement just pushes the control to the next line of the loop. This statement is used in the place where the program cannot be left blank.

Syntax:

    if condition:

        pass

Suppose we have a loop or a function that has to implement later, in that case we cannot leave the loop empty. Because empty body will leads to error, so we use the pass statement to construct a body that does nothing.

Example:

Python program to demonstrate pass.

```
a=int(input("Enter a number"))
if a<=100:
    pass   #do nothing
```

Output:

Enter a number20

When the input "a" is get from user, it checks whether "a" is less than or equal to 100. The condition is "True", so the body of "if" loop will get executed. The body of the "if" loop contains only the pass statement which does not perform any operation. So the output only contains only one line (to get input from user).

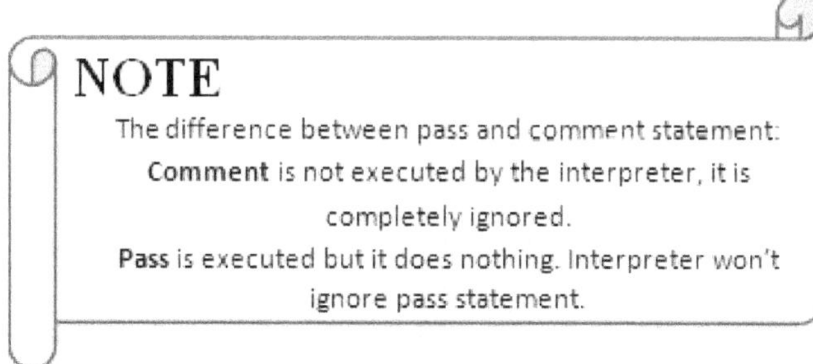

SUMMARY

•	Control statements are used to control the flow of the program. Some of the control statements in python are if, for, while.

•	The process of repeating a set of statements is known as looping or iterating. The looping statements in python are for and while.

- A for loop is used when we want to execute a statement or a set of statements a particular number of times. Generally range( ) function is used in this looping.
- A while loop is used for executing a statement or a set of statements again and again when a condition is True.
- The break statement is used to exit completely from the current loop.
- The continue statement transfer the control completely to the next iteration of the loop leaving the remaining statement in the loop.
- The pass statement is a null statement, it won't perform any action.

ILLUSTRATIVE PROBLEMS

1)   Write a program to check the output of relational operators:

The relational operators are >, <, <=, >=, = =, != and the resultant output will be True or False. This program follows a **sequential flow.**

```
x = 50
y = 62
print('x > y  is',x>y)
print('x < y  is',x<y)
print('x == y is',x==y)
print('x != y is',x!=y)
print('x >= y is',x>=y)
print('x <= y is',x<=y)
```

Output:

```
x > y  is False
x < y  is True
x == y is False
x != y is True
x >= y is False
x <= y is True
```

2) Write a program to check the output of the logical operators

The logical operators are and, or , not and the resultant output will be Boolean values True or False. This program follows a **sequential flow.**

```
x = True
y = False
print('x and y is',x and y)
print('x or y is',x or y)
print('not x is',not x)
```

Output:

```
x and y is False
x or y is True
not x is False
```

3)   Write a program to find whether the given number is odd or even

The odd numbers are1,3,5,7,9,….. and even numbers are 2,4,6,8,….. If the number is modulo with 2 and if the resultant output is 0 then the number is even otherwise odd. This program follows **alternative execution (if….else…).**

```
number = int(input("Enter a number"))
if (number % 2 ==0):
   print ('The  number is even ')
else:
   print ('The  number is odd ')
```

Output:

Enter a number 3 5

The number is odd

4) Write a program to check whether the given number is positive, negative or zero.

This program is to check if the number is positive, negative of zero. If the number is greater than zero the it is a positive number, if it is equal to zero then it zero otherwise(both are false) it is negative number. For this program **chained if (if....elif....else..)** used.

```python
number=int(input("Enter a number"))
if number > 0:
   print('It is a Positive number')
elif number==0:
   print('The number is zero')
else:
   print('It is a Negative number')
```

Output:

Enter a number 10

It is a Positive number

5)   Write a program to compare two values is equal or not.

This program is to check whether the two values are equal not. Here, = = operator is used to check the equality. This program use **alternative execution (if....else....).**

```python
x='hai'
y='Hai'
if x == y:
   print( 'x and y are equal')
else:
   print ('x and y are not equal')
```

Output:

x and y are not equal

6)   Write a program to print number from 1 to n

This program is to print all the natural numbers from 1 to n. For this **while loop** is used.

```python
n=int(input("Enter the value of n"))
i=0
while i<n:
   i=i+1
   print(i)
```

Output:

Enter the value of n5

1

2

3

4

5

7)   Write a program python program to get sum of n numbers using while loop.

This program is to get summation of numbers from 1 to n using **while loop,** (i.e., sum of 4 is 1+2+3+4=10).

```python
n=int(input("Enter the value of n"))
```

```
i=1
sum=0
while i<=n:
  sum=sum+i
  i=i+1
print(sum)
```
Output:
Enter the value of n4
10

8) Write a program to print prime number from a range

Prime number is a natural number greater than one which has only factors are 1 and itself. The prime numbers are 2, 3, 5, 7, 11, 13, …. This program is to print all the prime numbers within the range. To execute this program **for loop** is used.

```
From = int(input('Enter lower range: '))
To = int(input('Enter upper range: '))
print('Prime numbers between', From, 'and', To,'are:')
for n in range(From,To + 1):
  if n> 1:
    for i in range(2,n):
      if (n % i) == 0:
        break
    else:
      print(n)
```
Output:
Enter lower range: 10
Enter upper range: 20
Prime numbers between 10 and 20 are:
11
13
17
19

9) Write a program to find whether the person is eligible to vote

This program is to check whether a person is eligible to vote or note. The person who age is 18 or greater than 18 is eligible for vote. In order to check this condition alternative execution (if…else…) is used.

```
age=int(input("Enter the age"))
if age>=18:
  print("Eligible to vote")
else:
  print("Not eligible to vote")
```
Output:
Enter the age21
Eligible to vote

10) Write a program to find sum and average of items in a list using range( ) function.

This program is to create a list, then insert value into the list using append method. Then find the sum and average of element in that list. This program **use for loop and range( )** function to insert value into that list.

```
l=[]
```

```python
n=int(input("Enter total number of items in list"))
for i in range(0,n):
   items=int(input("Enter items in list"))
   l.append(items)
print("The list is",l)
sum=0
for i in range(0,n):
   sum=sum+l[i]
print("Sum of list is",sum)
avg=sum/n
print("Average of list is",avg)
```

Output:

Enter total number of items in list4
Enter items in list2
Enter items in list4
Enter items in list3
Enter items in list7
The list is [2, 4, 3, 7]
Sum of list is 16
Average of list is 4.0

11)   Write a program to find factorial of n number using while loop

This program is to factorial of n numbers, factorial means product of multiplying a series of integer in descending order. For example, 4!= 4 x 3 x 2 x 1 which is 24. This program use **while loop** to get the same.

```python
n=int(input("enter the number\n"))
i=1
fact=1
while(i<=n):
   fact=fact*i
   i=i+1
print("The factorial of",n,"is",fact)
```

Output:

enter the number
4
The factorial of 4 is 24

12)   Write a program to find sum of digit of a number

This program is to sum all the digits of a number say if the number is 125 then the output 8 (1+2+5). This program use **while loop** to get the output.

```python
n=int(input("enter a number\n"))
sum=0
while(n>0):
   a=n%10
   sum=sum+a
   n=n//10
print("The sum of digits of the number is", sum)
```

Output:

enter a number
125
The sum of digits of the number is 8

13) Write a program to reverse the digits of a number.

This python program is to reverse the sum of digits of a number using **while loop.** Reversing the digits of the number means placing the digits in reverse order. For example if the number is 125 then the resultant output will be 521, which is the reverse of 125.

```
n=int(input("enter a number\n"))
rev=0
while(n>0):
    a=n%10
    rev=rev*10+a
    n=n//10
print("The reverse of the number is",rev)
```

Output:
enter a number
125
The reverse of the number is 521

14) Write a program to find whether the given number is Armstrong number or not.

An Armstrong number is the sum of the cubes of its digits is equal to the number itself. Armstrong numbers are 153, 371, etc. For example, $153 = 1^3+5^3+3^3 = 1+125+27 = 153$. Such numbers are known as Armstrong numbers. This program use **while loop** to get the result.

```
n=int(input("enter a number\n"))
x=n
sum=0
while(n>0):
    a=n%10
    sum=sum+a*a*a
    n=n//10
if(sum==x):
    print("It is an Armstrong number")
else:
    print("It is not an Armstrong number")
```

Output:
enter a number
153
It is an Armstrong number

15) Write a program to find whether the given number is palindrome or not

Palindrome number is a number which remains the same even if it is reversed. Some of the examples of palindrome are 212, 56765, 12321 even if the number is reversed the number will be same. This program use **while and if** to check whether the number is palindrome or not.

```
n=int(input("enter a number\n"))
temp=n
sum=0
while(n>0):
    a=n%10
    sum=sum*10+a
    n=n//10
```

```
if(sum==temp):
  print("The given number is palindrome")
else:
  print("The given number is not palindrome")
```

Output:

```
enter a number
12321
The given number is palindrome
```

16) Write a program to find Fibonacci series

Fibonacci series or sequence is a set of numbers that start with 0 and 1 and then is the sum of two preceding numbers. The Fibonacci series is 0, 1, 1, 2, 3, 5, 8,…. This program use '**for loop**' to print Fibonacci series from 0 to n.

```
a=0
b=1
n=int(input("Enter the number of terms: "))
print("Fibonacci Series are")
print(a)
print(b)
for i in range(1,n):
  c=a+b
  print(c)
  a=b
  b=c
```

Output:

```
Enter the number of terms: 6
Fibonacci Series are
0
1
1
2
3
5
8
```

17) Write a program to find whether the given number is prime or not

Prime number is a natural number greater than one which has only factors are 1 and itself. Example for prime number are 2, 3, 5, 7, 11, …. This program is to check whether the given number is prime or not. In this cases, '**for**' and '**if**' statements are used.

```
n=int(input("Enter a number"))
for i in range(2,n):
  if(n%i==0):
    print("The number is not a prime")
    break
else:
  print("The number is a prime number")
```

Output:

```
Enter a number7
The number is a prime number
```

18) Write a program to find whether the number is divisible by 6 or not

The prime factors of 6 are 2 and 3. So if a number is divisible by 6 then it should also be divisible by 2 and 3. This is the divisibility rule for 6. Here, **alternative execution** is used with relational and logical operator in it.

```
n=int(input("Enter a number"))
if((n%2==0)and(n%3==0)):
    print("The number is divisible by 6")
else:
    print("The number is not divisible by 6")
```

Output:
```
Enter a number12
The number is divisible by 6
```

19)   Write a program to print odd and even elements of a list into two different lists.

The number whose modulo by 2 is zero then that number is even others are odd. The even numbers are 2, 4, 6, 8,... and the odd number are 1,3,5,7,9,.... This program uses '**for loop**' and '**if...else...**' to print odd and even elements in two different lists.

```
l=[]
n=int(input("Enter number of elements:"))
for i in range(1,n):
    b=int(input("Enter element:"))
    l.append(b)
even=[]
odd=[]
for j in l:
    if(j%2==0):
        even.append(j)
    else:
        odd.append(j)
print("The even list",even)
print("The odd list",odd)
```

Output:
```
Enter number of elements:8
Enter element:1
Enter element:2
Enter element:4
Enter element:14
Enter element:31
Enter element:5
Enter element:8
The even list [2, 4, 14, 8]
The odd list [1, 31, 5]
```

20)   Write a program to calculate simple interest

The formula to calculate simple interest is SI=(p n r)/100 where, p is principle, n is time taken and r is the rate of interest. This program follows a **sequential flow**.

```
p=float(input("Enter the principle amount:"))
n=int(input("Enter the time(years):"))
r=float(input("Enter the rate:"))
```

```python
simple_interest=(p*n*r)/100
print("The simple interest is:",simple_interest)
```
Output:
```
Enter the principle amount:300000
Enter the time(years):2
Enter the rate:10.20
The simple interest is: 61200.0
```
21) Write a program to print inverted Triangle

This program is to print inverted star pyramid using **for loop**.
```python
n=int(input("Enter number of rows: "))
for i in range(n,0,-1):
    print((n-i) * ' ' + i * '*')
```
Output:
```
Enter number of rows: 5
*****
 ****
  ***
   **
    *
```

22) Write a program to print the multiplication table of any number n.

This program is to print multiplication table using **for loop**.
```python
n=int(input("Enter the table"))
for i in range(1,11):
    print(n,"X",i,"=",n*i)
```
Output:
```
Enter the table5
5 X 1 = 5
5 X 2 = 10
5 X 3 = 15
5 X 4 = 20
5 X 5 = 25
5 X 6 = 30
5 X 7 = 35
5 X 8 = 40
5 X 9 = 45
5 X 10 = 50
```

23) Write a python program to find the sum of the series: $1+ 1/2^2 + 1/3^2 + ... + 1/n^2$
```python
n=int(input("Enter the value of n"))
sum=0
for i in range(1,n+1):
    a=1/(i**2)
    sum=sum+a
print("The sum is:",sum)
```
Output:
```
Enter the value of n2
The sum is: 1.25
```

Here, the value of n is 2 so, 1+(1/(2**2)) is 1.25.

24) Write a python program to print the capital and small letters of English alphabet.

The ASCII value of capital letters starts from 65 and ends at 90. The ASCII value of small letters starts from 97 and ends at 122. Using for loop all the letters are printed recursively.

```
print("The capital letters are :")
for i in range(65,91):
    print(chr(i),end="")
print()
print("The small letters are :")
for i in range(97,123):
    print(chr(i),end="")
```

Output:
The capital letters are :
ABCDEFGHIJKLMNOPQRSTUVWXYZ
The small letters are :
abcdefghijklmnopqrstuvwxyz

ADDITIONAL PROBLEMS

1) Write a python program to reverse the order of words
2) Write a python program to get the Least Common Multiple (LCM) of two number
3) Write a python program to find the total number of vowels in the string
4) Write a python program to find the sum of the series: 1+ 1/2 + 1/3 + ... + 1/n
5) Write a python program to display the composite number of the range
6) Write a python program to find the sum of the series: 1/2+ 2/3 + ... + n/n+1
7) Write a python program to find sum of square and cubes of numbers in the range.
8) Write a program to find whether the number is divisible by 10 or not
9) Write a program to print the following pattern:
   ```
   * * * * *
   * * * *
   * * *
   * *
   *
   ```
10) Write a program to print the following pattern:
   ```
   *
   * *
   * * *
   * * * *
   * * * * *
   * * * *
   * * *
   * *
   *
   ```

11) Write a program to print the following pattern:

```
1
1 2
1 2 3
1 2 3 4
1 2 3 4 5
```

12) Write a program to convert meter into centimeter

13) Write a program to convert feet into centimeter

14) Write a program to print all the perfect squares of the range.

15) Write a program to calculate Body Mass Index (BMI)

16) Write a program print number which are divisible by 5 not by 10

REVIEW QUESTIONS

1) What are the types of control statements available in Python?

2) What are the looping statements available in Python?

3) What is the difference between break and continue statement?

4) What are Boolean values?

5) Write the syntax for if with example?

6) Write the syntax and flowchart for if else.

7) Write the syntax and flowchart for chained if.

8) Write the syntax for while loop with flowchart

9) Write the syntax for for loop with flowchart.

10) What is parameter and list down its type?

11) What is the purpose of pass statement?

12) Define Inline if...else

13) Explain nested if...else statement

14) What is the difference between selection and iterative statements?

15) Explain the need of range( ) function

MULTIPLE CHOICE QUESTIONS

1) What will the output for the following code:

```
for i in range(0,4):
    print(i, end="\t")
```
   a) 0 1   2   3
   b) 0 1   2   3   4
   c) 1 2   3   4
   d) 1 2   3

2) If there is only one parameter in the range( ) function of for loop, then what it will be:
   a) step
   b) begin
   c) end
   d) None of these

3) What will be the output for the following code:

```
for i in range(0,4)
```

```
    print(i,end="\t")
```
a)   0 1   2   3
b)   0 1   2   3   4
c)   syntax error
d)   "\t"

4) What will be the output for the following code:

```
a=10

if a>=10:

    pass
```
a)   Syntax error
b)   No output, Do nothing
c)   pass
d)   None of these

5) How many times "python" get printed.

```
while True:

    print("python")
```
a)   1
b)   0
c)   countless times, leads to infinite loop
d)   Syntax error

6) How many times "python" get printed.

```
while False:

    print("python")
```
a)   1
b)   0
c)   countless times, leads to infinite loop
d)   Syntax error

7) What will be the output for the following code:

```
a="python"

for i in a:

    if i=='h':

        break

    print(i,end="\t")
```
a)   h
b)   p y t h o n
c)   p y t   o   n

d) py t

8) What will be the output for the following code:

```python
while 1:
    print("hai")
    break
```
a) syntax error
b) print "hai" countless times, infinite loop
c) hai
d) No output

9) What will be the output for the following code:

```python
a="hai"
for i in range(len(a)):
    i="h"
    print(i,end="\t")
```
a) syntax error
b) h
c) h h   h
d) h a   i

10) What is the output for the following statement?

```python
>>> True or not False
```
a) True
b) False
c) 0
d) 1

11) Which statement is used to skip the current iteration and to go to the next
    iteration?
a) break
b) pass
c) skip
d) continue

TRUE OR FALSE

1) The elif and else are optional statements.
2) Indentation in program denotes the block.
3) It is not necessary to end conditional statement with colon.

4) The else statement is only used with if statement.
5) A while loop will get executed only when the condition is True.
6) Multiple elif statements cannot be used in python.
7) The break and continue statement can be used outside the loop.
8) Pass statement is used instead of comment statement.
9) The range( ) function is used to iterate over the sequence.
10) The condition or expression in the control statement is comparison or logical operator.

FILL IN THE BLANK

1) A statement inside another statement is known as __________.
2) If the condition of the while loop will never becomes False then that lead to __________ loop.
3) The indented statement in python is also known as __________.
4) Python consider all zero and null as __________ and non-non-zero and null as __________.
5) The pass statement is also known as __________.
6) The else if statement in python is __________.
7) Pressing Ctrl+C will create __________.
8) The __________ looping statement is used to execute a set of statement a particular number of times.
9) The switch case in python is done by using multiple __________ statement.
10) Fill in the blank to create a for loop to print sum of numbers from 1 to 10.

```
sum=0

for i in _________:

        sum=sum+_________

print(sum)
```

ANSWERS

MULTIPLE CHOICE QUESTIONS

1) a
2) b
3) c
4) b
5) c
6) b
7) d
8) c
9) c
10) a
11) d

TRUE OR FALSE

1) True
2) True
3) False
4) False
5) True
6) False
7) False
8) False
9) True
10) True

FILL IN THE BLANK

1) Nested statement
2) Infinite
3) Block
4) False, True
5) NOP
6) elif
7) keyboard Interrupt
8) for
9) elif
10) range(1,11), i

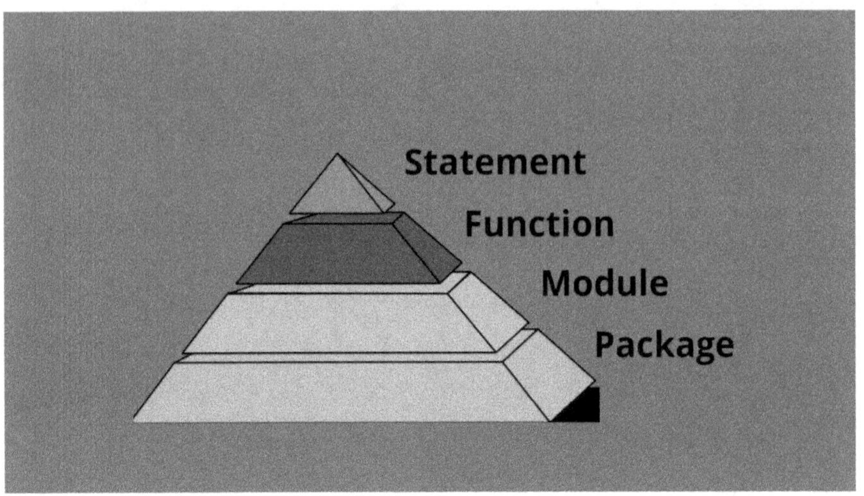

CHAPTER 6: FUNCTION, MODULES AND PACKAGES

This chapter describes about function, module and package in detail. Some simple statements together form a function. Functions and statements forms a module, collection of modules, directories and package itself forms packages. The main purpose of functions, modules and packages are code reusability.

CHAPTER OUTLINE

Function: Pre defined function, user defined function, User-defined function: Function definition, function call, flow of execution, parameter and argument, recursive function, fruitful function, scope, function composition, Lambda function, Documentation strings – Module: Predefined module, User defined module – Package.

OBJECTIVE

After completing this chapter you will be able:

- To know about function and how to define the function.
- To known the usage of fruitful functions.
- To understand the scope of the variable.
- To know how to use predefined functions and modules.
- To know how to create user defined functions and modules.
- To understand the working of recursive function.
- To work with lambda functions.
- To know about modular design
- To know about module and how to create it.
- To use the functions of predefined module.
- To know about built-in functions and module

- To known about packages.
- To learn about some commonly used python module.

6.1 FUNCTION

A collection of statements together form a function. A function is a group of re-usable code that can be called to perform some specific task or action. It is also known as methods, sub-routines, procedures, etc. Functions require arguments to perform their tasks. When a task of the called function is done, the result will be send back to the part of the program that called that function. Function allows transferring control back and forth between the codes. The main advantage of using function is code reuse.

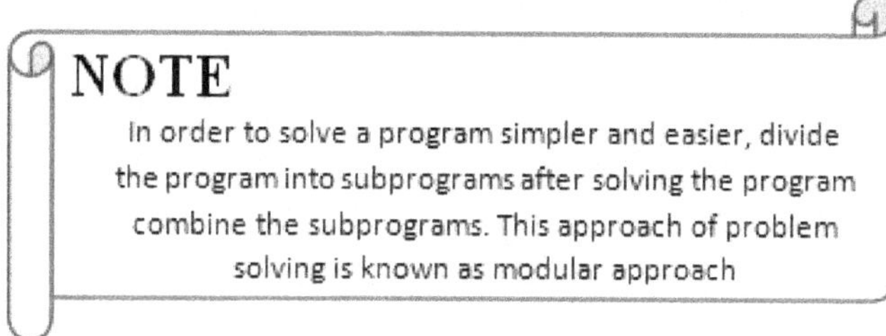

This function is of two types, they are:
- Predefined function
- User defined function

6.2 PREDEFINED FUNCTION

Predefined function is also known as built-in function. These functions are already available in Python. The working of these function are already predefined to the software. Some of the predefined functions are print( ), input( ), int( ), reverse( ), sqrt( ), pow( ), float( ), type( ), dir( ), len( ), help( ), abs( ), range( ), etc.

We can call them directly and use this function into our program, for some function we can use by importing its module in the program. This is used by calling the function name with arguments.

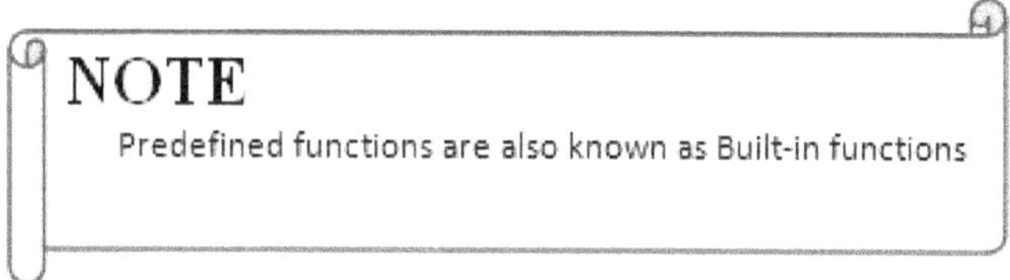

- **help( )** : The help( ) is a predefined function in python to get the documentation of symbols, type, keywords, topics, classes, modules etc. The help( ) function in inter-active helps utility starts up on the console.
Example:
>>> help()
help> symbols
Here is a list of the punctuation symbols which Python assigns special meaning to. Enter any symbol to get more help.

!=	*=	<<	^
"	+	<<=	^=
"""	+=	<=	_

```
%              ,          < >              _
% =            -           ==              `
&              -=          >              b"
&=             .           >=             b'
'              ...         >>             j
'''            /           >>=            r"
(              //          @              r'
)              //=         J              |
*              /=          [              |=
**             :           \              ~
**=            <           ]
```

help> J
Imaginary literals
****

Imaginary literals are described by the following lexical definitions:
   imagnumber ::= (floatnumber | intpart) ("j" | "J")
An imaginary literal yields a complex number with a real part of 0.0. Complex numbers are represented as a pair of floating point numbers and have the same restrictions on their range. To create a complex number with a nonzero real part, add a floating point number to it, e.g., "(3+4j)". Some examples of imaginary literals:
   3.14j 10.j   10j   .001j 1e100j 3.14e-10j
Related help topics: complex, cmath
help>

                In order to return back to python interpreter, type "quit" command.
help> quit
     You are now leaving help and returning to the Python interpreter. If you want to ask for help on a particular object directly from the interpreter, you can type "help(object)". Executing "help('string')" has the same effect as typing a particular string at the help> prompt.
•   **input( ):** The input( ) is a .function which is already available in python. This function is used to get input from the user during runtime.
Example:
>>> input("Enter your name")
Enter your nameJeni
'Jeni'
•   **print( ):** The print( ) function is another built-in function which used to print the output. We can also print multiple value using print( ) function.
Example:
>>> print("Hai Jeni")
HaiJeni
>>> a=10
>>> print(a)
10
•   **type( ):** This function is used to find which data type the variable is.
Example:
>>> type(a)
<type 'str'>
Example:
•   **len( ):** To find the length of the sequence.

```
>>> a='hai'
>>> len(a)
3
```

- **int( ):** The int( ) is one type of type conversion function which is used to convert any numeric data type to integer:

Example:
```
>>> z=23.1
>>> int(z)
23
```

- **min( ) and max( ):** The min( ) and max( ) are the function used to find minimum and maximum value respectively.

Example:
```
>>> min(3,5,1)
1
>>> min('hai','and')
'and'
>>> max(20,10,45,1)
45
```

- **sqrt( ):** The sqrt function is part of separate module called math. This function is used to perform square root of a number.

Example:
```
>>> import math
>>> math.sqrt(9)
3.0
```

In this expression, sqrt(9) is a function invocation. It is also known as a function call. The sqrt function is part of separate module called math. To use this function we have to import its module first. The math module has many other mathematical functions. These include trigonometric, logarithmic, and many other mathematical functions.

- **pow( ):** The pow( ) is a built-in function of math module which is used to display the exponential or power of a number. Here, pow(2,3) is 2^3 =2 x 2 x 2= 8.

Example:
```
>>> import math
>>>math.pow(2,3)
8.0
```

These are the some of the examples for built-in functions in python. Some functions perform an action but don't return a value such functions is known as void functions. The Void functions might display something on the screen or might have some other effect, but they don't have a return value.

6.3 USER DEFINED FUNCTION

User can define or create new functions such type of function is known as user defined function. This can be done by using, function signature, that includes def keyword followed by sequence of statements.

Syntax:
```
def function_name ( parameter list ) :      # Function signature
     """docstring"""
     statement(s)     # Body of function
```

This is how a user defined function is created. It contains def keyword followed by function name; parameter is passed to that function. Function definition should end with colon (:) and indented statement after that.

6.3.1 Function definition

Function definition is a way of creating a user defined function. The above is syntax of function definition. This function definition includes:

- Function signature
- Function body

Example:

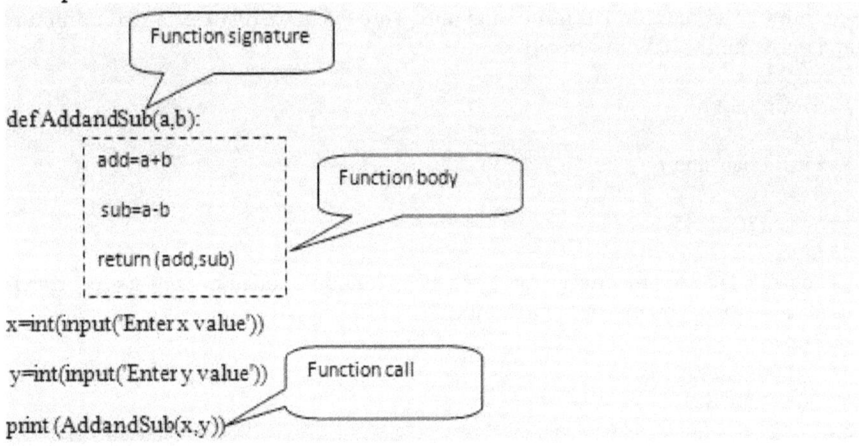

Function signature:

The first line of the user defined function is known as Function signature. It is also known as function header. This signature includes keyword, function name, parameter(s) and should end with colon.

Example for function signature:

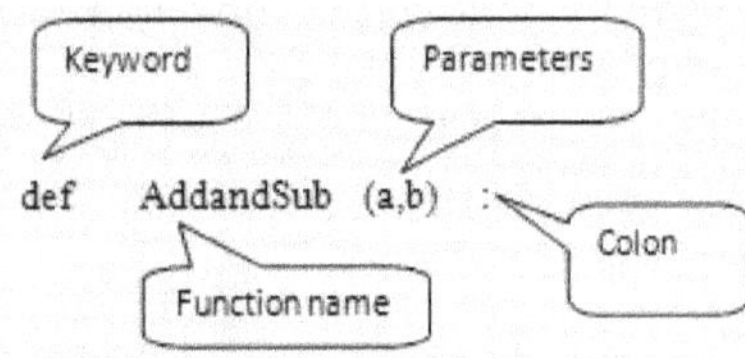

Here,

- The 'def' is a reserved word in python. This word tells that a new function is about to defined. The def is placed in the beginning of a function definition.
- The function is called by using that name so user has to name the function.
- One or more parameter which is separated by comma. These parameters are enclosed in parentheses.
- Finally colon (:) to end the function signature.

Function body:

The indented statement after the function signature is function body. It contains,

- Documentation string (docstring) is an optional part. It is used to describe what the function does.
- A function should contain at least one Statement. All the statements are indented by using tab or 4 spaces.
- An optional return statement that will return a value from the function. It will transfer the control back to the point and return the result.

6.3.2 Function Call

Calling the function by passing an argument is known as function call. The function call is used to invoke the function. When a function is invoked the control jumps to the called function. Now the statements of the called function will get executed. Normally interpreter reads the function but it won't execute it until it is called, in order to execute a function it has to get called it. In the above example, **AddandSub(x,y)** is the function call and **(x,y)** is the argument passed to the function. The argument can be an expressions or values which are passed as an input to the function.

Once the function is called it take values from the calling function and return back some values to the called function. Whenever a function is called, the control passes to the called function and the execution of the calling function is temporarily stopped. After the completion of the called function, the control returns back to the calling function and executes the next statement.

Output:

Enter x value10

Enter y value4

(14, 6)

From the above example it is clear that, the function operates on the value of the calling function and returns the result back to calling function using return statement.

6.3.3 Flow of execution

This represents how the flow of control for the program that is in which order the program executes and produces the output. The function call is known as **calling function** and the function which the calling function calls is known as **called function**. Normally the flow of control in python will be:

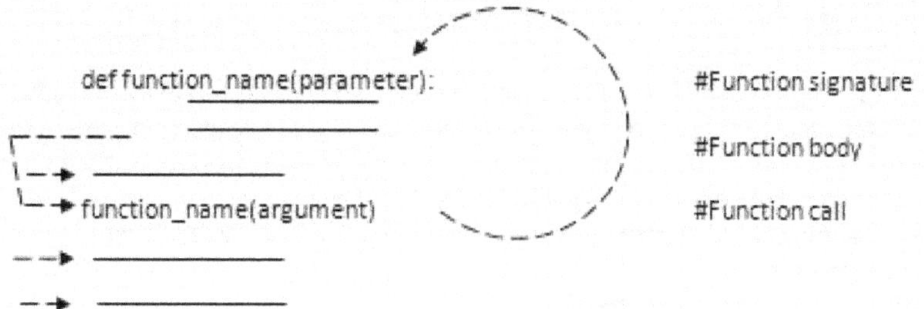

- First it there is any import statement will get executed. This includes all the feature of that module in to the program.
- Next the control flows to the next line of the statement; if that line is a function statement then it won't get executed. The will only get executed when it is called.

Let's now discuss the order of execution with an example:

Example:

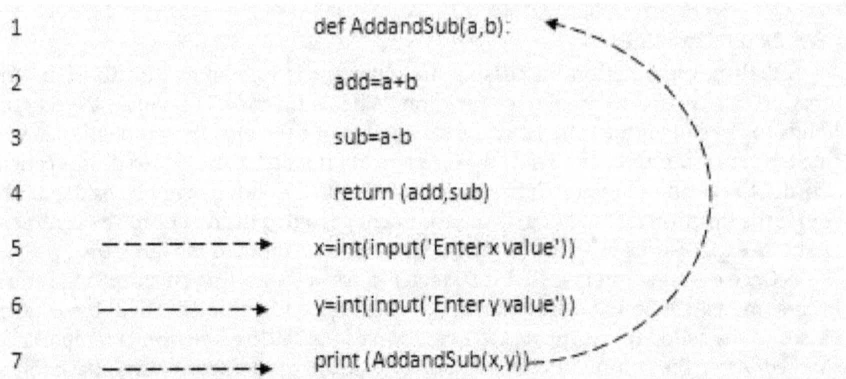

The flow of execution is: 1, 5, 6, 7, 1, 2, 3, 4,7.

- In the above program, the interpreter reads the first line but it won't execute it. Because the first line is function, the function will only get executed when it is called.
- Now the control goes to end of the function, Line 5 got executed and get input x from the user. Next, line 6 got executed and gets value of y from user.
- After line 6, control goes to line 7, which is a function call. It calls a function name AddandSub with argument a and b.
- Now, line 1 is executed and the body of that function will also get executed. Finally this function will return the result and return the control back to called function in line 7.

Output:
Enter x value10
Enter y value4
(14, 6)

From this output, it is clear that how the flow of execution of this program is done. First it get the input x and y from the user as 10 and 4 respectively. Then those values are passed as an argument to the function to call a function. Once the function is called, the control goes to the called function and executes the body of the function. As a result addition and subtraction is done and displays the value as result by using return statement.

6.3.4 Parameter and argument

Parameter:

The parameters are values or variables specified within the pair of parentheses in the function definition. In general, the variable passed during function definition is known as parameter. A function definition may have one or more parameters. Parameter is the name given to the function definition. The parameter receives values when the function is invoked. It is just like a variable, but the value of the parameter is defined when it is called. The caller of the function gives values into the function by using these parameters.

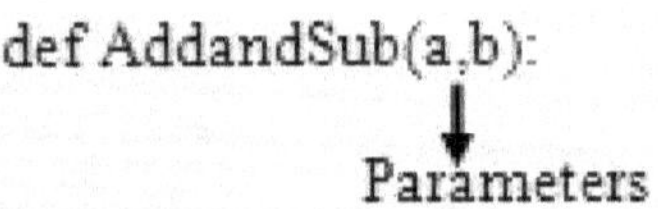

In the above example, a and b are passed to the function AddandSub as parameters. The parameter list may be empty. An empty parameter list indicates that no value is passed into the function by

the caller. There are two types of Parameters:
- Formal Parameters
- Actual Parameters.

Argument:
The values or expression given in the function call is known as argument. The value or expression which is passed to the called function is called argument. When a function is called it take some value the calling statement. The argument must be in same order as that in parameter. In the above example x and y are the arguments of the function.

print AddandSub(x,y):

↓

Argument

In this x and y are the argument used to call the function AddandSub.

The types of argument are:
- Required arguments
- Keyword arguments
- Default arguments
- Variable-length arguments

Required arguments: The argument passed to the function based on the position order.

Keyword arguments: This argument is related to the function call.

Default Argument: It is an argument that assumes a default value if the value is not passed in function call.

Variable length Argument: It is also known as arbitrary argument, here asterisk (*) is placed before the variable name. The variable length argument is used when the user do not known how many arguments has to be passed during function call.

6.3.5 Recursive function

When the solution is a recurrence relation we have to use recursion. Recursion is the ability to solve recurrence relation. The function calling itself again and again with a value is known as recursive function. Example for recursive functions are factorial, Fibonacci, etc.

Example:

In order to find factorial(n) we have to find factorial(n-1) this is known as recurrence relation. The figure 6.1 explains the flows of recursive function. Factorial is defined for non-negative integers as:

n! = n*(n-1)*(n-2)* ...... 3*2*1 and 0! is 1.

For all recursive function there are two cases, they are:
- Base case
- Recursive case or Inductive case

In recursive function we have to identify what is the base case and recursive case.

```
1   def factorial(n):
2        if n==1:
3          return 1
4        else:
5          return n*factorial(n-1)
6   n=int(input("Enter a value"))
7   print (factorial(n))
```

Here, Base case is n = = 1

      Base case solution is return 1

      Recursive case is n = = 1 is false

      Recursive case solution is return n*factorial(n-1)

Flowchart for recursive function

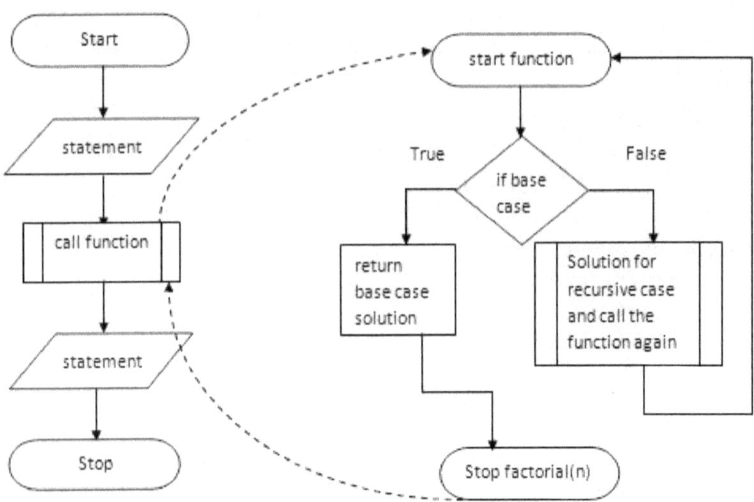

Figure 6.1: Flow chart for recursive function

Base case:

      Base case is a case for which the solution can be stated non-recursively. This is the solution for the simpler version of the problem. This part is also known as stopping or terminating condition. In the above example **if n==1** is the base case and **return 1** is the solution for that base case.

Recursive case:

      It is the case for which the solution can be stated in terms of a small version of itself. This part redefines the problem into simpler version of the original problem. In the above example **if n ==1** is **False** then that is the recursive case. The solution for recursive case will return a subprogram of itself i.e. **return n*factorial(n-1).**

Flow of execution:

- The first line of this program is read but it won't get executed because function will only get executed when it is called.
- Now the control goes to line 6 and get input from user.
- Then the next line factorial(n) got executed which is a function call. This function call calls the function named factorial by passing n as argument.
- Next, line 1 got executed which passed the parameter to the body of the program. Once the function got executed, the body of the function will start the execution.
- Here, if the base condition is True, it will return 1 and stops.
- If the condition is False, the recursive case solution n*factorial(n-1) will be executed. This solution recursively calls the function again.
- When it satisfies the base case, the result of that recursive function will be

displayed.
Output:
Enter a value5
120
5!=5*4*3*2*1
Here,factorial(5)= 5* factorial(4)
                 = 5*4* factorial(3)
                 = 5 * 4 * 3 * factorial(2)
                 = 5 * 4 * 3 * 2 * factorial(1)
                 = 5 * 4 * 3 * 2 * 1 * factorial(0)
                 = 5 * 4 * 3 * 2 * 1 * 1
                 = 5 * 4 * 3 * 2 * 1
                 = 5 * 4 * 3 * 2
                 = 5 * 4 * 6
                 = 5 * 24
                 = 120

This is the order in which the factorial got executed. This is the best example for recursive function. The recursive function should contain at least one base case otherwise it lead to infinite recursion.

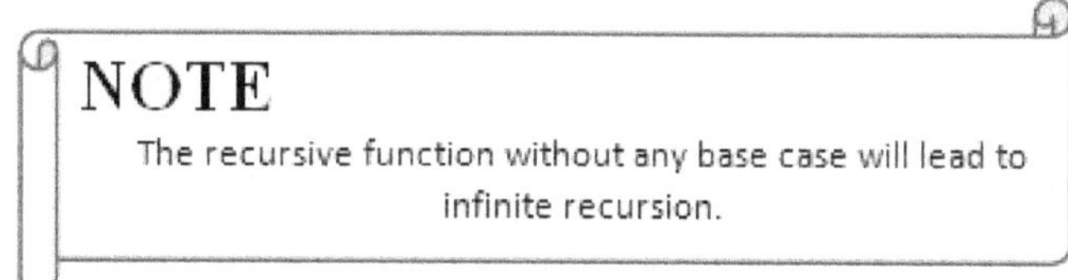

6.3.6 Fruitful Functions

The function that returns a value is known as fruitful functions otherwise it is known as void function. The return keyword is used to return the value of the expression. Once the return statement is executed, it immediately exits that function. Without the return statement the default value None is returned.
Syntax:
return
Example:

```
def sub(a,b):
  c=a-b
  return c
print(sub(10,5))
```

Output:
5

If there is no return statement in a function then the function will return None object.
Example:

```
def add(a,b):
  c=a+b
print(add(10,5))
```

Output:
None

The function can also return more than one value at a time.

Example:
```
def calculator(a,b):
    c=a+b
    d=a-b
    return c,d
print(calculator(10,5))
```
Output:
(15, 5)

> **NOTE**
> Namespace is a space that holds some names and their object binding. It is a mapping of names to the associated object.

In a function, multiple values can be returned using return keyword.
```
def cal(a,b):
    return a+b, a-b
add,sub=cal(10,4)
print("Addition is :",add,"and Subtration is :",sub)
```
Output:
Addition is : 14 and Subtration is : 6

6.3.7 Local and Global scope

The scope is the position of the program from where a namespace can be accessed directly. It is a region of the code in which it is accessible. Parameter names and any variable names that is assigned inside the function, are local to the function in which they are defined. This means that the name can only be used inside the body of a function. We call the body of the function the scope of the parameter names. The function is said to create a local scope, whereas names defined outside the function have a global scope. Changing the local values inside the function has no effect on the global scope. The order of precedence in which the scope of the name executed in python will be based on LEGB rule. This rule is used for the scope of the variable.

- L → Local
- E → Enclosing
- G → Global
- B → Built in

The names or variables defined within the body of the function are **local** to that function. The namespace inside a class or function is known as local namespaces. In function parameters are also local to that function. If the name is not found locally then it is searched for its definition such scope is known as **enclosing** scope. If the name or variables defined outside the function, classes and objects then the scope of that name is **global** scope to that function. The name that appears outside the function, class is called global names and that namespace is known as global namespaces. Python has some built in names which can be accessed anywhere in the script such scope is known as **built in** scope. In python programming Local and global scope are the two scope which are used more often.

Example:
```
x=20
def scope():
```

```
  y=10
  add=x+y
  print ('add:',add)
scope()
add= x+y
print (add)
```
In the above example, x is global scope and y is local scope. We can access x throughout the program but the limit of y is within that function. If we access y outside the function it will display Name error.

Output:

add: 30

Traceback (most recent call last):

 File "C:/Python27/6.py", line 7, in <module>

  add= x+y

NameError: name 'y' is not defined

Example:

```
a='python'
def scope():
  a='learn'
  print ('Local scope :',a)
scope()
print ('Global scope:',a)
```
Is the above program name a is used locally and globally.

Output:

Local scope: learn

Global scope: python

The value will not get override by other and from this example it is clear that local namespace has higher precedence over global namespace. So local scope will get executed first followed by global scope will get executed.

The keyword global is used to change the value of the local variable as global. Using global keyword before any variable name will change the scope of that variable global.

```
a='learn'
def sample():
  global a
  a='python'
  print("Local scope of a is : ", a)
sample()
print("Global scope of a is : ", a)
```
Output:

Local scope of a is : python

Global scope of a is : python

In the above example, variable 'a' is assigned both inside and outside the function with values 'python' and 'learn' respectively. But, the value 'python' inside the function is assigned as global.So the scope of 'a' got changed with the global value as 'python'.

6.3.8 Function Composition

The Function composition is a process of combining functions. In this, the result of one function is passed as an argument to the next function. In other word calling one function within other is known as function composition. The return value of one function is passed as parameter to another. This function composition is denoted by f(g(x)). Here x is the argument of g, that g's result is passed as argument to f. Where f and g are function, the return value of function g is passed to function f.

Example:

Write a program to find average of four numbers using function composition

```
def avg():
  return sum(a,b,c,d)/4
def sum(a,b,c,d):
  return a+b+c+d
a=10
b=10
c=5
d=15
print ('average is',avg())
```

Here one function calls another one function and the value is passed to itself, that means function avg( ) calls another function sum( ) and the value of that function is passed the function avg. This is known as function composition.

Output:

average is 10.0

From the value of sum( ) is passed to avg( ) and that performs average of four numbers.

6.3.9 Lambda / anonymous Function

Lambda Function is a way of creating anonymous function. It is a function without a name so it is known as anonymous function. The anonymous functions are defined by using the keyword lambda. The lambda function does not contain a return statement. This functions are mainly used in combination of functions filter( ), map( ) and reduce( ).

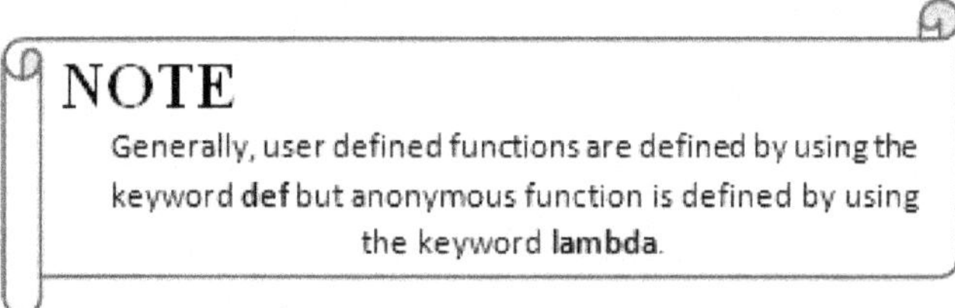

Syntax:

Lambda arguments : expression

The Lambda function can have any number of arguments but should have only one expression. The expression is evaluated and returned.

Example:

```
>>> x=lambda a: a+1
>>> print(x(2))
3
```

In the above example **lambda a: a+1** is the lambda function. Here, **a** is the argument and **a+1** is the expression. In this value of **a** is 2 is passed to the anonymous function, which return the result of expression 2+1 = **3**. It is used with built-in functions like filter( ), map( ), reduce( ), etc,.

Lambda function with map( )

The function is called with all the items in the list and it will return a new list which contains items returned as the result of the expression.

Syntax:

variable_name = (list (map (lambda parameters : operations , input_list_name)))

Example: Write a program using lambda function to display cube of a number using map( ).

```
>>> a=[1,5,9,0]
>>> b=list(map(lambda x:x*x*x,a))
>>> b
[1, 125, 729, 0]
```

Example:

```
>>> b=list(map(lambda x:x>0,a))
>>> b
[True, True, True, False]
```

Lambda function with filter( )

This function evaluates the expression and returns the items in the list if the expression is True. This function will not change the items in the list.

Syntax:

variable_name = (list (filter (lambda parameter : < condition>, input_list_name)))

Example: Write a program using lambda function to display the items which are greater than zero.

```
>>> a=[1,5,9,0]
>>> b=list(filter(lambda x:x>0,a))
>>> b
[1, 5, 9]
```

Example:

```
>>> b=list(filter(lambda x:x*x*x,a))
>>> b
[1, 5, 9]
```

6.3.10 Documentation String

Documentation string is also known as **docstrings**, it is same as comments. It is used to explain code in python. It is an optional part in the function body of a program. This is the first line after the function signature. It helps the reader to understand the code easily. It has syntax and it is more specific, this is to provide specifications of function. In program the documentation string is written within multiline comment which is by triple quotes.

Example:

```
def factorial(n):
    ''' This program is to find factorial of n number using recursive function'''
    if n==1:
        return 1
    else:
        return n*factorial(n-1)
n=int(input("Enter a value"))
print (factorial(n))
```

Here, the content inside the triple quotes is known as documentation strings. By using the built-in function help( ) we can get the description of the function. The help( ) function is used to get access to the docstrings. This function retrieves the content which is in the triple quotes.

NOTE

The help( ) function accepts the name of the function, class, module or method and print their details.

>>> help(factorial)
Help on function factorial in module __main__:
factorial(n)
   This program is to find factorial of n number using recursive function

From the above example, it is clear that help function is used to retrieve contents in the multiline comments. If there is more than one multiline comment, then first multiline comments will get displayed. Also by using _ _doc_ _ attribute of the function we can access the docstring.

Example:
>>> print(factorial.__doc__)
 This program is to find factorial of n number using recursive function

It is a good practice to add documentation string in the function.

6.3.11 Advantge of function

- The main advantage of using function is code reusability
- It breaks large problems into small parts that make the program easy.
- It is not necessary to write coding again and again, if we need the function to be executed just call the function with argument. It reduces the code duplication in the program.
- Python has many built-in functions which makes the program easier.
- It save time and memory space.
- It has high code Readability and code Reusability.

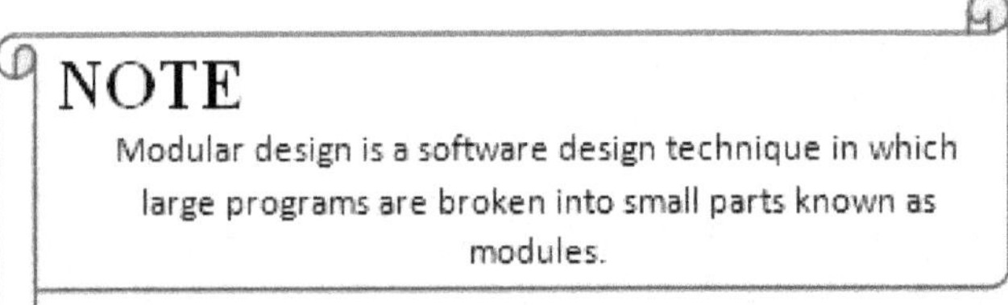

NOTE

Modular design is a software design technique in which large programs are broken into small parts known as modules.

6.4 MODULE

The Module is a file which contains a collection of related functions. It is a file with .py extension. Module helps to break a task into small subtasks of a reusable size. Using module in programming is known as modular programming. The modular design follows Top-down design process. The modules are stored in individual file. There are two types of module:

- Predefine module
- User defined module

Syntax:

import module_name

6.4.1 Predefined module

The predefined module is also known as built-in module; this module is already predefined to python. Python contains many functions, which are organized in libraries of code called modules. Some of the examples for built in module are math, date, clock, random, etc. To use the function in this module we have to import that module.

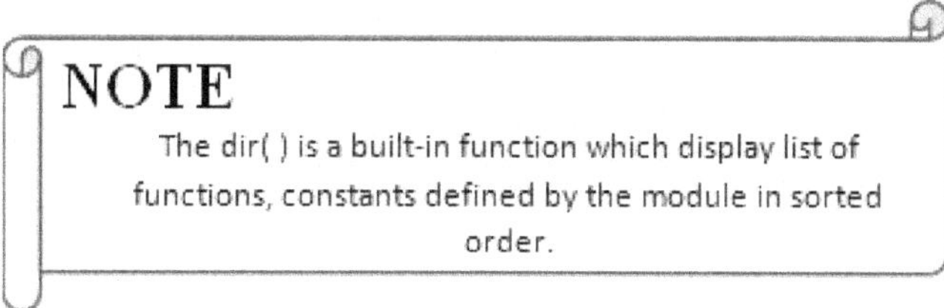

6.4.1.1 math module

Math module in python contains many mathematical functions which are used to perform mathematical calculations. It contains functions related to numeric, power, trigonometric, angular, constants, etc,. Some of the functions are sqrt( ), pow( ), sin( ), etc.

```
>>> import math
>>> math.sqrt(9)
3.0
```

Example:

```
>>> import math
>>> dir(math)
['__doc__', '__name__', '__package__', 'acos', 'acosh', 'asin', 'asinh', 'atan', 'atan2', 'atanh', 'ceil', 'copysign', 'cos', 'cosh', 'degrees', 'e', 'erf', 'erfc', 'exp', 'expm1', 'fabs', 'factorial', 'floor', 'fmod', 'frexp', 'fsum', 'gamma', 'hypot', 'isinf', 'isnan', 'ldexp', 'lgamma', 'log', 'log10', 'log1p', 'modf', 'pi', 'pow', 'radians', 'sin', 'sinh', 'sqrt', 'tan', 'tanh', 'trunc']
```

Example:

```
>>> sqrt(9)
Traceback (most recent call last):
  File "<pyshell#2>", line 1, in <module>
    sqrt(9)
NameError: name 'sqrt' is not defined
```

6.4.1.2 Random module

The random module in python is used to generate a pseudorandom number in the range. It is used to stimulation of games, application, etc. This module has many function, they are:

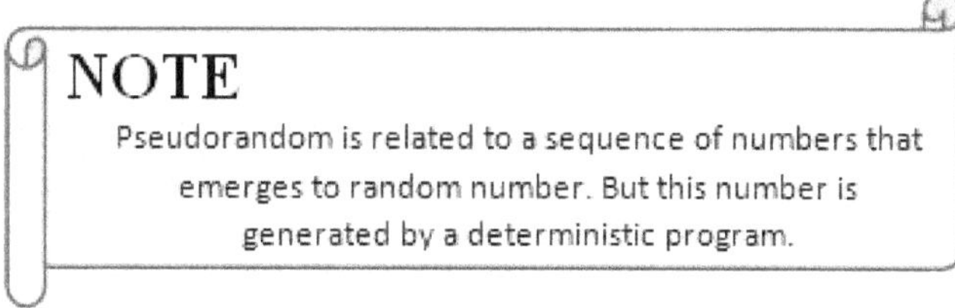


```
>>> import random
```

```
>>> dir(random)
['BPF', 'LOG4', 'NV_MAGICCONST', 'RECIP_BPF', 'Random', 'SG_MAGICCONST', 'System-
Random', 'TWOPI', '_BuiltinMethodType', '_MethodType', '_Sequence', '_Set', '__all__',
'__builtins__', '__cached__', '__doc__', '__file__', '__loader__', '__name__', '__package__',
'__spec__', '_acos', '_ceil', '_cos', '_e', '_exp', '_inst', '_log', '_pi', '_random', '_sha512',
'_sin', '_sqrt', '_test', '_test_generator', '_urandom', '_warn', 'betavariate', 'choice', 'ex-
povariate', 'gammavariate', 'gauss', 'getrandbits', 'getstate', 'lognormvariate', 'normal-
variate', 'paretovariate', 'randint', 'random', 'randrange', 'sample', 'seed', 'setstate',
'shuffle', 'triangular', 'uniform', 'vonmisesvariate', 'weibullvariate']
```

Example:

The function random( ) will generate a random number between 0.0 and 1.0, i.e. including 0.0 to 2.0.

```
>>> import random
>>> print(random.random())
0.118210200091669354
```

Example:

The randint( ) function in the random module is used to generate a random integer number in the range.

```
>>> import random
>>> print(random.randint(0,9))
0
```

This function is used to print integer from the range 0 to 9 and the generated random number is 0. Here, any integer including 0 and 9 will be generated as random number.

Example:

The choice( ) function is a function in random module which chose a item from the sequence.

```
>>> import random
>>> a=[1,3,7,3.5,'hai','pen']
>>> print(random.choice(a))
7
>>> print(random.choice(a))
3.5
```

6.4.1.3 sys module

This module is used to get the system related in function. It is mainly used to locate the path of the program. This module contains variables and functions that relate to the operation of the operating system.

```
>>> import sys
>>> dir(sys)
['__displayhook__', '__doc__', '__excepthook__', '__interactivehook__', '__loader__',
'__name__', '__package__', '__spec__', '__stderr__', '__stdin__', '__stdout__', '_clear_
type_cache', '_current_frames', '_debugmallocstats', '_getframe', '_home', '_mercurial',
'_xoptions', 'api_version', 'argv', 'base_exec_prefix', 'base_prefix', 'builtin_module_
names', 'byteorder', 'call_tracing', 'callstats', 'copyright', 'displayhook', 'dllhandle',
'dont_write_bytecode', 'exc_info', 'excepthook', 'exec_prefix', 'executable', 'exit',
'flags', 'float_info', 'float_repr_style', 'getallocatedblocks', 'getcheckinterval', 'getde-
faultencoding', 'getfilesystemencoding', 'getprofile', 'getrecursionlimit', 'getrefcount',
'getsizeof', 'getswitchinterval', 'gettrace', 'getwindowsversion', 'hash_info', 'hexver-
sion', 'implementation', 'int_info', 'intern', 'last_traceback', 'last_type', 'last_value',
'maxsize', 'maxunicode', 'meta_path', 'modules', 'path', 'path_hooks', 'path_im-
```

porter_cache', 'platform', 'prefix', 'setcheckinterval', 'setprofile', 'setrecursionlimit', 'setswitchinterval', 'settrace', 'stderr', 'stdin', 'stdout', 'thread_info', 'version', 'version_info', 'warnoptions', 'winver']

Example:
```
>>> import sys
>>> sys.path
['C:\\Python27', 'C:\\Python34\\Lib\\idlelib', 'C:\\WINDOWS\\SYSTEM32\\python-34.zip', 'C:\\Python34\\DLLs', 'C:\\Python34\\lib', 'C:\\Python34', 'C:\\Python34\\lib\\site-packages']
```

6.4.1.4 time module

The time module is a built-in module in python which is used to get time and date. This module has many attributes for hour, minute, second and microsecond. This can be used in program by importing the module time. The functions in this module are:

```
>>> import time
>>> dir(time)
['_STRUCT_TM_ITEMS', '__doc__', '__loader__', '__name__', '__package__', '__spec__', 'altzone', 'asctime', 'clock', 'ctime', 'daylight', 'get_clock_info', 'gmtime', 'localtime', 'mktime', 'monotonic', 'perf_counter', 'process_time', 'sleep', 'strftime', 'strptime', 'struct_time', 'time', 'timezone', 'tzname']
```

Example:

Write a program to print the current local time using time module.

```
import time
local_time=time.localtime()
print("The local time is:\t",local_time)
```

This program will print the current year, month, date, hour, minute, second, etc.

Output:

```
The local time is:    time.struct_time(tm_year=2018, tm_mon=6, tm_mday=19, tm_hour=20, tm_min=23, tm_sec=15, tm_wday=1, tm_yday=170, tm_isdst=0)
```

6.4.1.5 calendar module

The calendar module has several methods to display monthly and yearly calendars. This module contains main function to display the date, month, year, etc, of calendar.

```
>>> import calendar
>>> dir(calendar)
['Calendar', 'EPOCH', 'FRIDAY', 'February', 'HTMLCalendar', 'IllegalMonthError', 'IllegalWeekdayError', 'January', 'LocaleHTMLCalendar', 'LocaleTextCalendar', 'MONDAY', 'SATURDAY', 'SUNDAY', 'THURSDAY', 'TUESDAY', 'TextCalendar', 'WEDNESDAY', '_EPOCH_ORD', '__all__', '__builtins__', '__cached__', '__doc__', '__file__', '__loader__', '__name__', '__package__', '__spec__', '_colwidth', '_locale', '_localized_day', '_localized_month', '_spacing', 'c', 'calendar', 'datetime', 'day_abbr', 'day_name', 'different_locale', 'error', 'firstweekday', 'format', 'formatstring', 'isleap', 'leapdays', 'main', 'mdays', 'month', 'month_abbr', 'month_name', 'monthcalendar', 'monthrange', 'prcal', 'prmonth', 'prweek', 'setfirstweekday', 'sys', 'timegm', 'week', 'weekday', 'weekheader']
```

Example:

Write a python program to display calendar of the year 2018 and June month.

```
import calendar
cal=calendar.month(2018,6)
```

```
print("calendar :\n",cal)
```
Here, month(theyear, themonth) is a function used to get the calendar of the month in the year.

Output:
```
calendar :
    June 2018
Mo Tu We Th Fr Sa Su
        1  2  3
 4  5  6  7  8  9 10
11 12 13 14 15 16 17
18 19 20 21 22 23 24
25 26 27 28 29 30
```

6.4.1.6 os module

A directory is a collection of files and sub directories. The os module in python has many useful built-in methods and functions to interact with the operating system. In order to use the functions in directory, we have to import os module first. The table 7.4 explains the methods of os directories in detail with example.

Example:
```
>>> import os
>>> dir(os)
['F_OK', 'MutableMapping', 'O_APPEND', 'O_BINARY', 'O_CREAT', 'O_EXCL', 'O_NOIN-
HERIT', 'O_RANDOM', 'O_RDONLY', 'O_RDWR', 'O_SEQUENTIAL', 'O_SHORT_LIVED',
'O_TEMPORARY', 'O_TEXT', 'O_TRUNC', 'O_WRONLY', 'P_DETACH', 'P_NOWAIT',
'P_NOWAITO', 'P_OVERLAY', 'P_WAIT', 'R_OK', 'SEEK_CUR', 'SEEK_END', 'SEEK_SET',
'TMP_MAX', 'W_OK', 'X_OK', '_Environ', '__all__', '__builtins__', '__cached__', '__doc__',
'__file__', '__loader__', '__name__', '__package__', '__spec__', '_execvpe', '_exists', '_exit',
'_get_exports_list', '_putenv', '_unsetenv', '_wrap_close', 'abort', 'access', 'altsep',
'chdir', 'chmod', 'close', 'closerange', 'cpu_count', 'curdir', 'defpath', 'device_encoding',
'devnull', 'dup', 'dup2', 'environ', 'errno', 'error', 'execl', 'execle', 'execlp', 'execlpe',
'execv', 'execve', 'execvp', 'execvpe', 'extsep', 'fdopen', 'fsdecode', 'fsencode', 'fstat',
'fsync', 'get_exec_path', 'get_handle_inheritable', 'get_inheritable', 'get_terminal_size',
'getcwd', 'getcwdb', 'getenv', 'getlogin', 'getpid', 'getppid', 'isatty', 'kill', 'linesep', 'link',
'listdir', 'lseek', 'lstat', 'makedirs', 'mkdir', 'name', 'open', 'pardir', 'path', 'pathsep',
'pipe', 'popen', 'putenv', 'read', 'readlink', 'remove', 'removedirs', 'rename', 'renames',
'replace', 'rmdir', 'sep', 'set_handle_inheritable', 'set_inheritable', 'spawnl', 'spawnle',
'spawnv', 'spawnve', 'st', 'startfile', 'stat', 'stat_float_times', 'stat_result', 'statvfs_re-
sult', 'strerror', 'supports_bytes_environ', 'supports_dir_fd', 'supports_effective_ids',
'supports_fd', 'supports_follow_symlinks', 'symlink', 'sys', 'system', 'terminal_size',
'times', 'times_result', 'umask', 'uname_result', 'unlink', 'urandom', 'utime', 'waitpid',
'walk', 'write']
```

Example:
```
import os
print(os.getcwd())
print(os.chdir('C:\Python34'))
print(os.listdir('C:\Python34'))
```
Output:
```
C:\Python27
None
['a.txt', 'b.txt', 'cx_Oracle-doc', 'cx_Oracle-wininst.log', 'DLLs', 'Doc', 'include', 'Lib',
```

'libs', 'LICENSE.txt', 'NEWS.txt', 'python.exe', 'pythonw.exe', 'README.txt', 'Removecx_Oracle.exe', 'Scripts', 'tcl', 'Tools']

These are the some of the methods of the os module to manage the file and sub directories.

6.4.1.7 Email module

This module is a internet related module which has functions related to message.

\>\>\> import email

\>\>\> dir(email)

['__all__', '__builtins__', '__cached__', '__doc__', '__file__', '__loader__', '__name__', '__package__', '__path__', '__spec__', 'message_from_binary_file', 'message_from_bytes', 'message_from_file', 'message_from_string']

6.4.1.8 Fractions module

This module contains functions related to mathematical calculation such as gcd, math, and many more.

Example:

\>\>\> import fractions

\>\>\> dir(fractions)

['Decimal', 'Fraction', '_PyHASH_INF', '_PyHASH_MODULUS', '_RATIONAL_FORMAT', '__all__', '__builtins__', '__cached__', '__doc__', '__file__', '__loader__', '__name__', '__package__', '__spec__', 'gcd', 'math', 'numbers', 'operator', 're', 'sys']

If we use a function inside the module without importing it, then error will be displayed. We can just import just some specific functions from a module. The syntax of using a specific function from a module is:

from module_name import function

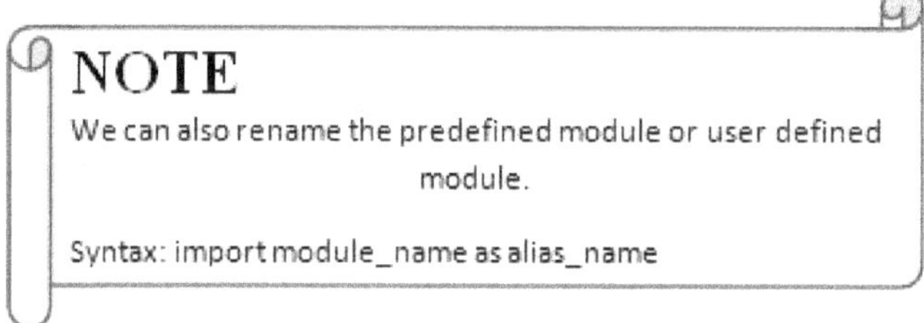

6.4.1.9 datetime module

The datetime module store information about date and time. It is used to get the current system date and time.

Example:

\>\>\> import datetime

\>\>\> dir(datetime)

['MAXYEAR', 'MINYEAR', '__builtins__', '__cached__', '__doc__', '__file__', '__loader__', '__name__', '__package__', '__spec__', 'date', 'datetime', 'datetime_CAPI', 'sys', 'time', 'timedelta', 'timezone', 'tzinfo']

6.4.2 User defined module

The module which is defined by user is known as user defined module. Any file contains python code can be imported as module. To create user defined module, write a program and save it with a filename with extension .py. Then import that file into the program.

Syntax:

import filename
filename.function_name(parameter)
Example:
        The below coding is saved as scientific.py

```
def square(a):
  square=a*a
  return square
def cube(a):
  cube=a*a*a
  return cube
def squareroot(a):
  squareroot=a**0.5
  return squareroot
```

Now to import that file as a module into the program, import that file and then mention the filename and function name to run that function.

```
>>> import scientific
>>> scientific.square(3)
9
>>> import scientific
>>> scientific.cube(3)
27
```

6.4.3 Importing modules

        In a programs Modules can be imported in many ways.
*   Using import module_name entire module is imported. Then using (.) dot operator the functions are used.
*   For including specific function of the module, from module_name import function1[, function2, ……, functionN] is used.
*   We can import and rename the entire module in that program by import module_name as new_module_name.
*   The module_name import * is used to import all name and function except the names begins with underscore (_).

6.4.4 Advantge of module

*   We can divide large code into small subtasks.
*   We can reuse the code.
*   Improvement or changing of code is much easier.

6.5 PACKAGES

        Package is a directory which contains collection of modules. It is a hierarchical file directory structure that has functions, modules and other packages within it. In order to consider that directory as package we have to use a file called _init_.py. A python package must contain an additional file known as _init_.py. All directories which contain file named _init_.py are considered as packages in python. It is not mandatory to write something in the _init_.py file, this file can be empty. We can put several modules into a package. The main purpose of packages is for code reusability, it is a collection of modules that has common purposes.
        Steps to create a python package:
*   Create a directory and insert the package.
*   Insert necessary classes, function or modules into that directory.

- Create _ _init_ _.py file in that directory.

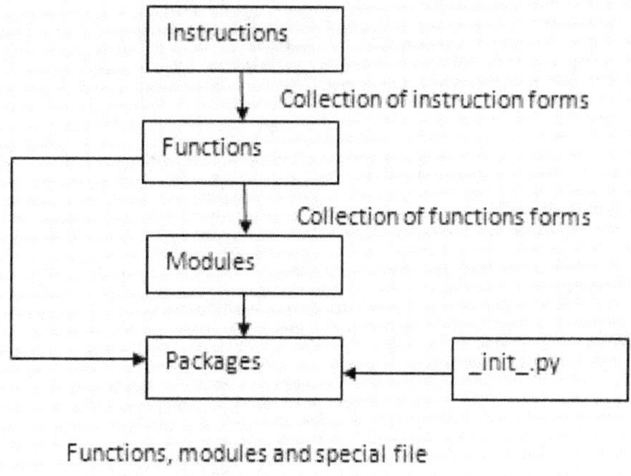

Functions, modules and special file
(_init_.py) forms a package

The above diagram shows the hierarchy from instruction to package.

Example:

    Let us create a package program for a calculator program to perform basic calculations with some modules. The directory name is the package name which is calculator. This directory must contain a file named "_init_.py". This "_init_.py" file will get executed when the package is imported, it file can be empty or contain codes. This directory contains two modules named incdec and muldiv and many other files. The module incdec contain files such as addition.py and subtract.py and module muldiv contains files such as multiply.py and division.py. The pictorial representation of calculator package is shown below.

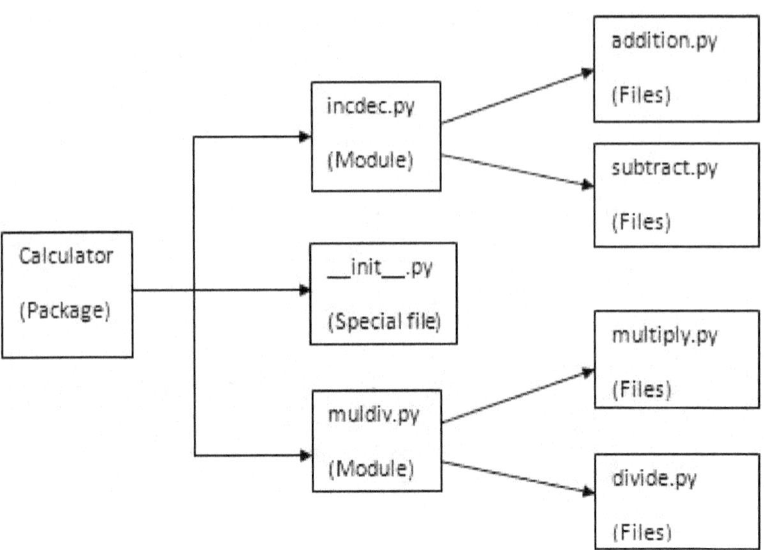

The file addition.py contains:

```python
def add(a,b):
    c=a-b
    return c
```

The file subtract.py contains:

```python
def subtraction(a,b):
    sub=a-b
    return sub
```

The file multiply.py contains:

```python
def multiplication(a,b):
    mul=a*b
    return mul
```

The file divide.py contains:

```python
def division(a,b):
    div=a/b
    return div
```

To import the module incdec and muldiv:

```python
>>>from calculator import addition, subtract
>>> addition.add(6,2)
4
>>> subtract.subtraction(6,2)
4
```

In interactive shell:

```python
>>> import calculator
>>> calculator
<module 'calculator' from 'C:/Python27/calculator/__init__.py'>
```

The above example is the calculator program in package which contains many function, modules and special file _ _init_ _.py.

SUMMARY

- A collection of statements together form a function. A function is a group of reusable code that can be called by name to perform some specific task.

•   Large programs are divided into subprograms in order to perform the task easily and effectively.

•   Built-in functions are the functions which are already defined to the interpreter. This function is already known as predefined function because the working of this function is already predefined to the interpreter.

•   User defined functions are the functions which are defined or created by the user.

•   The import statement is a statement used to import a module into the program.

•   Documentation string is also known as docstrings, it is same as comments. It is used to explain code in python.

•   The function calling itself with a value is known as recursive function.

•   The two cases in recursive function are base case and recursive case.

•   The return statement is used to return the value of the expression.

•   Namespace is a space that holds some names and their object binding.

•   Scope is the position of the program from where a namespace can be accessed directly. It is a region of the code in which it is accessible.

•   The scope rule in python is LEGB (Local, Enclosing, Global, Built-in).

•   The names defined within the body of the function are local to that function. The namespace inside a class or function is known as local namespaces.

•   If the name defined outside the function, classes and objects then the scope of that name is global scope to that function.

•   Module is a file which contains a collection of related functions. Using module in programming is known as modular programming.

•   Math module in python contains many functions which are used to perform mathematical calculations. Functions such as sqrt( ), pow( ), etc.

•   The random( ) function in random module is used to generate a random number in the range [0,1).

•   Package is a directory which contains collection of modules. It is a hierarchical file directory structure that has functions, modules and other packages within it.

ILLUSTRATIVE PROGRAMS

1.   Write a python program to print current formatted date and time.

The asctime( ) function in time module will get the current local formatted date and time.

```
import time
local_time=time.asctime()
print("The current local time :\t",local_time)
```

Output:

The current local time :   Tue Jun 19 20:27:58 2018

2.   Write a python program to find GCD of two numbers.

GCD (Greatest Common Divisor) is the greatest number that divides two or more numbers. It is also known as HCF (Highest Common Factor) or GCF (Greatest Common Factor). In this program gcd(a,b) function of fractions module is used to calculate the GCD of a and b.

```
import fractions
m=int(input("Enter a number"))
n=int(input("Enter another number"))
```

```
gcd=fractions.gcd(m,n)
print("The GCD of two number is:\t",gcd)
```
Output:
```
Enter a number12
Enter another number4
The GCD of two number is:    4
```
3. Write a python program to find the power or exponentiation of a number using the predefined function.

The Power of a number can be defined as base multiplied to itself n times. Here n represent the exponent. This program is to find the power or exponentiation of a number i.e., baseexp. This program can be implemented by using pow(a,b) function in math module2n.
```
import math
base=int(input("Enter the base"))
exp=int(input("Enter the exponent"))
power=math.pow(base,exp)
print("The power of a number is:\t",power)
```
Output:
```
Enter the base2
Enter the exponent3
The power of a number is:    8.0
```
Here, the base is 2 and exponent is 3, 23=2 x 2 x 2 which is 8.

4. Write a python program to find the square root of a number using the predefined function.

This program is to find square root of a number using sqrt( ) function in math module.
```
import math
a=int(input("Enter a number"))
square_root=math.sqrt(a)
print("The square root of a number is:\t",square_root)
```
Output:
```
Enter a number9
The square root of a number is:    3.0
```
Here, the sqrt of 9, i.e., $\sqrt{9}$ =3

5. Write a python program to guess a random number within a range.

This program is to guess and find out whether the random number generated by the system is guessed correctly by the user or not. In this program a random number from 0 to 50 is generated.
```
import random
random_number=random.randint(0,50)
print(random_number)
guess=int(input("Enter user guess"))
if random_number==guess:
  print("You have guessed correctly")
else:
  print("You have guessed wrong")
  print("The random number generated is ",random_number)
```
Output:
```
Enter user guess26
```

You have guessed wrong
The random number generated is 24

6. Write a python program to find Fibonacci series of nth term of a number using recursive function.

The Fibonacci series is a sequence of integers, the first and second integers are 0 and 1. The next term is the sum of immediate preceding two terms. Therefore the Fibonacci series is 0, 1, 1, 2, 3, 5, 8, 13, 21, 34, ……..

$$
fib(n) = \begin{cases} 0 \\ 1 \\ fib(n-1) + fib(n-2) \end{cases}
$$

```python
def fib(n):
  if n==0:
    return 0
  if n==1:
    return 1
  else:
    return fib(n-1)+fib(n-2)
n=int(input("Enter number of terms"))
print(n,"th Fibonacci term is",fib(n))
```

Output:

Enter number of terms7
7 th Fibonacci term is 13
Here, the Fibonacci series of 7 terms are 0   1   1   2   3   5   8   13.

7. Write a python program to create a user defined function to calculate sum of n numbers.

```python
def cal(n):
  sum=0
  for i in range(1,n+1):
    sum=sum+i
  print("sum is:",sum)
n=int(input("Enter the value of n"))
cal(n)
```

Output:

Enter the value of n10
sum is: 55

8. Write a python program to find LCM of two numbers using user defined function.

```python
def lcm(x, y):
  if x > y:
    greater = x
  else:
    greater = y
  while(True):
    if((greater % x == 0) and (greater % y == 0)):
      lcm = greater
      break
```

```
    greater += 1
  return lcm
num1=int(input("enter the value of num1"))
num2=int(input("enter the value of num2"))
print("The L.C.M. of", num1,"and", num2,"is", lcm(num1, num2))
```

Output:
```
enter the value of num110
enter the value of num25
The L.C.M. of 10 and 5 is 10
```

9. Write a python program for simple calculator.

```
def add(a,b):
  add=a+b
  return add
def sub(a,b):
  sub=a-b
  return sub
def mul(a,b):
  mul=a*b
  return mul
def div(a,b):
  div=a/b
  return div
print("select your choice")
print("1.addition")
print("2.subtraction")
print("3.multiplication")
print("4.division")
choice = input("Enter choice(1/2/3/4):")
n1 = int(input("Enter the value of a: "))
n2 = int(input("Enter the value of b:"))
if choice == '1':
  print(n1,"+",n2,"=", add(n1,n2))
elif choice == '2':
  print(n1,"-",n2,"=", sub(n1,n2))
elif choice == '3':
  print(n1,"*",n2,"=", mult(n1,n2))
elif choice == '4':
  print(n1,"/",n2,"=", div(n1,n2))
else:
  print("Invalid input")
```

Output:
```
select your choice
1.addition
2.subtraction
3.multiplication
4.division
Enter choice(1/2/3/4):2
Enter the value of a: 12
Enter the value of b:6
```

12 - 6 = 6

10. Write a python program to find area of circle using random number generation.

```
import random
radius=random.randint(0,20)
print("radius is ",radius)
Pi=22/7
area=Pi*radius*radius
print("The area of circle is ",area)
```

The area of circle is (pi* r2) Π r2 (pi* r2). In this program radius of the circle is created randomly using randint( ) function and calculated the area of the circle.

Output:

radius is 16

The area of circle is 804.5714285714286

11. Write a python program to calculate volume of sphere using random number generation.

```
import random
radius=random.randint(0,20)
print("radius is",radius)
volume=(4/3)*(22/7)*(radius**3)
print("The volume of sphere of is ",volume)
```

Output:

radius is 8

The volume of sphere of is 2145.523809523809

12. Write a python program to find the number is positive, negative or zero using user defined function.

```
def number(n):
   if n>0:
     return 'positive number'
   elif n<0:
     return 'negative number'
   else:
     return 'zero'
n=int(input("enter a number"))
print(number(n))
```

Output:

enter a number-2

negative number

13. Write a python program to get the year, week number and day of the week for the given date using built-in function.

```
import datetime
a= datetime.date(2018,6,22)
year,week_num,day_of_week = a.isocalendar()
print("Year is: %d \nWeek Number is: %d \nDay of the Week is: %d\n " %
(year,week_num, day_of_week))
```

Output:

Year is: 2018

Week Number is: 25

Day of the Week is: 5

14. Write a python program to find whether the given year is leap year or not using

calendar module.

```
import calendar
year=int(input("Enter a year"))
if calendar.isleap(year):
  print("leap year")
else:
  print("Not a leap year")
```

Output:

```
Enter a year2020
leap year
```

15. Write a python program in which function is defined and calling that function prints hello world.

```
def pro():
  a='hello world'
  return a
print(pro())
```

Output:

```
hello world
```

16. Write a python program in which function is defined and calling that function prints the string parameter given to function.

```
def pro(a):
  return a
a='hello world'
print(pro(a))
```

Output:

```
hello world
```

17. Write a python program to get the value of pi from the predefined module.

```
from math import pi
print("The value of pi is:",pi)
```

Output:

```
The value of pi is: 3.141592653589793
```

18. Write a python program to solve Tower of Hanoi problem using recursive function.

```
def Tower_of_Hanoi(n,source, destination,auxillary):
  if n==0:
    return
  elif n==1:
    print('Move that disk from',source,'to',destination)
  else:
    Tower_of_Hanoi(n-1,source,auxillary,destination)
    print('Move that disk from',source,'to',destination)
    Tower_of_Hanoi(n-1,auxillary,destination,source)
n=int(input("Enter the number of disk"))
moves=(2**n)-1
print("Number of moves is:\t", moves)
print(Tower_of_Hanoi(n,1,3, 2))
```

Output:

```
Enter the number of disk3
Number of moves is:       7
```

Move that disk from 1 to 3
Move that disk from 1 to 2
Move that disk from 3 to 2
Move that disk from 1 to 3
Move that disk from 2 to 1
Move that disk from 2 to 3
Move that disk from 1 to 3
None

19. Write a python program to shut down your computer.

```python
import os
ans= input("Do you want to shut down your computer ? (y/n): ")
if ans == 'n':
    exit();
else:
    os.system("shutdown /s /t 1")
```

20. Write a python program to reverse a string without using built-in function.

```python
def reverse(str):
    rev=''
    i=len(str)-1
    while i>=0:
        rev+=str[i]
        i-=1
    return rev
str=input("Enter the string to reverse")
print("The reversed string is",reverse(str))
```

Output:

Enter the string to reversewelcome
The reversed string is emoclew

ADDITIONAL PROGRAMS

1. Write a python program to find the number odd or even using user defined function.
2. Write a python program to swap two numbers using user defined function.
3. Write a python program to convert hour into minute using user defined function.
4. Write a python program to calculate GCD of two numbers using recursive function.
5. Write a python program to calculate power or exponentiation of two numbers using recursive function.
6. Write a python program to get square root of a number using recursive function.
7. Write a python program to find greatest among three numbers using recursive function.
8. Write a python program to calculate circumference of circle using random module.
9. Write a python program to display the next month using predefined module.
10. Write a python program to add two numbers using lambda function.
11. Write a python program to reverse the number using recursive function.
12. Write a python program to find factor of number using function.
13. Write a python program to demonstrate scope of the variable.

REVIEW QUESTIONS

1) Define function.
2) What are pre-defined functions? Give example.
3) What is return statement?
4) How a function is defined by user?
5) What are the advantages of function?
6) What is lambda function?
7) Explain about function composition.
8) What is mean by documentation string?
9) Explain about dir( ) function
10) What is module? Explain its advantages.
11) How to create a user defined module?
12) Explain about math and random module.
13) What is scope?
14) What is package? Explain its purpose.
15) Write a program to display the calendar using predefined function.
16) What is _ _init_ _.py in python?
17) What is function call?
18) What is fruitful function?
19) Explain the difference between recursion and iteration.
20) What is void function?

MUTIPLE CHOICE QUESTIONS

1. The advantage of function is:
   a. Reuse code
   b. Reduce duplication of code
   c. Clarity of code
   d. All the above
2. The use of return statement is:
   a. Exit the function
   b. Initiate the function
   c. To return null value
   d. None of these
3. Which keyword is used to create anonymous function?
   a. def
   b. lambda
   c. return
   d. None of these
4. What is the output of the code?

```
def add():
    pass
    add()
```

   a. Defines the function add, Does nothing
   b. Print None
   c. Display error
   d. None of these
5. Which keyword is used to define the user defined function.

    a.   lambda
    b.   import
    c.   def
    d.   return

6. What attribute is used to find the name of the module?
    a.   _ _ doc_ _
    b.   _ name _
    c.   Module_name
    d.   None of these

7. What is the built-in function that displays the identifiers or name in list defined inside the module?
    a.   dir()
    b.   list()
    c.   doc()
    d.   reload()

8. The statement which invoke function is:
    a.   import
    b.   Function definition
    c.   Function call
    d.   dir( )

9. What is the output for the code?

```python
import math
a=math.ceil(10.23)
print(a)
```

    a.   10
    b.   11
    c.   10.23
    d.   10.25

10. What is the output of the program?

```python
a=abs(-10.25)
print( a)
```

    a.   10.25
    b.   10
    c.   -10.25
    d.   11

TRUE OR FALSE

1. Documentation string should be in single line statement.
2. User defined function should begin with def keyword.
3. The function should contain return statement otherwise error will be displayed.
4. The function will get executed only when it is called.
5. The documentation string is the optional statement in the function.
6. The function signature should end with colon.
7. The return statement can be put outside the function.
8. We can access the object anywhere in the program if the object is assigned as global.
9. The lambda function is the function without any name.
10. The import * imports all names except the name begins with underscore.

11. A recursive function takes less time and memory than non recursive function.
12. The string which is mentioned inside the triple quote is known as docstrings.
13. The standard library contains installed module.

FILL IN THE BLANKS

1. Documentation string is also known as _________
2. Lambda function is also known as _________
3. If there is no return statement then the output will be _________
4. The recursive function without base case will leads to _________
5. To use the module in the program _________ statements must be used.
6. The _________ give explanation of the program.
7. The function has to _________ before it is got called.
8. The function definition contains _________ and _________
9. The special file in all package is _________
10. The documentation strings in the function can be accessed by _________ attribute.
11. The values passed to a function call are known as _________.

ANSWERS

CHOOSE THE CORRECT ANSWER
1. d
2. a
3. b
4. a
5. c
6. b
7. a
8. c
9. b
10. a

TRUE OF FALSE
1. False
2. True
3. False
4. True
5. True
6. True
7. False
8. True
9. True
10. True
11. False
12. True
13. True

FILL IN THE BLANKS
1. docstrings
2. anonymous
3. none object

4. infinite recursion
5. import
6. documentation string
7. define
8. function signature, function body
9. _ _init_ _.py
10. _ _ doc_ _
11. arguments

CHAPTER 7: FILES AND FILE HANDLING

This chapter discusses about files and file handling concepts in detail. In the previous chapters inputs are given by input devices such as keyboard and mouse by using input( ) function, this data is processed and displays the output on the screen. These types of programs are called transient. But in this chapter the input data are combined and placed in a file, and then by using python programs we are reading the data from that file, This file is then processed and display output. These types of programs are called persistent. This chapter also discuss about handling the python file.

CHAPTER OUTLINE

Files- File directory, file path and file name - Opening and closing a file - File access mode - Reading and writing a file - File position - File operations – File attributes, Command line arguments – Sys module, OS module - Databases: Pickling.

OBJECTIVE

After covering the chapter, the you will be in a position:

- To know about files and types of files.
- To know about file operations
- To know about open and close file
- To know about various modes of file
- To know about reading and writing files
- To study about various functions and methods of file.
- To know about command line arguments.
- To understand about file name, file path and file directories.
- Understand the usage of 'with' keyword.

7.1 FILES

When the program gets executed, the data gets stored in Random Access Memory (RAM). When the lifetime of the program ends or when the system shutdown all the data will get lost. In order to avoid the data lost and to store data permanently; we have to store these data as file in some memory. The files are collection of data which is stored in memory location for future use. It is the named location in a disk to store information. These files are stored in some storage devices such as a disk, CD, or flash memory. File is a stream of bytes; the file can be used in any applications where data has to be store permanently.

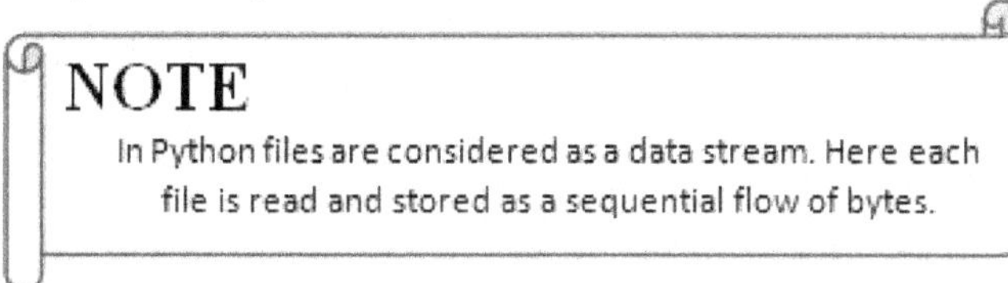

The files are categorized into two, they are:
- Text files
- Binary files

Text Files

The text file is simple text file whose data can be characters, words, numbers, or symbols. This file is in human readable, not machine readable format. It occupies more memory space; the text file is with the extension **.txt**. The procedure to create text file is:

IDLE –> File –> New File – >Type the content – Save the notepad with the extension .txt

Binary Files

The binary file contains binary data which can be only understandable by machine. The interpreter converts the given data into binary file. The binary file occupies lesser memory space than text file. It is a collection of bytes which is of the form of 0's and 1's. It is also known as character streams.

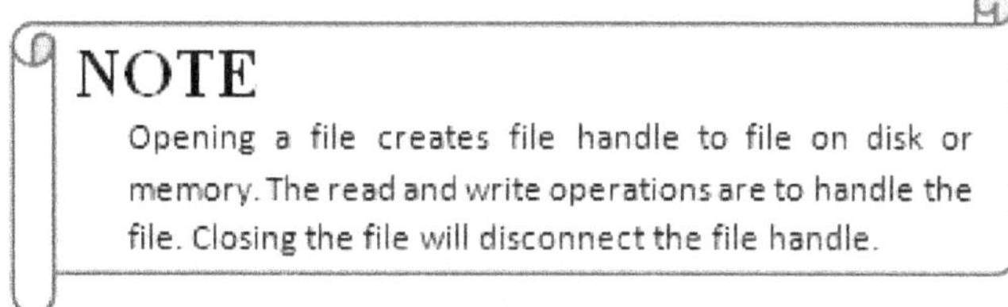

To perform some actions in text file we have to perform the following steps:
- Open a file
- Performs some action (read or write)
- Close a file

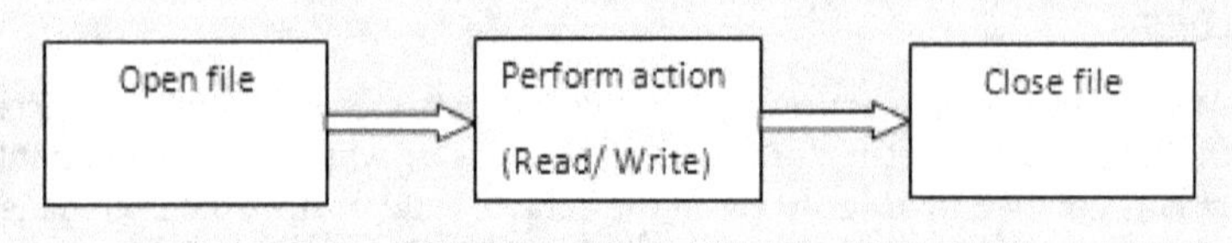

Figure 7.1   Steps for performing operations in file

All the above three steps has to be followed in order to perform some operations in the text file in python. First, the file had to be opened. This will establish a connection between the file object in the Python program and the data stored on the disk. Next, operation is performed for the file object, operations such as read or write to the file is done. This process involves taking data from the disk and storing them in a string in the Python program, or vice versa. After all the action is completed, the final step is to close the file. The figure 7.1 shows the step by step performance of file.

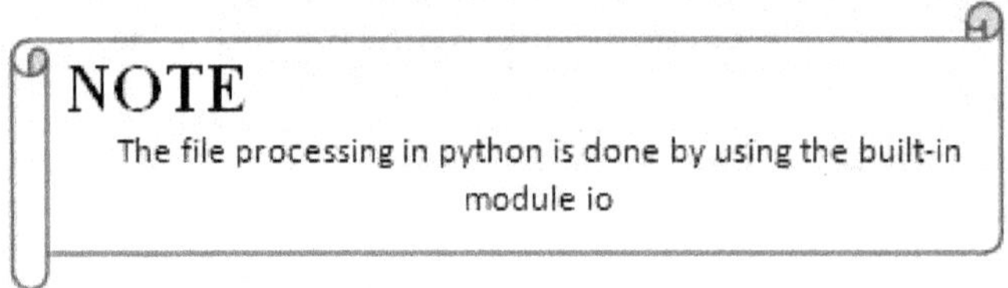

Example:
```
>>> import io
>>> dir(io)
['BlockingIOError', 'BufferedIOBase', 'BufferedRWPair', 'BufferedRandom', 'BufferedReader', 'BufferedWriter', 'BytesIO', 'DEFAULT_BUFFER_SIZE', 'FileIO', 'IOBase', 'IncrementalNewlineDecoder', 'OpenWrapper', 'RawIOBase', 'SEEK_CUR', 'SEEK_END', 'SEEK_SET', 'StringIO', 'TextIOBase', 'TextIOWrapper', 'UnsupportedOperation', '__all__', '__author__', '__builtins__', '__cached__', '__doc__', '__file__', '__loader__', '__name__', '__package__', '__spec__', '_io', 'abc', 'open']
```

In Python open function is used to open a text file, which includes file pathname or file name and a mode of operation to access. This function will open a connection to the file on memory and returns a file object. The syntax for opening a file is:

Syntax:
```
file_object=open("file_name","access_mode")
```
Example:

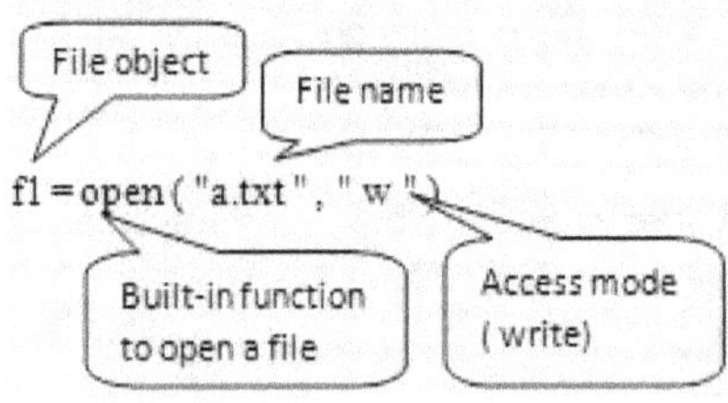

In the above example f1 is the file object, open( ) is the built in function to open a file, file_name is the name of the file which you like to perform the operation and access_mode is the mode in which the operations has to be done. To write a file, we have to open it with mode 'w' as a second parameter.

• File object is created as object for the text file. In python program, file is represented by a value. This value does not have the contents of the file but it act as an intermediate through which user can access the contents of the file. The file object act as an intermediate where we can see the file.

• open( ) is a built-in function to open a file.

• File path or File name is the full address location of the file or name of the file respectively.

• Access mode is the mode in which the file has to be accessed. The access modes are read, write, append, etc.

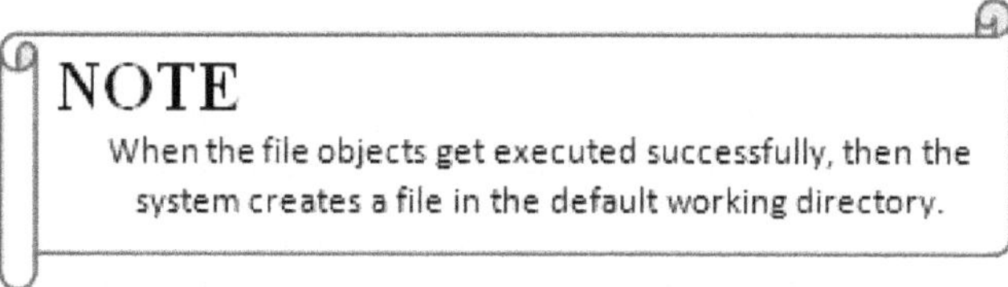

7.2 FILE DIRECTORY, FILE PATH AND FILE NAME

All the files are placed in the directories, these directories are also known as folders. The python opens the file from its default directory, which is also called as current directory. In default python checks the file in the current directory to perform some operation. In order to known the current working directory os.getcwd() method is used.

Example:
>>> import os
>>> os.getcwd()
'C:\\Python34'

In the above example os means operating system which is the module. The os.getcwd( ) is a method to get current working directory. Here, cwd means current working directory which is also known as file path. This will display the current working directory ('C:\\Python34').

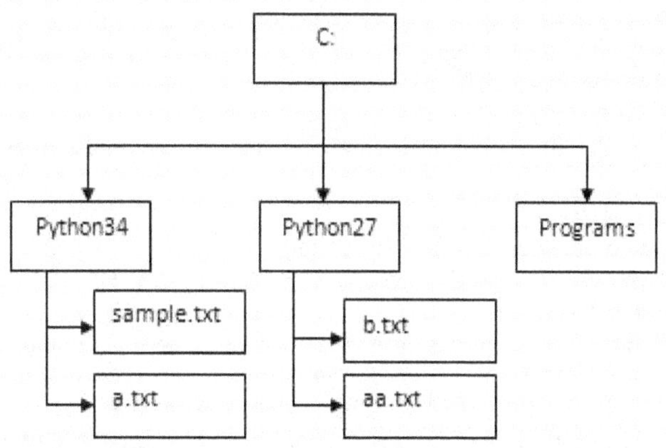

Figure 7.2: Tree structure of files

A string that identifies a file or directory is called as file path. The file path should be mentioned within the quotes. The file path is also known as pathname. The figure 7.2 shows the tree structure of files. The file path begins with root folder, in the figure " C: " is the root folder.

Example:
>>> input=open("C:\\Python34\\a.txt ","r")

In the above example "C:\\Python34\\a.txt" is the path of the file. There are

two types of file path:
- Relative path
- Absolute path

>>> input=open("a.txt","r")

The filename, "a.txt" is a relative path because it relates to the current working directory.

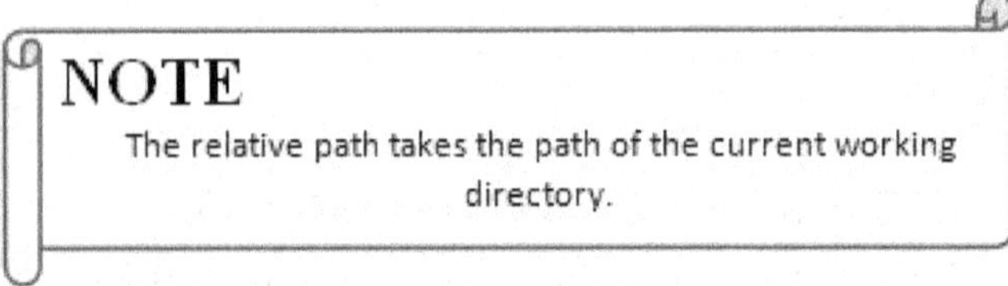

>>> input=open("C:\\Python34\\a.txt ","r")

The absolute path starts with the root node and has complete directory. The path with '\\' is not depending on the current directory is known as absolute path.

>>> os.path.exists("C:\\Python34\\a.txt")
True

In the current directory, "C:\\Python34\\a.txt" is present so True is displayed.

Example:

>>> f=open("E:/aaaa/rev/a.txt")

In the above example, the current directory is E:/aaaa/rev, the filename a.txt that refer to E:/aaaa/rev/a.txt. A path that begins with '/' does not depends on the current directory. It is called an absolute path. To find the absolute path to a file, you can use os.path.abspath

Example:

>>> import os
>>> os.path.abspath("rev/a.txt")
'C:\\Python34\\rev\\a.txt'

In order to see all the file of the current directory, use listdir(path).

Example:

>>> os.listdir(os.getcwd())
['a.txt', 'cx_Oracle-doc', 'cx_Oracle-wininst.log', 'DLLs', 'Doc', 'include', 'Lib', 'libs', 'LICENSE.txt', 'NEWS.txt', 'python.exe', 'pythonw.exe', 'README.txt', 'Removecx_Oracle.exe', 'Scripts', 'tcl', 'Tools']

In the above example, os.listdir(os.getcwd( )) method display all the files in the directory. Here, os.getcwd( ) is used to get the path of current directory and list of file in that path will get displayed by using os.listdir(path) method.

If we try to access a file in the read mode then python will check whether the file is present in the current working directory, if so it will read the file else display IOError. If the access mode is w (write) and if the file is already present python will overwrite the file. If the file is not present then the python will create a new file in that current directory.

Example:

>>> f2=open("c.txt","r")
Traceback (most recent call last):
  File "<pyshell#9>", line 1, in <module>
    f2=open("c.txt","r")

FileNotFoundError: [Errno 2] No such file or directory: 'c.txt'

If only the file name is mentioned then the python will check the file from its current working directory. To check whether the file name or path exists use os.path.exists(path) methods, It will return True if present else return False.

7.3 OPENING AND CLOSING A FILE

In order to perform some task in file first that file has to be opened. After performing the task that file has to be closed. Python has built-in function to open and close the file.

7.3.1 OPENING A FILE

For performing some operation in file first we have to open it. To open a file a built-in function called open( ) is used in python. This function takes file name as the first argument. The second argument is the access mode in which the file has to get accessed. The syntax for opening a file is:

Syntax:

file_object=open("file_name"[,"access_mode"])

Here, file_name is the string that specifies the file and access_mode is the mode in which the file has to get accessed. The access_mode is a optional parameter.

Example:

f1=open("b.txt","w")

OPENING FILE IN READ MODE AND WRITE MODE

If we try to open a file in read mode which is does not exist then it leads to error.	If we try to open a file in write or append mode which is not exists then it a new file is created in that name.

7.3.2 CLOSING A FILE

When all the operations are done and outputs are obtained, the file should be closed, if the file is not closed properly then all the data will get lost. To free the memory space or to release the resource a built-in function called close( ) is used. It closes the file and releases the memory space and also saves the file. Once the file is closed we cannot perform any updations for that file.

Syntax:

file_object.close()

Example:

f1=open("b.txt","w")

f1.close()

By using file object we have to close the file. Once we close the reference object of the file, the reference object is reassigned to other file. This process will clean up the memory space using garbage collector.

> **NOTE**
>
> Reading or writing the file which is already closed will leads to ValueError.

Example:
```
>>> f1=open("b.txt","w")
>>> f1.close()
>>> f1.write('hai')
Traceback (most recent call last):
  File "<pyshell#18>", line 1, in <module>
    f1.write('hai')
ValueError: I/O operation on closed file.
```

7.4 FILE ACCESS MODE

The file access mode says about what operation has to be performed when the file is opened. The operations that can be performed are read, write or append. These operations are known as the access mode of the file. The table 7.1 explains the access modes of file in detail.

> **NOTE**
>
> **File Handle:** It denotes in which position the cursor is currently in. It states from which position the data has to be read and write. It is also known as **file pointer**.

MODE	SYMBOL	DESCRIPTION	FILE HANDLE
Read only	r	This mode is used to read the file. If the file does not exist IOError is raised. It is the default access mode.	At the beginning of the file.
Read & write	r+	This mode is used to read and then write. If the file does not exist IOError is raised.	At the beginning of the file.
Write only	w	This mode is used to write the file. If the file already exists then it will override else a new file is created.	At the beginning of the file.
Write & read	w+	If the file already exists then write mode will override the file else a new file is created.	At the beginning of the file.
Append only	a	This mode is used to open the file for writing. Data will be inserted at the end if already exists else new file is created.	At the end of the file.
Append & read	a+	In this mode data is appended and then readed. Data will be inserted at the end, if the file exists else new file is created.	At the end of the file.
Read in binary	rb	This mode open the file in read only mode but in binary format.	At the beginning of the file.
Read & write in binary	rb+	This mode opens the file for reading and then writing in binary format.	At the beginning of the file.
Write in binary	wb	This mode opens the file for writing in binary format. The file will be overridden if exists else a new file is created.	At the beginning of the file.
Write & read in binary	wb+	This mode opens the file for writing and reading in binary format	At the beginning of the file.
Append in binary	ab	In this mode data append in binary format. Data will be added at end If the file exists else data inserted in new file.	At the end of the file.
Append & read in binary	ab+	In this mode data is appended and readed in binary format. If the file already exists then the data will add at the end else data will inserted in a new file.	At the end of the file.

Table 7.1 File access mode

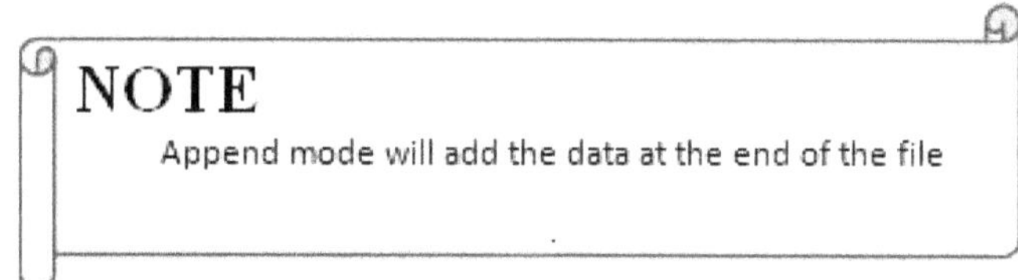

For further example consider two text file named 'a.txt' and 'b.txt'.

a.txt: hai!!!

        how are you.............

b.txt: hello.......

        I am fine

Example:

```
>>> fl=open("b.txt","r")
>>> f1
<_io.TextIOWrapper name='b.txt' mode='w' encoding='cp1252'>
```

Here f1 is the file object which holds information such as file name, access mode of file and encoding.

Example:
```
>>> f1=open("a.txt")
>>> f1
<_io.TextIOWrapper name='a.txt' mode='r' encoding='cp1252'>
```
In the above example, file named a.txt is opened but the access mode is not specified. So python considered the access mode as read which is the default access mode.

7.5 READING AND WRITING A FILE

Reading and writing are the operations performed in the file. The output obtained will be in the form of string. In order to perform read or write operation, first we have to open the file. Python has built-in functions to read and write the files.

7.5.1 READING FROM A FILE

First we have to open the file in r (read only) or r+ (read and write) mode to read a file in order to read the content of the file. This mode is used to read the existing file. There are three functions are used to read the data from a file:

- **read( ):** This function is used to read all the bytes of the file. The syntax for reading the bytes of a file is:

Syntax:
```
file_object.read([x])
```
Here, x is the total number of bytes or size that has to be read in a file. The x is a numeric argument, it is the optional parameter. If x is not mentioned all the bytes of the file up to EOF (End of File) will be read.

Example:
```
>>> f1=open("a.txt","r+")
>>> f1.read()
'hai!!!\nhow are you............'
```
Here, \n indicated the new line in file. If we again read this file we will get an empty string, because file handler is now at the end of the file.

Example:
```
>>> f=open("sample.txt","r")
>>> str='hello'
>>> f.write(str)
```

```
Traceback (most recent call last):
  File "<pyshell#12>", line 1, in <module>
    f.write(str)
io.UnsupportedOperation: not writable
```

From the above example, it is clear that if we try to write the file which is in read mode then it will leads to error.

Example:

```
>>> f1=open("b.txt","r+")
>>> f1.read(6)
'hello.'
```

In the above example, 6 byte from the text file "b.txt" is read. Now the file handler is in seventh byte.

Example:

```
>>> f1.read()
'......\nI am fine'
```

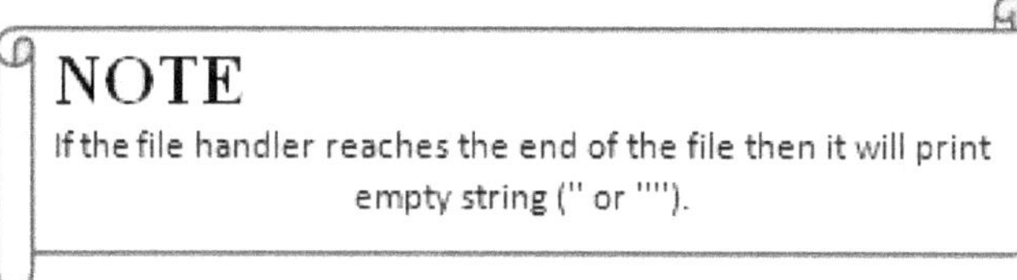

Example:

```
>>> f1.read()
''
```

- **readline( ):** This function is to read individual lines of the file. This function will read only one line and display it as string. The syntax of this function is:

Syntax:

```
file_object.readline(x)
```

Example:

```
>>> f1=open("a.txt","r+")
>>> f1.readline()
'hai!!!\n'
```

Even if the total number of bytes is not mention, it will only read a line from the file and display it.

- **readlines( ):** This function reads all the lines of the file up to the EOF. The output of this function will be list of strings. The syntax of this function is:

Syntax:

```
file_object.readlines(x)
```

Here, x is the optional argument; it represents the size of string to be displayed.

Example:

```
>>> f1=open("a.txt","r+")
>>> f1.readlines()
['hai!!!\n', 'how are you............']
```

The method readlines( ) will present all the lines in the file. In the output, \n represents new line.

NOTE

If we try to read a file which does not exist in read mode then it will leads to FileNotFoundError.

Example:
>>> f=open("chapter.txt","r")
Traceback (most recent call last):
  File "<pyshell#13>", line 1, in <module>
    f=open("chapter.txt","r")
FileNotFoundError: [Errno 2] No such file or directory: 'chapter.txt'

But if we open a file in write mode, even it does not exit then python will create a new file with the given name on its own.

Opening the file using 'with' keyword

The 'with' keyword can be used to open the file and close automatically after the process is done in python. This keyword will close the file properly after using it. It is not necessary to close the file explicitly using close( ) function.

Example:
```
with open("sample.txt","r") as f:
  for i in f:
    print(i)
```
Output:
how are you
>>> f.read()
Traceback (most recent call last):
  File "<pyshell#1>", line 1, in <module>
    f.read()
ValueError: I/O operation on closed file.

From this example, it is clear that using the 'with' keyword the file is opened and closed automatically.

7.5.2 WRITING TO A FILE

The write( ) function is used to write the file in text format or binary format. To write a file we have to open the file in write (w) mode or append (a) mode. If we open a file in write mode and if the file is already exists then the data will be overridden. If the file is not available then a new file is created. Two functions are used to write a file:

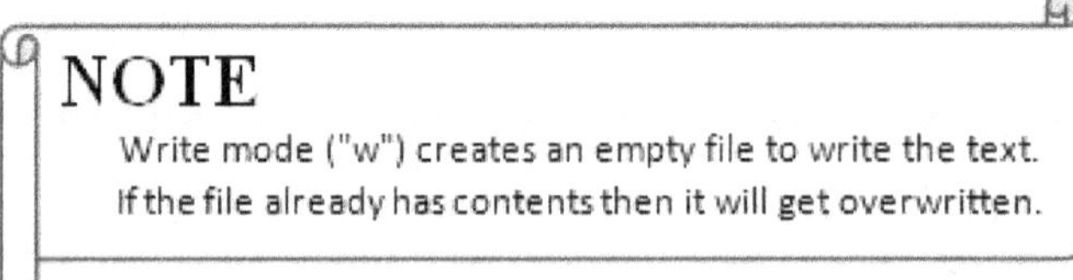

NOTE

Write mode ("w") creates an empty file to write the text.
If the file already has contents then it will get overwritten.

•   **write( ):** This function is used to insert all the string in the opened file. The write method does not add newline. The syntax for this function is:
Syntax:
file_object.write(str)
Example:
>>> f6=open("b.txt","w")

```
>>> s='hai'
>>> f6.write(s)
>>> f6.close()
```
      Now to view the contents of the file, open the file in r mode and read it.
```
>>> f6=open("b.txt","r")
>>> f6.read()
'hai'
```
- **writelines( ):** This function will insert multiple lines at a time. This will insert a list of string to the file. The syntax of this function is:

Syntax:

file_object.writelines(str)

Example:
```
f6=open("b.txt","w+")
>>> f=['hai\n','how\n']
>>> f6.writelines(f)
>>> f6.close()
>>> f6=open("b.txt","r")
>>> f6.read()
'hai\nhow\n'
```

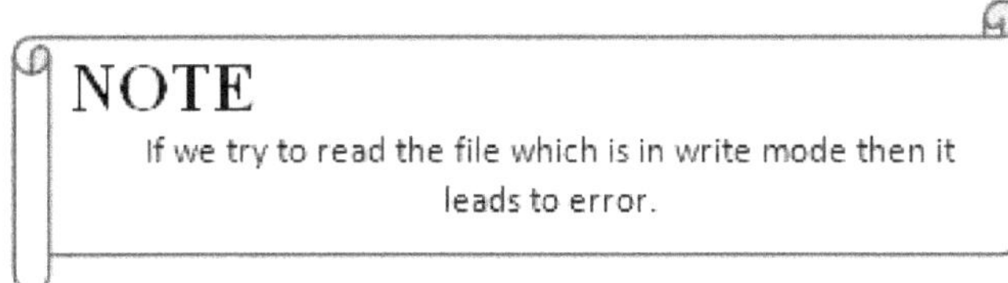

Example:
```
>>> f=open("sample.txt","w")
>>> f.read()
Traceback (most recent call last):
  File "<pyshell#15>", line 1, in <module>
    f.read()
io.UnsupportedOperation: not readable
```
      From the above example it is clear that we cannot read the file which is in write mode.

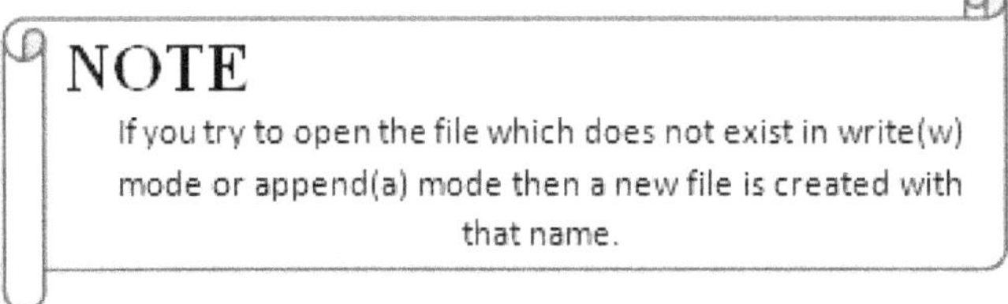

7.5.3 APPENDING TO A FILE

      Adding the data at the end of the file is known as appending. To appending something into a file, open the file with append mode ('a' or 'a+'). The append mode will not override the file; it will add the data at the end of the existing file.

Syntax:

file_object.open("file_name","a")

Example:
>>> f1=open("b.txt","r")
>>> f1.read()
'hai\nhow\n'
The file name "b.txt" contains strings 'hai\nhow\n'
>>> f1=open("b.txt","a")
>>> f1.write('are you')
>>> f1.close()
Now that file is opened in append mode ("a"). Here, 'are you' is added at the end of that file.
>>> f1=open("b.txt","r")
>>> f1.read()
'hai\nhow\nare you'

Finally, from the above example it is clear that the string 'are you' is added at the end of the file and the output is 'hai\nhow\nare you'. Here, \n indicates new line.

7.6 FILE POSITION

Various methods are used to known and change the position of file handler. The methods are:

1. tell( )
2. seek( )

> **NOTE**
>
> Reading is a sequential operation. When a file is opened the position of file handler is position 0 which is the starting position. After the read, the file handler moves forward.

• **tell( ):** This method tells the current position of file handler in that file. Initially the file handler will be in 0 position i.e., in the first byte of the file.
Example:
>>> f1=open("z.txt","r")
>>> f1.tell()
0L

From the above example it is clear that, initially when we open a file, the file handler is in the position 0.
Example:
>>> f1=open("z.txt","r")
>>> f1.read(2)
'ha'
>>> f1.tell()
2L

Here, 2 bytes has been read from the file and now the file handler is in second position.
• **seek( ):** This method is used to change the current position of the file handler. Initially, file handler reads from the position 0. We have to pass an argument to seek( )

method in order to change the position. This argument is the position in which the file handler has to move.

Example:

```
>>> f1=open("z.txt","r")
>>> f1.read()
'hai'
>>> f1.tell()
3L
>>> f1.seek(0) # to change the current position of the file handler
>>> f1.tell()
0L
```

Example:

```
>>> f1.read()
'hai'
>>> f1.tell()
3L
>>> f1.seek(2)
>>> f1.read()
'i'
>>> f1.tell()
2L
```

In the above example, seek(2), moves the file handler to the position 2.

7.8 FILE METHODS

The python has many built-in files to manipulate the data of the file. The table 7.2 explains the methods of file in detail.

METHOD	DESCRIPTION	SYNTAX
open( )	Open a file	file_object.open("file_name"," mode")
read( )	Read entire file into a single string	file_object.read()
read(n)	Read n number of bytes	file_object.read(n)
readline( )	Read next line	file_object.readline()
readlines( )	Read entire file and display it into list of strings	file_object.readlines()
write( )	Write string s into file	file_object.write("string")
writelines( )	Write all line strings in list onto the file	file_object.writelines("string")
close( )	Manual close the file opened file to release the resources. It will not do any process if the file is already closed.	file_object.close()
next( )	It returns the next line from the file.	file_object.next()
fileno( )	This method returns the integer file description.	file_object.fileno()
flush( )	This method will automatically flush the files while closing. It will force the unsaved data that is in the internal buffer.	file_object.flush()
iatty( )	This method return True if the file is connected to any terminal devices otherwise return False.	file_object.isatty()
truncate( )	It truncates the file size to the given size.	file_object.truncate([size])

Table 7.2 Methods of file

Example:

```
f=open("sample.txt","r+")
print("Current position",f.tell())
print(f.readlines())
print("Current position",f.tell())
print("File descriptor",f.fileno())
print("Truncate",f.truncate(5))
f.seek(0,0)
print(f.read())
f.flush()
f.close()
```

Output:

Current position 0

['The files are data which is stored in memory location for future use.\n', 'These data can be a text files, binary files or in other formats and these files is stored in some storage medium such as a disk, CD, or flash memory.\n', 'These data are given as input from users through input devices such as the keyboard, mouse, etc.\n']

Current position 321

File descriptor 3

Truncate 5

The f

From the above example it is clear that, tell( ) methods tells the current location of pointer or file handler. The readlines( ) method read all the data and display in the form of list of strings. The fileno( ) return the descriptor of the file and truncate(5) method keep only the data of 5 bytes and delete or truncate the remaining.

7.9 SYS MODULE AND COMMAND LINE ARGUMENTS

We can pass some command line arguments to your python programs during execution. The values of the command line control, the program from outside. For using command line argument we have to import **sys** module. And these command line arguments are access through **sys.argv**.

Here, argv[ ] is used to access the command line argument. This argument list starts from 0, sys.argv[0] is the file name. The command line argument in file has two uses, they are:
- sys.argv will return list of command line arguments
- len(sys.argv)   will return the count or number of command line arguments.

Example:
```
import sys
print("The file name is %s"%(sys.argv[0]))
```
Output:
```
The file name is C:\Python34\7.py
```
The above example is to get sys.argv[0] which is the file name.

Example:
```
import sys
f=open(sys.argv[1],"r+")
f1=open(sys.argv[2],"w+")
while True:
  f2=f.readline()
  if f2=="":
    break
  f1.write(f2)
f.close()
f1.close()
```
To run the script open terminal or command prompt:
```
C:\Python27>sys.py z.txt y.txt
```
Here, sys.argv[0] is the script (sys.py), sys.argv[1] is z.txt and sys.argv[2] is y.txt. In command prompt the first argument is always the script name and remaining are the arguments passed to the program. In this, z.txt and y.txt are inputs passed to the script through command line argument while running the program.

7.10 FILE OBJECT ATTRIBUTES

File object attributes are the attributes of file object which is used to get information about the file object. The table 7.3 shows the file object attribute with example.

Example:
```
>>> f=open("sample.txt","r+")
```

ATTRIBUTES	DESCRIPTION	EXAMPLE	OUTPUT
Name	This attribute is used to get the name of the file	>>> f.name	'sample.txt'
Mode	This attribute is used to know what mode the file is.	>>> f.mode	'r+'
Closed	This attribute will return True if the file is closed else return False.	>>> f.closed	False
Softspace	This attribute will return False, if space explicitly required, otherwise it will return True.	>>>f.softspace	False

Table 7.3 File attributes

7.11 OS DIRECTORIES

A directory is a collection of files and sub directories. The os module in python has many useful built-in methods and functions to interact with the operating system. In order to use the functions in directory, we have to import os module first. The table 7.4 explains the methods of os directories in detail with example.

Example:

```
>>> import os
>>> dir(os)
['F_OK', 'MutableMapping', 'O_APPEND', 'O_BINARY', 'O_CREAT', 'O_EXCL', 'O_NOIN-
HERIT', 'O_RANDOM', 'O_RDONLY', 'O_RDWR', 'O_SEQUENTIAL', 'O_SHORT_LIVED',
'O_TEMPORARY', 'O_TEXT', 'O_TRUNC', 'O_WRONLY', 'P_DETACH', 'P_NOWAIT',
'P_NOWAITO', 'P_OVERLAY', 'P_WAIT', 'R_OK', 'SEEK_CUR', 'SEEK_END', 'SEEK_SET',
'TMP_MAX', 'W_OK', 'X_OK', '_Environ', '__all__', '__builtins__', '__cached__', '__doc__',
'__file__', '__loader__', '__name__', '__package__', '__spec__', '_execvpe', '_exists', '_exit',
'_get_exports_list', '_putenv', '_unsetenv', '_wrap_close', 'abort', 'access', 'altsep',
'chdir', 'chmod', 'close', 'closerange', 'cpu_count', 'curdir', 'defpath', 'device_encoding',
'devnull', 'dup', 'dup2', 'environ', 'errno', 'error', 'execl', 'execle', 'execlp', 'execlpe',
'execv', 'execve', 'execvp', 'execvpe', 'extsep', 'fdopen', 'fsdecode', 'fsencode', 'fstat',
'fsync', 'get_exec_path', 'get_handle_inheritable', 'get_inheritable', 'get_terminal_size',
'getcwd', 'getcwdb', 'getenv', 'getlogin', 'getpid', 'getppid', 'isatty', 'kill', 'linesep', 'link',
'listdir', 'lseek', 'lstat', 'makedirs', 'mkdir', 'name', 'open', 'pardir', 'path', 'pathsep',
'pipe', 'popen', 'putenv', 'read', 'readlink', 'remove', 'removedirs', 'rename', 'renames',
'replace', 'rmdir', 'sep', 'set_handle_inheritable', 'set_inheritable', 'spawnl', 'spawnle',
'spawnv', 'spawnve', 'st', 'startfile', 'stat', 'stat_float_times', 'stat_result', 'statvfs_re-
sult', 'strerror', 'supports_bytes_environ', 'supports_dir_fd', 'supports_effective_ids',
'supports_fd', 'supports_follow_symlinks', 'symlink', 'sys', 'system', 'terminal_size',
'times', 'times_result', 'umask', 'uname_result', 'unlink', 'urandom', 'utime', 'waitpid',
'walk', 'write']
```

METHODS	DESCRIPTION	EXAMPLE	OUTPUT
os.mkdir( )	This method will create new directory in the declared path. If the path is not declared then new directory is created in the current working path.	>>>os.mkdir("1_sampl e")	>>>It create a directory named "1_sample"
os.getcwd( )	This method will display the current working directory in the form of string.	>>> os.getcwd()	'C:\\Python27'
os.getcwdb( )	This method will display the current working directory in the form of binary.	>>> os.getcwdb()	b'C:\\Python27'
os.chdir()	This method changes the current working directory.	>>> os.chdir ('C:\Python34')	>>> It change the directory to 'C:\Python34'
os.rmdir( )	This method removes or deletes the current working directory.	>>> os.rmdir ('C:\\Python27')	>>> It remove this 'C:\\Python27'
os.listdir( )	This method list all the files and subdirectories in the current directory.	>>> os.listdir ('C:\Python34')	['a.txt', 'b.txt', 'DLLs', 'cx_Oracle-doc', 'Doc', 'cx_Oracle-wininst.log', 'include', 'Lib', 'libs', 'LICENSE.txt', 'NEWS .txt', 'python.exe', 'pythonw.exe', 'README.txt', 'Removecx_Oracle.exe', 'Scripts', 'tcl', 'Tools']
os.rename( )	This method will rename the existing file name with the new one.	>>>os.rename("sample .txt","samp.txt")	>>> The file "sample.txt" is renamed as "samp.txt".
os.remove( )	This is used to remove the existing file.	>>> os.remove("a.txt")	>>> a.txt is removed

Table 7.4 Methods of OS directories

Example:
```
import os
print(os.getcwd())
print(os.chdir('C:\Python34'))
print(os.listdir('C:\Python34'))
```
Output:
```
C:\Python27
None
['a.txt', 'b.txt', 'cx_Oracle-doc', 'cx_Oracle-wininst.log', 'DLLs', 'Doc', 'include', 'Lib', 'libs', 'LICENSE.txt', 'NEWS.txt', 'python.exe', 'pythonw.exe', 'README.txt', 'Removecx_Oracle.exe', 'Scripts', 'tcl', 'Tools']
```

These are the some of the methods of the os module to manage the file and sub directories.

7.12 PICKLE

Pickle is a module in python; it is used to store non-strings or byte stream in a database. The pickle is for long term storage. The picking is to write a list or a dictionary to a file. To take all data type use pickle module. Pickling is used to convert a python object like list, dictionary, etc. into a byte streams. It translates any type of object into a string suitable for storage in a database, and again translates strings back into objects. The Pickle methods are used to store the contents to the file and retrieve their values from the file. In pickling multiple objects can be stored and restored in

the same time. The two main methods of pickle are:
- dumps( ) - It is to write object for the file.
- loads( ) - It is to read and return object from the pickle data stored in the file.

To use the methods of pickle, first we have to import pickle module.

Example:
```
>>> import pickle
>>> a=('hai',1)
>>> pickle.dumps(a)
```
Output:
```
"(S'hai'\np0\nI1\ntp1\n."
```
Example:

Pickling and unpickling is same as that of copying the object.
```
>>> t=('a',4)
>>> s=pickle.dumps(t)
>>> z=pickle.loads(s)
>>> z
('a', 4)
```

The value of t is now stored in z, even though z has the same value as t it is not the same object.
```
>>> t==z
True
>>> t is z
False
```

From this it is clear that the purpose of dumps and loads in python.

7.12.1 Pickling

The dumps is to dump or write string. The pickle.dumps takes object as a parameter and returns a string representation as output. Before writing, the data are converted into byte stream. This process is known as pickling which is done by using dump( ) method.

Syntax for dump:
```
pickle.dump(data,file_object)
```
Example:
```
import pickle
f1=open("sample.txt","wb")
pickle.dump(['hai','hello'],f1)
pickle.dump({'a':'hai','b':'hello'},f1)
f1.close()
```

In the above example a list and dictionary is created in file object f1, using dump( ) method of the pickle module. This process is known as pickling. Here, while opening the file 'wb' mode is used because in pickling, writing of data into byte streams take place.

7.12.2 Unpickling

While reading, conversion of byte stream to original data takes place. This process is known as unpickling which is done by using load( ) method.

Syntax:
```
pickle.load(file_object)
```
Example:

```
import pickle
f1=open('sample.txt','rb')
a=pickle.load(f1)
b=pickle.load(f1)
print(a,b)
f1.close()
```

Here, while opening the file 'rb' mode is used because in unpickling read of byte streams take place which is then converted into data.

Output:
['hai', 'hello'] {'b': 'hello', 'a': 'hai'}

In the above example, unpickling is done which read and return object from the pickle data stored in the file.

SUMMARY

•   In transient program inputs are given by input devices such as keyboard and mouse by using input( ) function, this data is processed and displays the output on the screen.

•   In persistent program, the input data are combined and placed in a file. It is a permanent storage file.

•   The two types of files type are text file and binary file. The default file type is text file.

•   The open( ) is a built-in function to open a file and close( ) function is used to close the file.

•   The relative path is a file name which is in the current working directory.

•   The absolute path starts with the root node and has complete directory. The path with \\ which is not depending on the current directory is known as absolute path.

•   In order to perform some task in file first that file has to be opened. After performing the task that file has to be closed. Python has built-in function to open and close the file.

•   File object attributes are the attributes of file object which is used to get information about the file object.

ILLUSTRATIVE PROGRAMS

1.   Write a python program to display all the contents of the file.

```
file= open("sample.txt", "r")
print("Contents of file :\t",file.read())
file.close()
```

Output:
Contents of file : how are you

2.   Write a python program to display the content of the file and also count number of lines in that file.

```
file= open("C:\\Python34\\sample.txt", "r")
print("The content of the file is:\n",file.read())
file.seek(0)
count=0
for i in file:
  line=i.split('\n')
  count=count+1
```

```
print("The total number of line is:\t",count)
file.close()
```
Output:
The content of the file is:
 If the data are immutable strings, aliasing can save on memory.
But aliasing is not always a good thing.
It has side effects.
The total number of line is: 3

3. Write a python program to copy the content of one file to another file and display the content.
```
file_in = open("input.txt", "r")
file_out = open("output.txt", "w")
print("Content of input file is:\t",file_in.read())
file_in.seek(0)
contents = file_in.readlines()
file_out.writelines(contents)
file_out = open("output.txt", "r")
print("Content of copy file is:\t",file_out.read())
file_in.close()
file_out.close()
```
Output:
Content of input file is: Hai, How are you??
Content of copy file is: Hai, How are you??

4. Write a python program to demonstrate file position
```
file= open("input.txt", "r")
print("Current position is: ",file.tell())
file.read() # After the read file handler reaches the end of the file
print("Now position is: ",file.tell())
print("Changing the position....................")
file.seek(0) #To change the position
print("Now position is: ",file.tell())
file.seek(10) #To change the position
print("Now position is: ",file.tell())
file.close()
```
Output:
Current position is: 0
Now position is: 20
Changing the position...................
Now position is: 0
Now position is: 10

5. Write a python program to add the string at the last of the given file and display the entire file.
```
f1=open("input.txt","a+")
f1.write('Fine')
f1.seek(0)
print("The content is ",f1.read())
f1.close()
```
Output:
The content is Hai, How are you??

Fine

6. Write a python program to count the occurrences of string in the file

```python
f1=open("sample.txt","r")
wordcount={}
for word in f1.read().split():
  if word not in wordcount:
    wordcount[word] = 1
  else:
    wordcount[word] += 1
f1.close();
print ("%-30s%s " %('Words' , 'Count'))
for key in wordcount.keys():
  print ("%-30s%d " %(key , wordcount[key]))
```

Output:

Words	Count
is	1
effect.	1
good	1
always	1
But	1
If	1
has	1
the	1
save	1
can	1
thing.	1
immutable	1
aliasing	2
a	1
on	1
It	1
memory.	1
side	1
are	1
data	1
strings,	1
not	1

7. Write a python program to find frequently used word in the file.

```python
file=open("sample.txt","r")
count={}
for word in file.read().split():
  if word not in count:
    count[word] = 1
  else:
    count[word] += 1
file.close();
freq=0;
for key in count.keys():
  if count[key]>freq:
```

```
    freq=count[key]
print('The most frequently used word is')
for key in count.keys():
  if count[key]==freq:
    print(key)
```
Output:
```
The most frequently used word is
aliasing
```
8.   Write a python program to check whether there is a drive in the computer.
```
import os
print("True in output means the drive is present otherwise False")
print(os.path.exists("I:\\"))
```
Output:
```
True in output means the drive is present otherwise False
True
```
9.   Write a python program to display the content of the file and get the length of the file.
```
f=open("sample.txt","r")
x=f.read()
print("The contents in file is:\n",x)
print("The length of file is",len(x))
f.close()
```
Output:
```
The contents in file is:
 how are you
The length of file is 11
```
10. Write a python program to get the total size of the files in a particular drive.
```
import os
size=0
drive=input("Enter the drive name or path\t")
for i in os.listdir(drive):
  size=size+os.path.getsize(os.path.join(drive,i))
print("Total size of files in", drive,"is",size)
```
Output:
```
Enter the drive name or path C:
Total size of files in C: is 831821
```
12. Write a python program to demonstrate file attributes.
```
file=open("sample.txt","r")
print("The file attributes are name, mode and closed")
print("The file name is: ",file.name)
print("The file access mode is: ",file.mode)
print("The file is closed \ not ?: ",file.closed)
```
Output:
```
The file attributes are name, mode and closed
The file name is:  sample.txt
The file access mode is:  r
The file is closed \ not ?:  False
```
13. Write a python program to get a file from user and print the longest word.
```
def longest_word(filename):
```

```
    with open(filename, 'r') as i:
        words = i.read().split()
    maxim= len(max(words, key=len))
    return [word for word in words if len(word) == maxim]
f=input("Enter the name of the file to be processed")
print("The longest word is:\t",longest_word(f))
```
Output:
Enter the name of the file to be processedsample.txt
The longest word is: ['immutable']

14. Write a python program to list all the files and directories of the current working directory.
```
import os
print("The files in the current working directory are")
print(os.listdir())
```
Output:
The files in the current working directory are
['7.py', 'a.txt', 'b.txt', 'cx_Oracle-doc', 'cx_Oracle-wininst.log', 'DLLs', 'Doc', 'file_copy', 'file_copy.txt', 'include', 'input.txt', 'Lib', 'libs', 'LICENSE.txt', 'NEWS.txt', 'output.txt', 'python.exe', 'pythonw.exe', 'README.txt', 'Removecx_Oracle.exe', 'sample.txt', 'Scripts', 'tcl', 'Tools']

11. Write a python program to to read and display content of a text file in binary mode.
```
file=open("src.txt","rb")
r=file.read()
print("The contents in source file is:\n",r)
```
Output:
The contents in source file is:
 b'hai hai....\r\n'

ADDITIONAL PROGRAMS

1. Write a python program to count the number of vowels in the file.
2. Write a python program to copy and reverse the content one file to another file.
3. Write a python program to compare two files.
4. Write a python program to remove the last word of the given file.
5. Write a python program to count the number of characters in the file.
6. Write a python program to open file in binary format and display it.
7. Demonstrate pickling and unpickling.
8. Write a python program to sort the content of the given file.
9. Write a python program to search whether the word is in the file or not.
10. Write a python program to split each word of the file and display it.

REVIEW QUESTIONS

1. What is file? Explain the types of file.
2. What are the basic file operations available in python?
3. Explain about various access modes in python.
4. Explain about the file attributes in detail.
5. What are the functions for opening and closing a file?
6. Explain about file path and file name.
7. What is OS directory? Explain with example.
8. Differentiate seek( ) and tell( ) with example.

9. Explain the methods of file in detail.
10. Difference between readline( ) and readlines( ).
11. What is file directory?
12. Difference between opening a file in read and write mode.
13. Explain about 'with' keyword and its advantages.
14. Differentiate absolute path and relative path with example.
15. Explain about sys module and command line arguments.

MUTIPLE CHOICE QUESTIONS

1. Try to open the file in write mode which does not exist will leads to.
   a. FileNotFoundError
   b. Create a new file in that name
   c. IOError
   d. None of these
2. The file end with special character known as
   a. Newline (\n)
   b. End of File (EOF)
   c. space/tab
   d. None of these
3. Which method is used to change the position of the file handler
   a. chdir( )
   b. tell( )
   c. seek( )
   d. exists( )
4. Which method is used to delete a file?
   a. del( )
   b. delete( )
   c. remove( )
   d. exit( )
5. Which method is used to create a directory?
   a. mkdir( )
   b. mkdirs( )
   c. getdir( )
   d. makedirs( )
6. When a file is opened in append mode, the file pointer will be in which position.
   a. 0th position
   b. End of file
   c. 1st position
   d. Middle position
7. What is the syntax for closing a file
   a. file_object.close( )
   b. close(file_object)
   c. file_name.close( )
   d. close(file_name)
8. The responsibility of garbage collector is:
   a. Collect the entire object
   b. Collect the memory of the file
   c. Clean the directory

d. Clean up the unreferenced objects from memory

9. Which of the following is the default format while opening a file?
    a. Binary format
    b. Text format
    c. Image format
    d. None of these

10. Which of the following is correct for opening a file in w+ mode?
    a. It perform write only
    b. It performs write and read in binary format
    c. It performs read only
    d. It performs both write and read

11. Consider the file "C:\\Python34\\sample.txt" which has the text "how are you".
file= open("C:\\PYTHON34\\SAMPLE.TXT", "r")
print(file.read())
file.close()
Which of the following is correct, if the program is to display the content of the file?
    a. Syntax Error
    b. how are you
    c. Error, file path should be case sensitive.
    d. how

TRUE OR FALSE

1. The binary format can be read by both human and computer.
2. RAM memory is the permanent memory, the data will not loss even the system is shutdown.
3. The absolute path is the path with the root node.
4. The binary file takes less space than text file and it is so efficient.
5. The readline( ) method is to read all the lines of the file.
6. The append mode in file will create a new file in that name, if the file does not exists.
7. The seek( ) method is used to known the current position of file handler or pointer.
8. When the file is opened in append mode then the file pointer will be at the end of the file.
9. While opening a file using open( ) function, the access mode of file is an optional argument.
10. We can only open the file in text format.

FILL IN THE BLANKS

1. The file system is stored in the form of ___________ structure.
2. Fill in the blanks for the syntax of open( ) function.
file_object=open(____________,____________)
3. The ____________ function is used to release the resources.
4. The default access mode in file is ____________.
5. The ____________ method is used to get current working directory.
6. Try to open the file in read mode which does not exist will leads to ____________.
7. The ____________ method is used to know the current position of the file handler or pointer.

8. Fill in the blanks to print the content on the string from the file name "sample.txt".
   ___________ open("sample.txt","r") ___________ f:
      print(f.___________ ( ))
9. The ___________ attribute is used to get the access mode of the file.
10. The ___________ module in python has method related to directories.

ANSWERS

MUTIPLE CHOICE QUESTIONS

1. b
2. b
3. c
4. c
5. a
6. b
7. a
8. d
9. b
10. d
11. b

TRUE OR FALSE
1. False
2. False
3. True
4. True
5. False
6. True
7. False
8. True
9. True
10. False

FILL IN THE BLANKS
1. Tree
2. file name, access mode
3. close( )
4. read(r) mode
5. getcwd( )
6. IOError
7. tell( )
8. with, as, read
9. mode
10. os

CHAPTER 8: ERRORS AND EXCEPTION

Errors detected during the execution or runtime are known as exceptions. This chapter explains about errors such as syntax error, logical error and exceptions. This chapter also discuss about built-in exception and runtime exception and how to handle the exceptions. When an exception is raised, it has to get handled immediately otherwise the code will get terminated abnormally. For exception handling, the concepts such as try, except, finally, assert, else, raise are used.

CHAPTER OUTLINE

Errors: Syntax error, Logical error, Runtime errors (Exceptions) – Exception handling – try, except, finally, else, raise – Assertion

OBJECTIVE

After completing the chapter, you will be in a position:

- To known what is error and what are its types
- To understand about exceptions
- To known about built-in exception and user defined exception.
- To known about error handling
- To handle Try …. except…. finally statements
- To raise an exception
- To use assertion in python
- To create user defined exception

8.1 ERRORS

Some abnormal or unexpected behavior in the program leads to errors or exceptions. In this chapter we are going to cover about errors and exceptions and the ways

to handle exceptions. The figure 8.1 shows the types of errors in detail. In python programming there are three main kinds of errors:
- Syntax errors
- Logical errors
- Runtime errors (Exceptions)

NOTE

The interpreter can detect syntax errors during the translation phase and run-time errors during the execution phase.

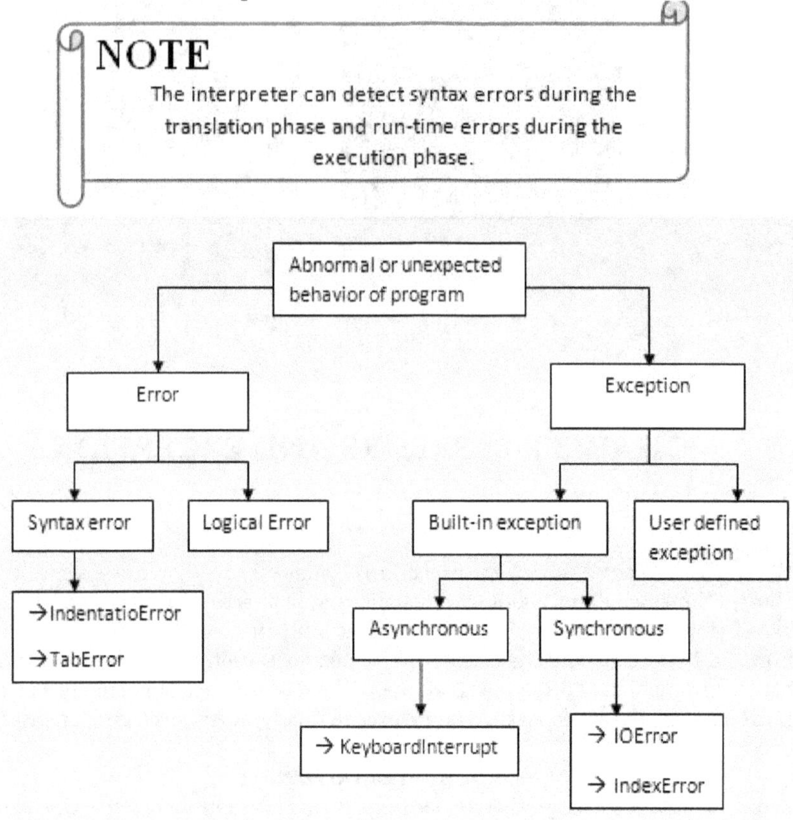

Figure 8.1 Types of errors

8.1.1 Syntax error

The syntax refers to the structure of the program, if the structure is not correct it leads to syntax error. The syntax error is also called as parser error, because this error will be raised when parser is not able to understand the code. This Syntax error is most common types of error. The program will get compiled only when all the syntax errors are corrected. These errors occur because of the usage of incorrect syntax in the program. If the interpreter finds any invalid program during execution, it will terminate the execution of the program and display the error. Some of the syntax errors are incorrect indentation, error while using the conditionals, or incorrect arguments.

These errors are very easy to clear if it is identified. Some of the ways to avoid syntax errors are:
1. Check whether the indentation is done properly.
2. Avoid using keyword as variable name.

3. Check whether there the statements such as while, if, def, else end with colon or not.

4. Put quotation marks for strings, a pair of quotation mark should be used.

5. Closing and opening parenthesis should be equal.

6. Check whether all block has at least one statement or not.

7. Check the spelling of the keywords.

Example:

if a=b

This is a type of syntax error due to the missing of colon (:) at the end of the conditional statement.

>>>(3+2)*((4/2)

Example:

The above example shows syntax error due to missing parenthesis in program.

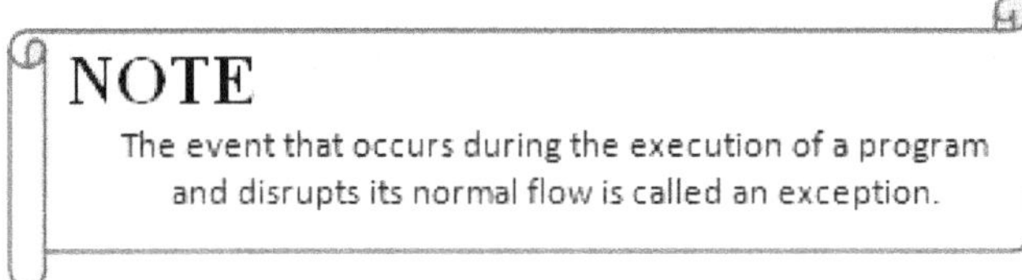

NOTE

The syntax error is also called as parser error, because this error will be raised when parser is not able to understand the code.

8.1.2 Logical errors

The logical errors are some different types of error that will result in some unpredictable outputs. These errors are more difficult to find and will affect the result of the program. The poor understanding of the problem or language will result in logical error. This error is only due to the mistake in logic, not because of any syntax error or exceptions.

NOTE

The event that occurs during the execution of a program and disrupts its normal flow is called an exception.

8.2 EXCEPTIONS

Errors detected during the execution time or runtime are known as exceptions. It is also known as runtime errors or unexpected errors. Even if the program is syntactically correct due to some exceptional event problem my arises during the execution of a program, such errors are known as exception. Few examples for exception are:

- ArithmeticError
- IndexError
- ZeroDivisionError
- FileNotFoundError

Example:
```
>>> a=[2,'1',9]
>>> a[4]
Traceback (most recent call last):
 File "<pyshell#10>", line 1, in <module>
   a[4]
IndexError: list index out of range
```

Here, IndexError is a type of error which raises when we try to access an element which is not in that index.

Example:
```
>>> 20/0
Traceback (most recent call last):
 File "<pyshell#1>", line 1, in <module>
   20/0
ZeroDivisionError: division by zero
```

This exception is raised because dividing a number by zero is not possible.

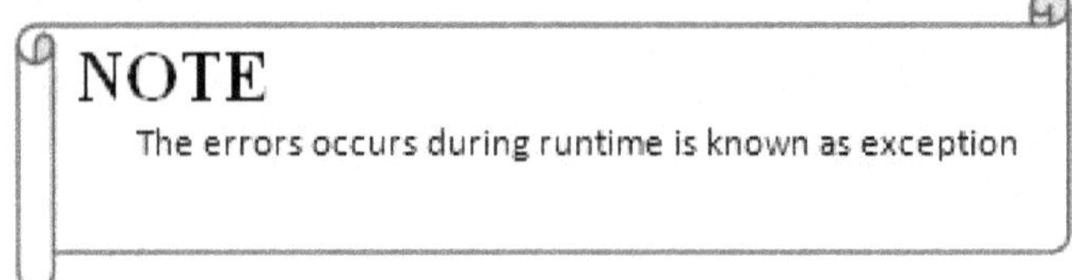

There are two types of exception, they are:

- Built-in exception
- User defined exception

8.2.1 Built-in exception

These are the exceptions that are already predefined to the system. The built-in exceptions in python are:
```
>>> dir(__builtins__)
```
['ArithmeticError', 'AssertionError', 'AttributeError', 'BaseException', 'BlockingIOError', 'BrokenPipeError', 'BufferError', 'BytesWarning', 'ChildProcessError', 'ConnectionAbortedError', 'ConnectionError', 'ConnectionRefusedError', 'ConnectionResetError', 'DeprecationWarning', 'EOFError', 'Ellipsis', 'EnvironmentError', 'Exception', 'False', 'FileExistsError', 'FileNotFoundError', 'FloatingPointError', 'FutureWarning', 'GeneratorExit', 'IOError', 'ImportError', 'ImportWarning', 'IndentationError', 'IndexError', 'InterruptedError', 'IsADirectoryError', 'KeyError', 'KeyboardInterrupt', 'LookupError', 'MemoryError', 'NameError', 'None', 'NotADirectoryError', 'NotImplemented', 'NotImplementedError', 'OSError', 'OverflowError', 'PendingDeprecationWarning', 'PermissionError', 'ProcessLookupError', 'ReferenceError', 'ResourceWarning', 'RuntimeError', 'RuntimeWarning', 'StopIteration', 'SyntaxError',

'SyntaxWarning', 'SystemError', 'SystemExit', 'TabError', 'TimeoutError', 'True', 'TypeError', 'UnboundLocalError', 'UnicodeDecodeError', 'UnicodeEncodeError', 'UnicodeError', 'UnicodeTranslateError', 'UnicodeWarning', 'UserWarning', 'ValueError', 'Warning', 'WindowsError', 'ZeroDivisionError', '__build_class__', '__debug__', '__doc__', '__import__', '__loader__', '__name__', '__package__', '__spec__', 'abs', 'all', 'any', 'ascii', 'bin', 'bool', 'bytearray', 'bytes', 'callable', 'chr', 'classmethod', 'compile', 'complex', 'copyright', 'credits', 'delattr', 'dict', 'dir', 'divmod', 'enumerate', 'eval', 'exec', 'exit', 'filter', 'float', 'format', 'frozenset', 'getattr', 'globals', 'hasattr', 'hash', 'help', 'hex', 'id', 'input', 'int', 'isinstance', 'issubclass', 'iter', 'len', 'license', 'list', 'locals', 'map', 'max', 'memoryview', 'min', 'next', 'object', 'oct', 'open', 'ord', 'pow', 'print', 'property', 'quit', 'range', 'repr', 'reversed', 'round', 'set', 'setattr', 'slice', 'sorted', 'staticmethod', 'str', 'sum', 'super', 'tuple', 'type', 'vars', 'zip']

The table 8.1 gives the explaination of built-in exceptions of python.

Exception	Reason for exception
Exception	It is the base class for all exceptions
AirthmeticError	Obtained if there is any error in arithmetic calculation.
AssertionError	When the assert statement fails
AttributeError	When an attribute assignment or refernece fails
EOFError	When there is no file pointer or any input( ) or raw_input( ) at the End of File
EnvironmentError	It is the base class for all exceptions that occur outside the python environment.
FloatingPointError	Obtained when the floating point operation fails
GeneratorExit	When a close( ) method is called
ImportError	When the imported module is not present
IOError	When any input or output operation fails
IndexError	When index is not found in the sequence
KeyError	Raised when the specific key is not available in directory
KeyboardInterrupt	Obtained when used interrupt the execution by pressing keys such as ctrl+c or del
MemoryError	When the system is running out of memory
NameError	Obtained when the variable is not available in the scope
NotImplementedError	If the abstract method is not implemented
OSError	For operating system fails or some error in operating system
OverflowError	When the operation exceeds out of the range
ReferenceError	Obtained when reference proxy accesses a garbage collected reference

Table 8.1: Built-in exceptions in python

The builtins module in python holds the exception. All exception classes are subtypes of the BaseException class. The figure 8.2 shows the hierarchy of exception classes.

1. BaseException
   a. Exception
   b. ArithmeticError
       i. FloatingPointError
       ii. OverflowError
       iii. ZeroDivisionError
   c. AssertionError
   d. AttributeError
   e. BufferError
   f. EOFError
   g. ImportError
   h. LookupError
       i. IndexError
       ii. KeyError
   i. MemoryError
   j. NameError
       i. UnboundLocalError
   k. OSError
       i. BlockingIOError
       ii. ChildProcessError
       iii. ConnectionError
       iv. BrokenPipeError
       v. ConnectionAbortedError
       vi. ConnectionRefusedError
       vii. ConnectionResetError
       viii. FileExistsError
       ix. FileNotFoundError
       x. InterruptedError
       xi. IsADirectoryError
       xii. NotADirectoryError
       xiii. PermissionError
       xiv. ProcessLookupError
       xv. TimeoutError
   l. ReferenceError
   m. RuntimeError
       i. NotImplementedError
   n. StopIteration
   o. SyntaxError
       i. IndentationError
       ii. TabError
   p. SystemError
   q. TypeError
   r. ValueError
       i. UnicodeError
       ii. UnicodeDecodeError
       iii. UnicodeEncodeError
       iv. UnicodeTranslateError
   s. Warning
       i. BytesWarning
       ii. DeprecationWarning
       iii. FutureWarning
       iv. ImportWarning
       v. PendingDeprecationWarning
       vi. ResourceWarning
       vii. RuntimeWarning
       viii. SyntaxWarning
       ix. UnicodeWarning
       x. UserWarning
   t. GeneratorExit
   u. KeyboardInterrupt
   v. SystemExit

Figure 8.2: Hierarchy of exceptions in python

8.2.2 User defined exception/Custom exception

The user defined exceptions are the exceptions which are created by the user. This exception can be done by creating a new class, by deriving classes from some built-in exceptions or from base exception class. The way of creating our own exception class or user defined exception is known as custom exception. The syntax for creating exception class is:

```
class UserDefinedError(Exception):
'''Base class of the exception'''
    #statements
raise UserDefinedError(<messages>)
```

Now create a user defined exception named CodeError and by calling the raise statement error message is generated.

Example:

```
class CodeError(Exception):
  def __init__(self, data):
    self.data = data
  def __str__(self):
      return repr(self.data)
try:
      raise CodeError(100)
except CodeError as ae:
```

    print ("Obtained error:", ae.data)
Output:
Obtained error: 100

When an exception is raised, it has to get handled otherwise the program terminated immediately. These exceptions in program are handled in two ways, they are:
- Exception handling
- Assertions

Let's now discuss about these in detail in forth coming sections.

8.3 EXCEPTION HANDLING

Even if the program is syntactically correct due to some exceptional event problem may arise during the execution of a program, such errors are known as exception. When an exception is raised it has to get handled immediately otherwise it will terminate abnormally. If any exception occurs, it has to handle by the programmer then program execution cannot get terminated abnormally. These errors can be handled by using exception handling techniques. The figure 8.3 shows the working of exception handler.

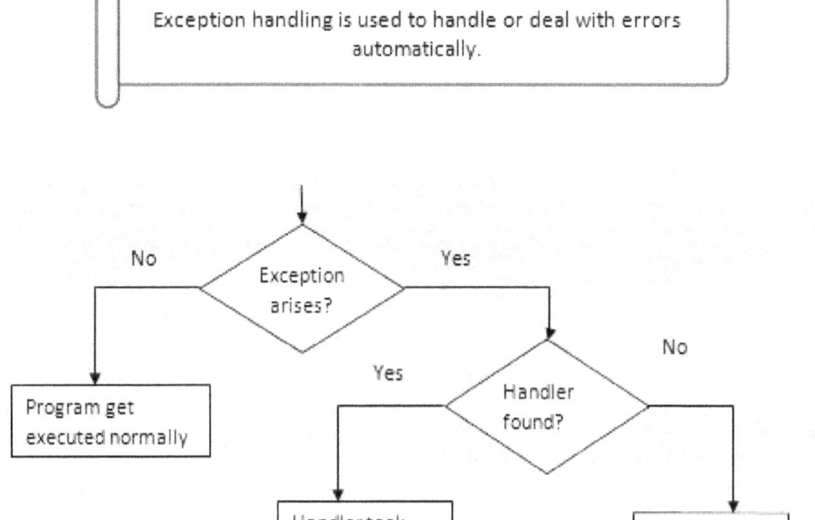

Figure 8.3: Exception handling

In order to overcome the runtime error, we are going for exception handling which contain some blocks to hold the runtime errors. The various blocks to handle exception are:
- try
- except
- raise

- finally

try: This block is created in order to catch the exception. It throws the exception if the code has runtime error. The try block contains one or more statement that can produce exception. If that operation fails or exception is thrown then, control goes to except block.

except: This block catches the exception thrown by except block and perform some action.

finally: This block is an optional block, which will get executed under all circumstances. This block is used to create some action whether the exception is raised or not.

raise: This statement is used to manually raise an exception

If you have any doubtful code just place these block in to the program and execute it.

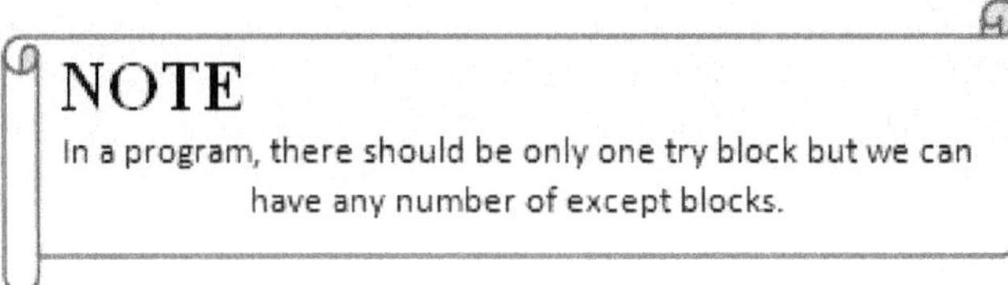

Syntax:

```
try:
    statement #actions to be performed
except <ExceptionType>:
    statement #Handle the exception
```

A try statement is a statement that is always available in exception handling. Inside the try block there are some codes that will raise an exception. The code for handling the exception is placed in except block. This is how exception is handled.

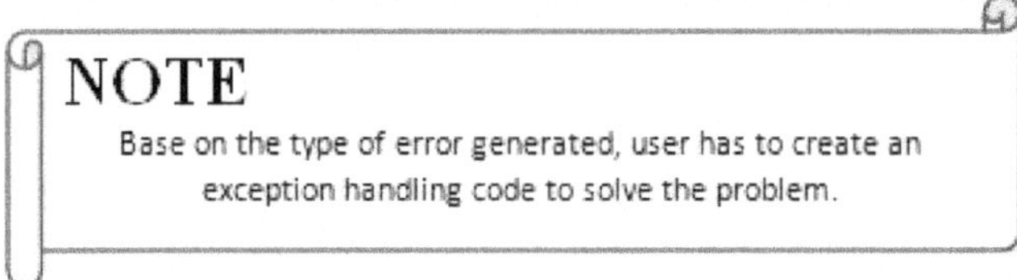

Example:

```
>>> a= int(input("Enter a number: "))
Enter a number: 6
```

Output:

```
>>> a= int(input("Enter a number: "))
Enter a number: 93.23
Traceback (most recent call last):
  File "<pyshell#6>", line 1, in <module>
```

From the above example it is clear that if the entered value is a floating point value then it will leads to exception. There are some ways to handle such exception.

Example:

```
try:
    n = int(input("Enter an integer: "))
except ValueError:
    print("Not a integer")
```

```
else:
    print ("It is a integer value")
```
Output:

Enter an integer: 6

It is a integer value

>>>

Enter an integer:

Not a integer

From the above example it is clear that, an exception known as ValueError is raised if we enter some value other than integer. If that exception occurs then control goes to except clause and executes the statement. There are many ways to handle exception, they are:

1. try...except
2. try...except without exception
3. try...except with multiple exception
4. try...except...finally
5. try... except...else
6. try...except.....except.....
7. try...raise..except..
8. assert

Let's now discuss about these types of exception handling in detail.

8.3.1 The try.......except clause with exception

The try....except clause is a type of exception handler, which is used to handle one exception in the except block.

Syntax:

```
try:
    Statements        # actions to be done
except exception:
    Statements        # if exception executes this block
else:
    Statement         # if no exception executes this block
```

Example:

```
a=int(input("Enter divident"))
b=int(input("Enter divisor"))
try:
    c=a/b
except ZeroDivisionError:
    print ("zero division error")
```

Output:

Enter divident5

Enter divisor0

zero division error

In the above example, the try block got executed first, if there is an exception except block will get executed

8.3.2   The except clause without exception

This type is used to handle any exception in the except block. We can also use except statement without specifying any exception in it.

Syntax:

```
try:
    Statements          # actions to be done
except:
    Statements          # if exception executes this block
else:
    Statement           # if no exception executes this block
```
Example:
```
try:
  a=open("ab.txt","r")
except:
  print ('no such file')
else:
  print ('file opened in read mode')
  a.close()
```
In the above program there is no particular exception mentioned in except block. If any exception is raised in try block the control automatically goes to except block and executes the statement.

Output:

no such file

8.3.3   The except class with multiple exceptions

This blocks used to handle multiple exceptions with except statement. We can also declare multiple exceptions in one except statement. Here a same except statement is used to handle multiple exceptions.

Syntax:
```
try:
    statement   #actions to be performed
except Exception1:
statement   #Handle the exception
except Exception2:
    statement   #Handle the exception

..........

..........
except ExceptionN:
    statement   #Handle the exception
else:
    statement   # If no exception executes this block
```
Syntax:
```
try:
    Statements          # actions to be done
except (exception1[,exception2,...exceptionN]]]):
    Statements          # if exception executes this block
else:
    Statement           # if no exception executes this block
```
Example:
```
a=int(input("Enter the value of a"))
b=int(input("Enter the value of b"))
try:
  c=a/b;
except(ArithmeticError, ZeroDivisionError):
```

```
    print ("Has Exception")
else:
    print ("Has no exception")
Output:
Enter the value of a10
Enter the value of b5
Has no exception
>>>
Enter the value of a10
Enter the value of b0
Has Exception
```

8.3.4   The finally clause

The finally clause is an optional clause; this clause will get executed under all circumstances. The finally block is placed after the try block. This clause is followed after try statement, this clause is also known as clean-up or termination clause. This block is used to create some action whether the exception is raised or not. Mostly in finally block all the code that must need to execute is placed, whether the exception occurs or not, this finally block will get executed.

Syntax:

```
try:
    statement    #action to be done
except:
    statement    #if exception execute this block
finally:
    statement    # statement that must be executed
```

The finally block is executed after try or except blocks.

> **NOTE**
> The finally block is used for writing the statements which you want to execute whether exception occurs or not

Example:

```
a=int(input("Enter divident"))
b=int(input("Enter divisor"))
try:
    c=a/b
    print("No ZeroDivisionError")
except ZeroDivisionError:
    print ("Has ZeroDivisionError")
finally:
    print("you wrote a program to check whether there is any ZeroDivisionError")
Output:
Enter divident12
Enter divisor4
No ZeroDivisionError
you wrote a program to check whether there is any ZeroDivisionError
```

From the above example it is clear that, even if there is any exception or not, finally block got executed always, irrespective of the exception.

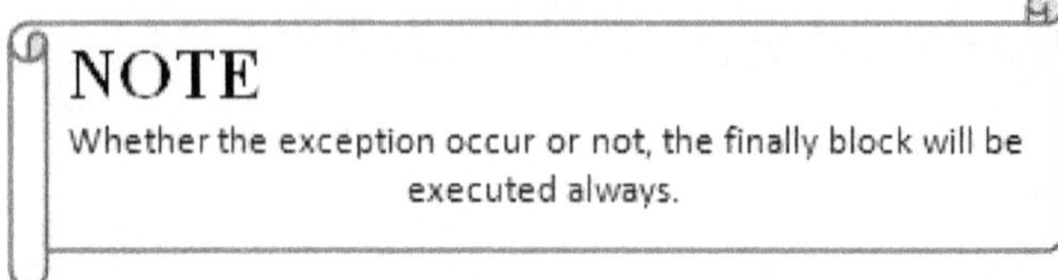

8.3.5 The else clause

The else clause is a clause used along with try....except clause. In this type, first the try block got executed. If there is an exception, except block will get executed otherwise (if no exception) else block will get executed.

Syntax:

try:

    Statements   # actions to be done

except exception:

    Statements   # if exception executes this block

else:

    Statement   # if no exception executes this block

    In try...except... else block, either 'except' or 'else' block will be executed.

Example:

Let's now discuss about IOError. The IOError is an exception is obtained when we try to open a file which is not exists.

```
try:
  a=open("i.txt","r")
except IOError:
  print ('no such file')
else:
  print ('file opened in read mode')
  a.close()
```

Output:

no such file

The open statement tries to open the file named "i.txt" in read mode and if there is no file, IOError exception is generated. Now the control goes to except block and if the raise exception is IOError except block will get executed otherwise control goes to else block. From the above example it is clear that we try to open a file which does not exist so the control goes to except block. Now the statement of the except block got executed and display the print statement.

Let's now discuss about ZeroDivisionError. The ZeroDivisionError is an exception obtained when we try to divide a number by zero or if we try to perform modulo by zero.

```
a=int(input("Enter divident"))
```

```
b=int(input("Enter divisor"))
try:
  c=a/b
except ZeroDivisionError:
  print ("zero division error")
else:
  print("the quotient is",c)
Output:
Enter dividend50
Enter divisor10
the quotient is 5.0
>>>
Enter dividend100
Enter divisor0
zero division error
```

In the above example, the try block got executed first, if there is an exception except block will get executed otherwise else block got executed.

8.3.6　Raising an Exception

We can raise or throw an exception explicitly several ways by using the raise statement. We can forcefully raise an exception by using raise keyword. This statement cause exception and if in case that exception is not handled then execution control gets stops. The syntax of this exception is raise keyword followed by exception class name and arguments.

Syntax:

raise [Exception[,arguments[,traceback]]]

Here, raise is a keyword, Exception is the type of exception, arguments are the optional part which is the value of exception argument and traceback is also an optional part.

Example:

```
>>> raise KeyboardInterrupt
Traceback (most recent call last):
  File "<pyshell#0>", line 1, in <module>
    raise KeyboardInterrupt
KeyboardInterrupt
```

Example:

```
a=input("Enter something")
try:
  print a
  raise NameError("Hello")
except NameError as e:
  print "An exception occurred"
  print e
Output:
Enter something6
6
An exception occurred
Hello
```

NOTE

To access the value "as" keyword is used and "e" is used as a reference variable which stores the value of the exception.

8.3.7 Assertions in Python

An assertion is a statement in python which is a sanity-check, it is like a raise-if statement. In assertion, an expression is tested and if the result is false then Assertion-Error exception is raised. This is mostly put at the beginning of a function to check whether the input is valid one or not. We cannot use assertion to find ZeroDivision-Error. For using assertion in python assert keyword is used.

Syntax:

assert Expression[, Arguments]

Assert keyword is used for assertion and if the assertion fails. Python uses ArgumentExpression as an argument for the AssertionError. We can also handle AssertionError exceptions by using try and except statement and it will terminate if not handle properly.

Example:

```
>>> a=10
>>> assert a<0, "a has to be a negative integer"
Traceback (most recent call last):
  File "<pyshell#22>", line 1, in <module>
    assert a<0, "a has to be a negative integer"
AssertionError: a has to be a negative integer
```

SUMMARY

• Some abnormal or unexpected behavior in the program leads to errors or exceptions.

• If the structure is not correct it leads to syntax error. It is also called as parser error, because this error will be raised when parser is not able to understand the code.

• The poor understanding of the problem or language will result in logical error.

• Errors detected that are during the execution or runtime are known as exceptions.

• When an exception is raised it has to get handled immediately otherwise it will terminate.

• The finally clause is an optional clause; this clause will get executed under all circumstances. The finally block is placed after the try block.

• The else block can be used to write some statements which we want to execute after try block in case here is no exception.

• We can raise or throw an exception explicitly several ways by using the raise statement. We can forcefully raise an exception by using raise keyword.

• An assertion is a statement in python which is a sanity-check, it is like a raise-if statement. In assertion, an expression is tested and if the result is false then Assertion-Error exception is raised.

raise: This statement is used to manually raise an exception   .

ILLUSTRATIVE PROGRAMS

1. Write a python program to demonstrate and handle ZeroDivisionError using try....except.

```python
a=int(input("Enter divident"))
b=int(input("Enter divisor"))
try:
    c=a/b
    print(c)
except ZeroDivisionError:
    print ("zero division error")
```

Output:
```
Enter divident10
Enter divisor0
zero division error
>>>
Enter divident10
Enter divisor5
2.0
```

2.   Write a python program to handle IOError using try....except...else clause.

```python
try:
    a=open("i.txt","r")
except IOError:
    print ('no such file')
else:
    print ('file opened in read mode')
    a.close()
```

Output:
```
no such file
```

3.   Write a python program to demonstrate finally clause.

```python
a=int(input("Enter divident"))
b=int(input("Enter divisor"))
try:
    c=a/b
    print("No ZeroDivisionError")
except ZeroDivisionError:
    print ("Has ZeroDivisionError")
finally:
    print("This program is to handle ZeroDivisionError")
```

Output:
```
Enter divident10
Enter divisor2
No ZeroDivisionError
This program is to handle ZeroDivisionError
```

4.   Write a python program to handle TypeError using try....except without exception.

```python
a=int(input("Enter a number"))
b=input("Enter another number")
try:
    c=a+b
    print(c)
except:
    print("Has TypeError")
```

Output:
Enter a number10
Enter another number55
Has TypeError
5. Write a python program to handle IndexError.
a=[1,6,7,2]
try:
   print(a[5])
except IndexError:
   print("List index out of range")
Output:
List index out of range

ADDITIONAL PROGRAMS
1. Write a python program to handle ArithmeticError
2. Write a python program to handle FloatingPointError using assertion.
3. Write a python program to handle ValueError.
4. Write a python program to handle ImportError.
5. Write a python program to demonstrate raise keyword.

REVIEW QUESTIONS
1. What are errors?
2. Explain about syntax and logical error.
3. What is exception?
4. Explain the type of exception with example.
5. What is exception handling? Explain the steps to handle exception.
6. What are built-in exceptions? Explain with example.
7. What is try….except in python?
8. What is known as assertion in python?
9. What are the advantages of exception?
10. How to raise an exception in python? Explain with example.
11. Explain about except clause with multiple exceptions.
12. Differentiate except clause with exception and without exception.
13. Write the syntax for exception handling?
14. Explain about user defined exception with example.
15. List some built-in exceptions in python.
16. Differentiate error and exception.

MUTIPLE CHOICE QUESTIONS
1. Which error occurs due to misunderstanding of the problem?
    a. Syntax error
    b. logic error
    c. Exception
    d. None of these
2. In exception handling, if there is no exception then which block will get executed.
    a. try
    b. except
    c. raise
    d. assert
3. Which of the following is not an optional block?
    a. try
    b. finally

    c. else
    d. None of these
4. Which keyword is used to generate exception?
    a. try
    b. except
    c. create
    d. raise
5. What kind of exception is obtained when a number is divided by zero?
    a. NameError
    b. AttributeError
    c. ZeroDivisionError
    d. TypeError
6. The exception can be raised forcefully using _________ keyword.
    a. exception
    b. assert
    c. raise
    d. try
7. An exception is _______
    a. an object
    b. a module
    c. a function
    d. None of these
8. Which of the following is not a standard exception in Python?
    a. ValueError
    b. AssignmentError
    c. NameError
    d. IOError
9. Which of the following is ArithmeticError?
    a. FloatingPointError
    b. OverflowError
    c. ZeroDivisionError
    d. All the above
10. What is the output for the following program?

```
a=10
b=5
if a>b
  print("a is greater")
print("b is greater")
```

    a. a is greater
    b. Syntax Error
    c. b is greater
    d. a is greater b is greater

TRUE OR FALSE

1. The assertion is raised when the assert statement fails.
2. Syntax error occurs because of the incorrect syntax or rules.
3. Exception occurs only when the program is syntactically wrong.
4. It is possible to get error during runtime even after the syntax of the program is correct.
5. The program will terminate immediately, if the exception is not handled.

6. An exception will not disturb the normal flow of the program.
7. Program should have only one except block.
8. The finally block always get executed.
9. Exceptions are created by inheriting exception class.
10. The else block will get executed only when there is no exception is raised from the try block.

FILL IN THE BLANKS

1. The process of handling the exception is known as ______________.
2. The error occurs while executing the program is known as ____________.
3. The KeyboardInterrupt is _____________ type of exception.
4. Exception in the program can be handled by using ____________ block.
5. The user defined exception is also known as ______________.
6. The ___________ block has statement which throws exception.
7. The ___________ statement manually creates an exception.
8. The two types of built-in exception are ______________ and _____________.
9. The _____________ error is only due to the mistake in logic, not because of any syntax error or exceptions.
10. The ______________ function is used to known built-in exceptions in python.

ANSWER

MUTIPLE CHOICE QUESTIONS

1. b
2. b
3. a
4. d
5. c
6. c
7. a
8. b
9. d
10. b

TRUE OR FALSE

1. True
2. True
3. False
4. True
5. True
6. False
7. False
8. True
9. True
10. True

FILL IN THE BLANKS

1. Exception handling
2. Exception
3. Asynchronous
4. try.... except
5. custom exception
6. try
7. raise

8.   Asynchronous and Synchronous
9.   logical error
10. dir(__builtins__)

ANNEXURE A: ADDITIONAL PYTHON PROGRAM

1. Write a python program to swap two number using temporary variables.

```
x=input("Enter  value of x")
y=input("Enter value of y")
print("Before swapping")
print("Value of x is ",x)
print("Value of y is ",y)
temp=x
x=y
y=temp
print("After swapping")
print("Value of x is ",x)
print("Value of y is ",y)
```
Output
```
Enter  value of x20
Enter value of y30
Before swapping
Value of x is  20
Value of y is  30
After swapping
Value of x is  30
Value of y is  20
```

2. Write a python program to find area and circumference of the circle.

```
r=int(input("Enter the radius of circle"))
a=3.14*r*r
c=2*3.14*r
print("The area of circle",a)
print("The circumference of circle",c)
```
Output:
```
Enter the radius of circle2
The area of circle 12.56
The circumference of circle 12.56
```

3. Write a program to print odd and even elements of a list into two different lists.

```
l=[]
n=int(input("Enter number of elements:"))
for i in range(1,n):
  b=int(input("Enter element:"))
  l.append(b)
even=[]
odd=[]
```

```
for j in l:
  if(j%2==0):
    even.append(j)
  else:
    odd.append(j)
print("The even list",even)
print("The odd list",odd)
```

Output:
```
Enter number of elements:8
Enter element:1
Enter element:2
Enter element:4
Enter element:14
Enter element:31
Enter element:5
Enter element:8
The even list [2, 4, 14, 8]
The odd list [1, 31, 5]
```

4. Write a program to find sum and average of items in a list using range( ) function.
```
l=[]
n=int(input("Enter total number of items in list"))
for i in range(0,n):
  items=int(input("Enter items in list"))
  l.append(items)
print("The list is",l)
sum=0
for i in range(0,n):
  sum=sum+l[i]
print("Sum of list is",sum)
avg=sum/n
print("Average of list is",avg)
```

Output:
```
Enter total number of items in list4
Enter items in list2
Enter items in list4
Enter items in list3
Enter items in list7
The list is [2, 4, 3, 7]
Sum of list is 16
Average of list is 4.0
```

5. Write a program to print the multiplication table of any number n.
```
n=int(input("Enter the table"))
for i in range(1,11):
  print(n,"X",i,"=",n*i)
```

Output:
```
Enter the table9
```

```
9 X 1 = 9
9 X 2 = 18
9 X 3 = 27
9 X 4 = 36
9 X 5 = 45
9 X 6 = 54
9 X 7 = 63
9 X 8 = 72
9 X 9 = 81
9 X 10 = 90
```

6. Write a python program to multiply two matrixes.

```python
a=[[1,2],[1,2]]
b=[[2,1],[2,1]]
c=[[0,0],[0,0]]
print("Multiplication of two matrix:")
for i in range(len(a)):
  for j in range(len(b)):
    for k in range(len(b)):
       c[i][j]=a[i][j]+a[i][k]*b[k][j]
for i in c:
  print(i)
```
Output:
```
Multiplication of two matrix:
[5, 4]
[5, 4]
```

7. Write a python program to find maximum element in the list.

```python
l=[]
n=int(input("Enter total number of elements/items in the list"))
for i in range(0,n):
  a=int(input("Enter the value"))
  l.append(a)
print(l)
max=l[0]
for i in range(1,n):
  if l[i]>max:
    max=l[i]
print("The maximum element in the list is ",max)
```
Output:
```
Enter total number of elements/items in the list5
Enter the value12
Enter the value3
Enter the value6
Enter the value78
Enter the value4
[12, 3, 6, 78, 4]
The maximum element in the list is  78
```

8. Write a python program to generate random number in a range.

```
import random
x=random.randint(0,9)
print("The random number is:\t",x)
```

Output:

```
The random number is:   7
```

9. Write a python program to find area of square using random number generation.

```
import random
side=random.randint(0,20)
print("radius is ",side)
area=side*side
print("The area of circle is ",area)
```

Output:

```
radius is  19
The area of circle is  361
```

10. Write a python program to print today's data and time by using built-in module.

```
import datetime
print(datetime.datetime.today())
```

Output:

```
2018-06-22 20:35:06.355912
```

11. Write a python program to display all the contents of the file.

```
file= open("sample.txt", "r")
print("Contents of file :\t",file.read())
file.close()
```

Output:

```
Contents of file :  how are you
```

12. Write a python program to display the content of the file and also count number of words of that file.

```
file= open("C:\\Python34\\sample.txt", "r")
print("The content of the file is:\n",file.read())
file.seek(0)
count=0
for i in file:
  line=i.split(' ')
  x=len(line)
  count=count+x
print("The word count is:\t",count)
file.close()
```

Output:

```
The content of the file is:
 If the data are immutable strings, aliasing can save on memory.
But aliasing is not always a good thing.
It has side effects.
The word count is:    25
```

13. Write a python program to check whether there is a drive in the computer.

```
import os
print("True in output means the drive is present otherwise False")
path=input("Enter the drive ")
print(os.path.exists(path))
```

Output:

```
True in output means the drive is present otherwise False
Enter the drive c:\
True
```

14. Write a python program to display all the characters of a string without whitespace

```
import re
a=re.findall(r'\w','1_pine apple')
print(a)
```

Output:

```
['1', '_', 'p', 'i', 'n', 'e', 'a', 'p', 'p', 'l', 'e']
```

15. Write a python program to extract year from date

```
import re
paragraph="This book was wrote on 12/08/1993 and published on 9/12/1995"
result=re.findall(r'\d{1,2}/\d{1,2}/(\d{2,4})',paragraph)
print (result)
```

Output:

```
['1993', '1995']
```

16. Write a python program to display only username from mail id.

```
import re
paragraph= "This mail is from xyz@gmail.com and  Please send mail to abc@yahoo.com, alex123@camp.com and ani@dcamp.com immediately."
mail_id = re.findall(r'([\w\.-]+)@[\w\.-]+', paragraph)
for ids in mail_id :
   print(ids)
```

Output:

```
xyz
abc
alex123
ani
```

17.   Write a python program to find factors of a number.

```
def factor(n):
  print("The factors of ",n,"are ")
  for i in range(1, n + 1):
    if n % i == 0:
      print(i)
x=int(input("Enter a number: "))
factor(x)
```

Output:

```
Enter a number: 6
The factors of 6 are
1
2
3
6
```

18. Write a python program to find compound interest (CI).

CI = P(1+(r/100)^n)

```python
def compound_interest(p, r, n):
    CI = p *((1 + r / 100)** n)
    print("Compound interest is", int(CI))
principle=int(input("Enter principle amount "))
rate=float(input("Enter the rate of interest"))
time=float(input("Enter the time peroid "))
compound_interest(principle, rate, time)
```

Output:

```
Enter principle amount 300000
Enter the rate of interest10.4
Enter the time peroid 2
Compound interest is 365644
```

19.   Write a python program to find sum of series 1 + 1/2 + 1/3 + ….. + 1/N.

```python
print("************************1 + 1/2 + 1/3 + ….. + 1/N ************************")
N=int(input("Enter the number of terms: "))
sum=0
for i in range(1,N+1):
    sum=sum+(1/i)
print("The sum of series is ",round(sum,2))
```

Output:

```
************************1 + 1/2 + 1/3 + ….. + 1/N ************************
Enter the number of terms: 4
The sum of series is  2.08
```

20.   Write a python program to find sum of series 1/1! + 2/2! + 3/3! + 4/4! +…….+ n/n!.

```python
print("******************* 1/1! + 2/2! + 3/3! + 4/4! +…….+ n/n! *******************")
N=int(input("Enter the number of terms: "))
sum=0
factorial=1
for i in range(1, N+1):
    factorial *= i
    sum = sum + (i/ factorial)
print("The sum of series is ",round(sum,2))
```

Output:

```
******************* 1/1! + 2/2! + 3/3! + 4/4! +…….+ n/n! *******************
Enter the number of terms: 4
The sum of series is  2.67
```

21. Write a python program to find sum of series $1^2+2^2+3^2+....+n^2$.

```
print("******************** 1²+2²+3²+....+n² ********************")
N=int(input("Enter the number of terms: "))
sum=0
for i in range(1, N+1):
    sum = sum + (i*i)
print("The sum of series is ",round(sum,2))
```

Output:

```
******************** 1²+2²+3²+....+n² ********************
Enter the number of terms: 4
The sum of series is  30
```

22. Write a python program to display a star pyramid pattern of n rows.

```
x = 0
n = int(input("Enter number of rows "))
for i in range(1, n+1):
  for j in range(1, (n-i)+1):
    print(end=" ")
  while(x != (2*i-1)):
    print("* ", end="")
    x = x + 1
  x = 0
  print()
```

Output:

```
Enter number of rows 7
*
* * *
* * * * *
* * * * * * *
* * * * * * * * *
* * * * * * * * * * *
* * * * * * * * * * * * *
```

23. Write a python program to display this pattern.

```
*
* *
*   *
* *
*
```

```
for row in range(5):
    for col in range(5):
        if ((row+col==2) or (col-row==2) or (row-col==2) or (row+col==6)):
            print("*",end=" ")
        else:
            print(end=" ")
    print(" ")
```

24. Write a python program to display this pattern for n rows.

```
7 6 5 4 3 2 1
7 6 5 4 3 2
7 6 5 4 3
7 6 5 4
7 6 5
7 6
7
n = int(input("Enter number of rows "))
for i in range(0, n):
   for j in range(n, i, -1):
      print(j , end="")
   print()
```

25. Write a python program to display this below alphabetic pattern for alphabet A - Z.

```
A
B C
D E F
G H I J
K L M N O
P Q R S T U
V W X Y Z 
n = int(input("Enter number of rows "))
count = 1
x = 65
for i in range(0, n):
   for j in range(0, count):
      alpha = chr(x)
      if alpha>'Z':
          break
      print(alpha, end=" ")
      x = x + 1
   count = count + 1
   print()
```

26. Write a python program to display this below diamond pattern.

```
*
* *
* * *
* * * *
* * *
* *
*

for i in range(0,4):
 print(" "*(4-i),end="")
 print(" *"*i)
for j in range(4,0,-1):
 print(" "*(4-j),end="")
 print(" *"*j)
```

27. Write a python program to find roots of Quadratic Equations.
(-b±√(b^2-4ac))/2a
```
a = float(input("Enter value of a "))
b = float(input("Enter value of b "))
c = float(input("Enter value of c "))
d = (b**2) - (4*a*c)
val1 = (-b -(d)**0.5)/(2*a)
val2 = (-b+(d)**0.5)/(2*a)
print("The two roots are",val1,"and", val2)
```
Output:
```
Enter value of a 4
Enter value of b 5
Enter value of c 3
The       two       roots       are       (-0.625-0.5994789404140899j)       and
(-0.625+0.5994789404140899j)
```

28. Write a python program to find ASCII value of the character.
```
char = input("Enter a character ")
ascii=ord(char)
print("The ascii value of the alphabet is",ascii)
```
Output:
```
Enter a character G
The ascii value of the alphabet is 71
```

29. Write a python program to convert kilometers into miles.
```
1 Kilometer = 0.621371 Mile
km = float(input("Enter value in kilometers "))
miles = km * 0.621371
print('%0.2f kilometers is equal to %0.3f miles' %(km,miles))
```
Output:
```
Enter value in kilometers 10
10.00 kilometers is equal to 6.214 miles
```

30. Write a python program to sort a list in descending order and ascending order.
```
n = int(input("Enter number of elements in the list "))
l=[]
for i in range(0,n):
    x=input("Enter items ")
    l.append(x)
print("Before sorting",l)
print("Descending order",sorted(l, reverse=True))
print("Ascending order",sorted(l))
```
Output:
```
Enter number of elements in the list 4
Enter items 3
Enter items 5
Enter items 2
Enter items 8
```

Before sorting ['3', '5', '2', '8']
Descending order ['8', '5', '3', '2']
Ascending order ['2', '3', '5', '8']

31. Write a python program to convert given number of days into years, weeks and days.

```
d=int(input("Enter total number of days:"))
leap_year=input("Is it a leap year ? Press y for Yes and n for No ")
if (leap_year=='y'):
    y=d/366
    a=d%366
    w=a/7
    d=a%7
    print("Years=",y,"\nWeeks=",w,"\nDays=",d)
elif (leap_year=='n'):
    y=d/365
    a=d%365
    w=a/7
    d=a%7
    print("Years=",y,"\nWeeks=",w,"\nDays=",d)
else:
    print('Say Yes or no')
```

Output:
```
Enter total number of days:56
Is it a leap year ? Press y for Yes and n for No n
Years= 0.15342465753424658
Weeks= 8.0
Days= 0
```

32. Write a python program to perform countdown.

```
n=int(input("Enter number to start countdown "))
while n>0:
    n=n-1
    print(n)
```

Output:
```
Enter number to start countdown 5
4
3
2
1
0
```

33. Write a python program to convert Celsius to Fahrenheit and vise versa.

```
temperture=float(input("Enter the celsius or fahrenheit for conversion"))
select=input("Press C for celsius / F for fahrenheit ")
if select=='C':
    celsius = (temperture)/1.8
    print(celsius)
elif select=='F':
    fahrenheit=(temperture*1.8)+32
```

```
   print(fahrenheit)
else:
   print("Enter correct choice")
```
Output:
Enter the celsius or fahrenheit for conversion56
Press C for celsius / F for fahrenheitC
31.11111111111111

34. Write a python program to print all prime number in that interval.
```
lower=int(input("Enter lower limit "))
upper=int(input("Enter upper limit "))
if lower==1:
   lower+=1
for a in range(lower,upper):
   k=0
   for i in range(2,a//2+1):
     if(a%i==0):
       k=k+1
   if(k<=0):
     print(a)
```
Output:
Enter lower limit 1
Enter upper limit 12
2
3
5
7
11

35.   Write a python program to get nth factorial.
```
def factorial(n):
   if n == 0:
     return 1
   else:
     return n * factorial(n-1)
num=int(input("Enter the value of n"))
print(factorial(num))
```
Output:
Enter the value of n 6
720

36. Write a python program to print only the odd numbers of the list.
```
L=[]
n=int(input("Enter total number of elements in the list"))
for i in range(0,n):
   L.append(input("Enter items"))
print("The list is",L)
print("The odd numbers in the list are")
for j in L:
```

```python
  if int(j)%2==1:
    print(j)
```
Output:
Enter total number of elements in the list4
Enter items3
Enter items7
Enter items4
Enter items9
The list is ['3', '7', '4', '9']
The odd numbers in the list are
3
7
9

37. Write a python program to print all the Armstrong number in that interval.
```python
lower=int(input("Enter lower limit "))
upper=int(input("Enter upper limit "))
for num in range(lower, upper + 1):
   sum = 0
   temp = num
   while temp > 0:
      digit = temp % 10
      sum += digit ** 3
      temp //= 10
   if num == sum:
      print(num)
```
Output:
Enter lower limit 5
Enter upper limit 2000
153
370
371
407

38. Write a python program to get Body Mass Index (BMI).
```python
height = float(input("Enter your height in mete: "))
weight = float(input("Enter your weight in kilogram: "))
bmi=weight / (height * height)
print("Your body mass index is: ",bmi)
```
Output:
Enter your height in meters: 1.58
Enter your weight in kilogram: 47
Your body mass index is: 18.82711103989745

39. Write a python program to print the current date and time using datetime module.
```python
import datetime
current=datetime.datetime.today()
print("Today date and time is",current)
```

```
print("Year is", current.year)
print("Month is", current.month)
print("Hour is", current.hour)
```
Output:
```
Today date and time is 2020-05-11 19:08:08.647112
Year is 2020
Month is 5
Hour is 19
```

40. Write a python program to find whether the entered number is prime or composite.
```
n=int(input("Enter a number"))
Flag=False
for i in range(2,n):
   if(n%i==0):
     Flag=True
     break
if(Flag==True):
   print(n,"is a composite number")
else:
   print(n,"is a prime number")
```
Output:
```
Enter a number8
8 is a composite number
```

41. Write a python program to print all the leap year in a range.
```
start=int(input("Enter a starting year"))
end=int(input("Enter a ending year"))
for i in range(start,end):
   if(i%4==0):
     print(i)
```
Output:
```
Enter a starting year1990
Enter a ending year2020
1992
1996
2000
2004
2008
2012
2016
```

42. Write a python program to encrypt a message by the key given.
```
msg=input("Enter the message to encrypt :")
key=int(input("Enter the key"))
i=0
while i<len(msg):
   x=msg[i]
   print(chr(ord(x)+key),end='')
```

```
    i=i+1
```
Output:
Enter the message to encrypt :The end
Enter the key4
Xli$irh

GLOSSARY

Access mode: It is the mode in which the file has to be accessed. The access modes are read, write and append. The default access mode is read.

Algorithm: Algorithm is a sequence of steps that tells us how to do something. Algorithm gives the logic of the program that is a step-by-step description of how to arrive at a solution.

Append: Adding the data at the end of the file is known as appending. To appending something into a file, open the file with append mode ('a' or 'a+'). This mode will add the data at the end of the existing file.

Arithmetic operator: These operators are used to perform arithmetic operations such as addition, subtraction, multiplication and division. The arithmetic operators in python are +, -, *, /, %, // and **

Assembler: The program in assembly language is converted into machine language by the help of assembler.

Assignment operators: This operator is used to store right hand side operand in the left hand side operand. It is used to assign value to the variables. The basic assignment operator is equal (=).

Associativity: If the operators are having same precedence then associativity decides the order in which the operator executes. It is of two types of associativity, they are left to right and right to left.

Bitwise operators: These are the operators performs bit level operation on operands. It operates bit by bit. The bitwise operators in python are &, |, ^, ~, << and >>

BOOLEAN (bool): It is a data type having two values known as 'True' or 'False'. It represents truth value in logic.

break: To exit from the current loop break statement is used.

Built-in exception: These are the exceptions that are already predefined to the system. Some of the built-in exceptions are NameError, IndexError, IOError, etc.

Byte code: Byte code is the fixed set of instructions that represents all operations which run on any operating system. Byte instructions are platform independent. The size of each byte code instructions is one byte. So it is named as byte code. This byte code is saved with an extension .pyc.

Comments: As programs get bigger and complicated, they will get more difficult to read. In order to get better understanding a text or note is added in the program, which is known as comment. The symbol '#'and extend to the end of the line is known as comments.

Comparison or Relational operators: Comparison operators are used to compare values or operands and return either True or False. The relational operators are ==, ! =, <, >, <= and >=.

Compiler: Compiler translates source code or instruction written in High Level Language (HLL) into machine language.

Complex: Complex number is a combination of real and imaginary part. It is in the form a+bi, whereas 'a' carries real part and 'bi' has imaginary part.

Computer: A computer is an electronic device that can accept data as input, process the data and produce information as output, and store the information for future use

continue: Skip the remaining statement and transfer the control to the next iteration of the loop.

Control flow: Control flow is a statement that determines the order of flow of a set of instructions or statements.

Dictionatries: Dictionaries are unordered sets; it has key-value pairs. The dictionary is represented by using curly brackets. i,e. { }. The dictionary contains key – value pairs, the items are accessed via keys and not via their position.

Directory: All the files are placed in the directories, these directories are also known as folders. The python opens the file from its default directory, which is also called as current directory.

Documentation string: It is also known as docstrings, used to explain code in python. It is an optional part in the function body of a program. It is written within multiline comment which is by triple quotes.

except: This block catches the exception thrown by except block and perform some action.

Exception: The errors detected during execution are known as exception. It isalso known as runtime error.

Expression: Expression is combination of literals, variable and operators that python evaluates to produce a value. An expression represents data items such as variables, constants and is interconnected with operators as per syntax of the language.

File Handle: It denotes in which position the cursor is currently in. It states from which position the data has to be read and write. It is also known as file pointer.

File object: File object is created as object for the text file. The file object act as an intermediate where we can see the file.

File path: A string that identifies a file or directory is called as file path. The file path should be mentioned within the quotes. The file path is also known as pathname.

Files: The files are collection of data which is stored in memory location for future use. It is the named location in a disk to store information.

finally: This block is an optional block, which will get executed under all circumstances. This block is used to create some action whether the exception is raised or not.

Floating point: It is written with decimal point. It has decimal part and fractional part. Decimal point separates the integer and fractional parts.

Flowchart: Flowchart is a diagrammatic or symbolic representation of process that illustrates the sequence of operations to be performed to arrive at a solution.

Flowcharting: The process of drawing flowchart is known as flowcharting.

For loop: It is used to execute a set of statement a particular number of times.

Function composition: The Function composition is a process of combining functions; in this the result of one function is passed as an argument to the next function.

Function definition: Function definition is a way of creating a user defined function. The function definition includes function signature and function body.

Function signature: The first line of the user defined function is known as Function signature; this signature includes keyword def, function name, parameter(s) and should end with colon.

Function: Function is a block of organized, reusable code that is used to perform some related action. Function provides better modularity and high degree of code reusability.

Garbage collection: Python has garbage collector for collecting object which is no longer referred.

Identity operators: These operators are used to compares the memory location of two objects, it finds whether both operands are same or not. The identity operators in python are is and not is.

IDLE: IDLE means Integrated Development and Learning Environment. The IDLE has python shell and python editor. It is a most popular and standard python development environment.

Indentation: The whitespace at the beginning of the line is known as indentation. User need to specify that indentation in 4 spaces or one tab. It is a space given to the flow control, block of codes for class and function definitions.

Infinite loop: If the condition of the iterative statement does not terminate properly then it leads to infinite loop.

Inline if...else: The 'inline if...else' is the easiest and conventional form of if...else condition which is mostly used to perform simple task.

In-place operators: The in-place operators are the assignment operators. The operators such as +=, -=, *=, /=, //=, %=, **=, >>= and <<= are called as in-place operators or shortcut operators.

Input: The process of entering data to the computer system. The input devices such as keyboard, mouse, scanner, MICR, OCR etc. takes data from user to the computer for processing.

Integer: Integers are whole numbers without decimal point. They can be positive or negative. Integers have unlimited size in python.

Interpreter: The interpreter does the translation and executes the program line by line.

Iterative control: Executes a set of statement repeatedly.

Keyword: In every programming language there are certain words which are reserved for some other purpose. These words are known as reserved words or keywords in python.

Lambda function: Lambda Function is a way of creating anonymous function. It is a function without a name so it is known as anonymous function.

Lists: List is an ordered sequence of values. Values in the list are called elements or items. It can be written as a list of comma-separated items (values) in square brackets [ ]. It is mutable.

Logical operators: Logical operator is used to check and compare two or more conditionals and the resultant is Boolean values. The logical operators in python are and, or and not.

Machine language: Machine Language is what the computer can understand but it is difficult for the programmer to understand.

Membership operator: Membership operator is used to check whether the value is belongs to the sequence or not. The membership operators are in and not in.

Modular programming: Using module in programming is known as modular programming.

Module: The Module is a file that contains a collection of related functions. Some of the built-in module are math, sys, so, calendar, etc.

Nested loop: Placing one loop inside the other loop is known as nested loop.

Object oriented: It uses both procedural oriented approach which has procedures or functions and has object oriented approach such as polymorphism, inheritance, etc.

Operating System: Operating System (OS) intermediates between user of computer and computer hardware. Windows XP, Windows 7, UNIX, MS-DOS and Mac OS X, are some examples of OS.

Operators: The operator is a symbol which is used to perform some operation with one or more operand. It is the constructs used to control or manipulate the value of operands.

Output: The process of producing results using the processing device for getting useful information.

Package: Package is a directory which contains functions, modules and other packages within it.

pass: Pass means null statement, nothing happens when pass is executed.

Pickle: Pickle is a module in python; it is used to store non-strings or byte stream in a database. The pickle is for long term storage.

Pickling: The pickle.dumps takes an object as a parameter and returns a string representation. Before writing the data are converted into byte stream. This process is known as pickling which is done by using dump( ) method.

Precedence: When an expression contains more than one operator, the order of evaluation depends on the order of precedence. Precedence defines the priority of an operator and guides the expression to be evaluated.

Predefined function: Functions which is already available to the python are called predefined or built-in function. Some of the built-in functions are pow( ), sqrt( ), abs(), etc.

Problem solving: The process of analyzing, understanding and solving the problem is known as problem solving.

Process: The processing of data is done by the processing unit known as Central Processing Unit (CPU)

Program: Program is a set of instructions to a computer to perform a task. Programming is telling computers what to do.

PROLOG: Prolog is a General purpose logic programming language. It associated with computational linguistics and Artificial Intelligence (AI).

Pseudocode: Pseudocode looks like programming language but it is not a real programming code. Pseudocode is a formal design tool developed with the structural programming.

PVM: PVM means Python Virtual Machine; it converts byte code into machine understandable code (0's and 1's). If there is any runtime error (Exception) then error message will be displayed otherwise this machine code is executed and results are displayed.

Python: Python is a high level general purpose, object-oriented scripting programming language which follows object oriented concept.

raise: This statement is used to manually raise an exception   .

Recursion: Function calling itself until the base condition is reached is known as recursion. In recursion there are two cases i.e., Base case and recursive case.

Recursive function: The function calling itself again and again until the base condition is reached. The recursive function has two cases: base case and recursive case.

Repetition: Repetition means a set of steps which are repeated over and over until some event occurs. It is commonly known as iteration. Set of steps processed again and again until the conditions fails.

Return statement: The return statement is used to return the value of the expression. Without return keyword None object is created.

Scope: Scope is the position or region of the code in which the object can be accessed directly.

seek( ): This method is used to change the current position of the file handler. This argument is the position in which the file handler has to move.

Selection control: Select and execute one set of statements among various alternatives

Selection: A selection is a decision that has to be made. In selection only one alternative steps is executed based on the condition. Selection is a decision making process.

Sequence: A sequence is a series of steps that occur one after other, in same order every time. Steps are executed in sequence that follow top to bottom or left to right approach.

Sequential control: Executes the program sequentially from first line to last line.

Sets: Set is an unordered collection of values of any data type. Sets are list without duplicate entries. In set every element is unique and it is mutable. Elements are separated by, enclosed with { }.

Software: Software is a collection of data and instructions which is responsible for controlling and managing the hardware components to accomplish a specified task.

Source code: Source code is the python code. This source code is saved with the extension .py. Translator converts this source code into byte code.

SQL: Structured Query Language (SQL) a typical Data Base Management System (DBMS) allows users to store, access, and modify data in an organized, efficient way. Originally, the users of DBMSs were programmers.

Statement: Instructions that a Python interpreter can executes are called statements. A script contains sequence of statements. Each and every line in a program is known as statement.

String: String is defined as a sequence or set of characters represented in quotation marks. The characters may be number, letters, whitespace character, other symbols or combination of these inside the quotes. The string is immutable.

tell( ): This method tells the current position of file handler in that file. Initially the file handler will be in 0 position i.e., in the first byte of the file.

try: This block is created in order to catch the exception. It throws the exception if the code has runtime error. The try block contains one or more statement that can produce exception. If that operation fails or exception is thrown then, control goes to except block.

Tuple Assignment: Tuple assignment allows variables on the left of an assignment operator and values of tuple on the right of the assignment operator. In tuple assignment number of variable is the left side should be equal to the number of value in the right side.

Tuple: A tuple is same as list, except that the elements in the tuple are enclosed in parentheses instead of square brackets. A tuple is an immutable list which means once a tuple has been created; you can't add elements to a tuple or remove elements from the tuple.

Unpickling: While reading, conversion of byte stream to original data takes place. This process is known as unpickling which is done by using load( ) method.

User defined exception: The user defined exceptions are the exceptions which are created by user.

User defined function: The functions which are defined or created by the user are called user defined function.

Vacuum tubes: The vacuum tube is a glass tube that contains electrodes for controlling electron flow and was used in early computers.

Value: Value is the basic units of data like number or string that a program manipulates. A name is given to a value by using an assignment statement, or simply an assignment.

Variables: Variable is a name given to the value to refer a memory location. A variable allows us to store a value by assigning it to a name.

While loop: It is used to execute a set of statement a particular condition is True.

'with' keyword: It can be used to open the file and close automatically after the process is done in python. It is not necessary to close the file explicitly using close( ) function.

ABOUT THE AUTHOR

Jenif D Souza W S

Jenif D Souza works an Assistant Professor and a Research enthusiast for the Department of Computer Science and Engineering at St. Joseph's College of Engineering. She has deep and immense teaching and research experience. She handles Python, C programming, Java, AI, OOPS and other courses for Graduate and Post Graduate students. A rank holder from Anna university for Master of Engineering (CSE), she authored many technical papers in several international and national conferences and journals.